D1474972

LATIN AMERICAN HISTORICAL DICTIONARIES SERIES

Edited by A. Curtis Wilgus

1. *Guatemala*, by Richard E. Moore, rev. ed. 1973.

2. *Panama*, by Basil C. & Anne K. Hedrick. 1970.

3. *Venezuela*, by Donna Keyse Rudolph & G. A. Rudolph. 1971.

4. *Bolivia*, by Dwight B. Heath. 1972.

5. *El Salvador*, by Philip F. Flemion. 1972.

6. *Nicaragua*, by Harvey K. Meyer. 1972.

7. *Chile*, by Salvatore Bizzarro. 1972.

8. *Paraguay*, by Charles J. Kolinski. 1973.

9. *Puerto Rico and the U.S. Virgin Islands*, by Kenneth R. Farr. 1973.

10. *Ecuador*, by Albert W. Bork & Georg Maier. 1973.

11. *Uruguay*, by Jean L. Willis. 1974.

12. *British Caribbean*, by William Lux. 1975.

13. *Honduras*, by Harvey K. Meyer. 1976.

14. *Colombia*, by Robert H. Davis. 1977.

15. *Haiti*, by Roland I. Perusse. 1977.

16. *Costa Rica*, by Theodore S. Creedman. 1977.

17. *Argentina*, by Ione Wright & Lisa M. Nekhom. 1978.

18. *French and Netherlands Antilles*, by Albert Gastmann. 1978.

19. *Brazil*, by Robert M. Levine. 1979.

20. *Peru*, by Marvin Alisky. 1979.

21. *Mexico*, by Donald C. Briggs & Marvin Alisky. 1981.

22. *Cuba*, by Donald E. J. Stewart. 1981.

Historical Dictionary
of
MEXICO

by
Donald C. Briggs
and
Marvin Alisky

Latin American Historical Dictionaries, No. 21

F
1204
.B74
WEST

The Scarecrow Press, Inc.
Metuchen, N.J., & London
1981

Library of Congress Cataloging in Publication Data

Briggs, Donald C   1931-
  The historical dictionary of Mexico.

  (Latin American historical dictionaries ; no. 21)
  Bibliography: p.
  1. Mexico--Dictionaries and encyclopedias.
I. Alisky, Marvin, joint author. II. Title.
F1204.B74 `   972'.00321   80-27320
ISBN 0-8108-1391-2

Copyright © 1981 by Donald C. Briggs
and Marvin Alisky

Manufactured in the United States of America

CONTENTS

Editor's Foreword (A. Curtis Wilgus)   v

Introduction   viii

THE DICTIONARY   1

Bibliography

   Pre-1910 Era   237

   Modern Era   246

EDITOR'S FOREWORD

This volume has been prepared by two scholars thoroughly familiar with Mexico from having lived, studied and carried on research there. Their personal and teaching interests embrace the country's history, culture and personality. Each has contributed facts relating to all of Mexico and together they have covered the whole panorama of the country's history from pre-Columbian times.

Professor Briggs has had a long interest in the Mexican Indians and their language. His wife was born in Mexico as was his oldest son. His mother-in-law grew up in a small native village of about 5000 people. On many of his visits to this community he lived with the Indians, being concerned mostly with their language and culture. At home with family groups he came to understand their present day problems and the larger problems of Mexico itself. Between 1956 and 1974 Professor Briggs visited the country almost yearly, residing altogether for about four years. Besides his observations in Mexico he visited on three occasions 14 countries in Europe--from France to Russia and from Sweden to Spain--where he observed society (especially minority groups) and languages for better comparison with Mexico. His language interest has led him to teach English as a second language to Spanish-speaking people, with the result that he has served as an advisor to the National Endowment for the Humanities and for the Southern Association of Colleges and Schools. He is also a consultant on Spanish textbooks for a New York publisher.

At present Dr. Briggs is Professor of Spanish and Latin American History at Miami Dade Community College, North Campus. He has taught at Broward Community College, Barry College, and Florida State University at Tallahassee. Born in Cleveland, he received his A. B. degree at Ohio State University (1954). His M. A. degree (1961) at the University of the Americas, Mexico City, was in Spanish literature. He has also studied at the National University of Mexico. He has a Doctor of Arts degree (1975) in Inter American Studies and wrote his dissertation on the manner in which Hidalgo is presented to Mexican youths in textbooks used in primary and secondary schools.

Professor Alisky is the author of the Historical Dictionary of Peru, Volume 20 in this series. He is Professor of Political Science at Arizona State University and the founder and first director for seven years of the Center for Latin American Studies. In 1957 he founded the University's Mass Communications Department, serving as chairman for eight years. He has taught at Indiana University, Trinity University and the University of California, Irvine and has been a Visiting Professor at Princeton and at the Hoover Institution, Stanford. He has served as Fulbright Professor in Nicaragua and Peru and has lectured for the United States Department of State in Cuzco, Arequipo and Lima. From 1957 to 1962 he was guest lecturer at the American Institute of Foreign Trade. In 1975 he was Associate Scholar at the Inter-Parliamentary Conference, La Paz, Baja California and in 1973 he was Associate at the Colegio de México.

With his interests in mass communication, Dr. Alisky has been news correspondent for the NBC radio network in Latin America and Spain, and news columinist for the Christian Science Monitor and other papers. His published works include more than 200 magazine, encyclopedia and yearbook articles and twelve books and monographs, as author and co-author, including Governors of Mexico and Who's Who in Mexican Government. For these publications he has been honored by various institutions in Latin America and the United States.

Professor Alisky has had a long-standing interest in the Mexican political scene. In 1962 he covered the meeting of President Kennedy and President Adolfo López Mateos for NBC. In 1974 he was in President Ford's advisory group when he and President Luis Echeverría met in Arizona. He has not only interviewed these two Mexican presidents but also presidents Miguel Alemán, Adolfo Ruiz Cortines, Adolfo López Portillo, as well as dozens of Cabinet members, directors of government corporations and agencies, and leaders of Mexican industrial, commercial and fine arts groups. Because of his intimate knowledge of recent events he has been invited to appear on several Mexican television "talk-shows."

Mexico is a country not easily understood. The authors of this volume were given the assignment of selecting material on a logical basis which would produce a balanced historical dictionary rather than an encyclopedia. This was not an easy task, but it has been satisfactorily accomplished.

A. Curtis Wilgus
Emeritus Director
School of Inter-American
    Studies
University of Florida

INTRODUCTION

I

  To better understand modern-day Mexico it is necessary to observe how attitudes were shaped by historical oc-
currences pre-dating the arrival of the Spaniards in the New
World and continuing right up to the eve of the Mexican Revolution of 1910. The great Indian civilizations, notably the
Aztec and the Mayan, were in many ways more advanced than
their European counterparts in such things as astronomy,
mathematics and city organization. Bernal Díaz del Castillo,
upon seeing Tenochtitlán for the first time, was awed by its
beauty and remarked that he had never seen a city in Spain
which could match the beauty of the capital of the Aztec Empire. The Aztecs and other Indian civilizations of New Spain,
as Mexico came to be known, were defeated and subjugated
by the Spaniards, ultimately undergoing an assimilation which
was almost total. Thus today, the Mexican people are pre-
dominantly a mixed, or mestizo, race. But even today this
fact continues to be a reality which was never completely accepted by the Indian side of the Mexican, even though his
European side predominates.

  Cortés, the conqueror of the Mexicans, is not generally liked in Mexico, although there can be little doubt that
he is respected. Cuauhtémoc is regarded as the national hero,
although this tragic monarch witnessed the destruction of an
empire which was his responsibility to preserve and maintain.
The very painful and tragic deliverance of Mexico's once-proud
Indian civilizations into the Spanish colonial era was not without profound suffering, as evidenced by a small, unobtrusive
plaque erected at the Plaza of the Three Cultures in Mexico
City and commemorating the final victory of the Spaniards
over the Aztecs in August of 1521: "What happened here was
not a defeat, but the painful birth of what today is the Mexican nation." The Indian was to be a second-class citizen in
his own land, but nevertheless was to serve as the most im-

portant link in establishing and maintaining an historic perspective between flourishing pre-Columbian civilizations and
the independent, nineteenth and twentieth century nation-state
of Mexico. It will always be impossible for Mexico to ignore
its indigenous past, just as it will be equally impossible to
abandon its European heritage. The dream of José Vasconcelos of a union of the Indian and white races evolving into
what he referred to as a "cosmic race," continues to be an
idealized concept in Mexico. The Revolution of 1910 once
again pays homage to the Indian, even though the wretched
condition of so many of them continues to contrast starkly
with so idyllic a portrayal.

The lack of capable leadership is a problem which has
plagued Mexico down through the centuries. It was the superstitions of Montezuma which played right into the hands of
Cortés and in large part resulted in the conquest of Mexico
by Spain. And when it appeared that Montezuma's own followers would prevent this conquest by killing their leader, it was
not to be. Cuitláuhuac, who drove the Spaniards from Tenochtitlán, was dead of smallpox only five months after becoming
emperor. Thus, it was a disease associated with the white
man which proved to be the demise of this brave Aztec leader.
Cuauhtémoc was in his early twenties when he became the last
Aztec monarch and only twenty-three when he was put to death
by the Spaniards. It was not necessary to be a successful
leader to be remembered favorably in Mexico. No better il-
lustration of this exists than in the case of Miguel Hidalgo y
Costilla, honored as the independence leader of his country.
His lack of military ability is acknowledged by many Mexicans
and just before his death he renounced the movement which
he had led and pleaded with the Spaniards for forgiveness.
His extreme pride contrasts with the humility of his successor, José María Morelos y Pavón, a capable leader who was
put to death by the Spaniards in 1815, signalling the end of
the independence movement begun by Hidalgo in 1810. Even
when Mexico did become independent, the likes of Agustín de
Iturbide and José Antonio López de Santa Anna did not augur
well for that country.

A measure of presidential respectability manifested
itself in Benito Juárez, although his efforts to make government work were at times too idealistic, such as when he refused to prod the legislature to limit debate in the passing
of important laws. The long rule of Porfirio Díaz benefited
Mexico superficially. Certainly in the matter of citizen safety
from brigandage, the amount of foreign capital invested in

Mexico and the stability of the peso, he was eminently successful. However, the injustices again suffered by the Indian, from the standpoint of confiscation of his lands and the lowering of his living standard, were factors resulting in Porfirio Díaz's exile and the first great social upheaval of the twentieth century--the Mexican Revolution of 1910.

Foreign interference has also shaped the present-day attitudes of the Mexican. Many nations took their turn at either confiscating Mexico's wealth, occupying the country or, as in the case of the United States, annexing large areas of territory. Spain attempted to resubjugate Mexico in 1829, France controlled her customs house off the port of Veracruz in 1838, the United States annexed more than half of Mexico's territory in the war from 1846 to 1848 and the French occupied the country under Maximilian from 1864 to 1866. As recently as 1914 the United States occupied Veracruz with a large contingent of marines. If the Mexican tends to be suspicious, it is more readily understandable in the light of these experiences with various foreign powers.

These then, are briefly some of the factors which have contributed to the forming of modern Mexico. To be ignorant of them is to have little or no understanding of the forces at work in that country today.

II

Mexico's territory resembles a funnel, with the wide end winding along a 1,900-mile border with the United States. South of the narrow end of that funnel, the Isthmus of Tehuantepec, tropical forest lands unfurl as the Chiapas highlands, running to the border with Guatemala. The western Baja California peninsula encloses the Gulf of California, and a dry southeastern corner becomes the flat Yucatán peninsula.

Mexico's 764,000-square-mile area is one-fourth the size of the continental United States. More than half of this mountainous nation rises over 3,200 feet above sea level, with the terrain ranging from deserts to swamps. Only 7 percent of the total land is under natural-rainfall cultivation but thanks to hydroelectric projects adding irrigation, 14 percent of Mexico's surface is now being cultivated for crops or grazed by livestock.

Demographic disequilibrium strains the distribution and

communication facilities.   More than half of all Mexicans live
in less than 14 percent of the national territory, the central
region or Valley of Mexico, with industrial payrolls overwhelmingly bunched in the metropolitan areas of Mexico City,
Monterrey, and Guadalajara, despite the government's programs to encourage decentralized industries.

Of the 1979 population of 69 million, 45 percent were
rural and small-town residents.   Of the urban majority, one-
fifth of them crowd into the three largest metropolitan areas.
Since 1973, the government has opened thousands of Family
Planning Centers, yet the population has continued to increase
at the rate of 3.6 percent a year.   Public health measures
have drastically reduced the death rate but the birth rate has
not been curtailed much.

Machismo, the cult of male virility, prompts the fa-
thering of large families.   Despite a government program to
promote "Responsible Parenthood" through broadcasts, comic
books, billboards, and newspaper and magazine articles and
advertisements, only one woman in four of child-bearing age
uses the free services of the Family Planning Centers.   Once
fatal diseases which kept the population stable have been
eradicated.   With a low death rate and a high birth rate,
life expectancy has risen from 46 years in 1940 to 65 years
in 1979.

The typical Mexican is a Spanish-Indian hybrid or
mestizo.   While seven out of ten adults are technically literate, nine out of ten get their basic daily news from radio.
Not even one adult in six regularly reads newspapers or magazines.

Contrasted with most other Latin American nations
with a small upper class, a small middle class, and a lower
class making up most of the population, Mexico now has one-
third of its citizens classified as middle class in terms of
income and social status.   Mexico's assets include its 60
billion barrels of oil reserves, and its expanding industry and
tourism.   Its liabilities include a population increasing faster
than its job market.

Despite the pressures of inflation and underemployment
in the 1970's, Mexico has progressed during this century into
a nation with urban residents increasingly utilizing consumer
goods and credit.

A mixture of a political pamphlet and a travel folder, this republic has been modernizing for decades through on-going institutionalized reforms called the Revolution, spelled with a patriotic capital "R" to distinguish it from the revolts prior to 1910. Launched seven years before the Bolsheviki began changing Russia by violent means, the Mexican Revolution has been the non-Marxist prototype or model for nationalistic social change in this century not only in Latin America but also in other underdeveloped regions of the world.

The 35-year dictatorship of Porfirio Díaz from 1876 to 1911 concentrated most of the land being cultivated or grazed in the hands of a few large landowning families, whose extensive farm-ranch estates (haciendas) employed 90 percent of the rural population. These peasant-farmers (campesinos) spent their lives working on the hacienda on which they were born, laboring for bare subsistence and remaining in lifelong debt to the owners, who illegally acquired from the dictatorship the communal farms (ejidos) which had belonged to the villages since the era before the Spanish conquest of the Aztec Empire.

Francisco I. Madero, an intellectual, gave the Revolution its political articulation in 1910. His slogan called for "Effective suffrage and no re-election." The campesino leader Emiliano Zapata voiced the needs of the peasants, calling for "Land, bread, and justice." No one personality dominated the Revolution. As in an Italian opera, various leaders seemed to be speaking all at the same time. In addition to Madero and Zapata, the voices of Generals Alvaro Obregón, Pancho Villa, and Plutarco Calles added dimensions to the Revolution, as did President Venustiano Carranza during 1915-1920.

Carranza had a constituent assembly draft the federal Constitution of 1917 at Querétaro, which broke with the past. Article 123 became the magna charta of organized labor, guaranteeing the right to organize, the right to strike, the right to an eight-hour work day, with extra pay for overtime. Article 27 on land divorced the subsoil mineral riches from the surface property ownership and declared those natural resources to be the property of the Mexican nation. Only with a government concession could any entity develop these subsoil resources.

The fighting phase of the Revolution erupted on November 20, 1910, and lasted almost a decade. During ten years of civil war, more than one million Mexicans out of a then stable population of only 15 million lost their lives in battles.

During the presidency of Lázaro Cárdenas from December 1934 to December 1940, the continuing social reforms came of age. Cárdenas organized the Mexican Federation of Labor (CTM) and the National Campesino Federation (CNC) in 1936, expropriated the railroads in 1937, and expropriated the oil industry in 1938. He created the government corporation Pemex to explore, drill, transport, refine, and market petroleum, giving Mexico the basic fuel and transportation needed for its coming industrialization.

When Miguel Alemán became president in 1946, the age of the generals as chief executives ended. All presidents since 1946 have been civilian attorneys, except for the civilian economist Adolfo Ruíz Cortines, president from 1952 to 1958.

The Institutional Revolutionary Party (PRI) has dominated government, retaining since its founding in 1929 the presidency, the cabinet ministries, all the state governorships, all senate seats in the federal Congress except one held since 1976 by the leader of the Popular Socialist Party (PPS). In the lower house of the federal Congress, the Chamber of Deputies, until 1964 all but a handful of seats went to the PRI. With the constitution amended to give minority-party seats based on percentages of the total vote, the conservative National Action Party (PAN) gained 20 to 25 seats. With the chamber enlarged as of 1979, the PRI won 296 of the 300 congressional district seats, and six minority parties had to share on a proportional basis the 100 seats created for them. With the executive branch continuing to dominate the legislative branch, the increase in opposition party seats remained more cosmetic than substantive.

Modern era entries in this volume include key cabinet ministers and other outstanding leaders during the presidencies of Alemán, Ruíz Cortines, López Mateos, Díaz Ordaz, Echeverría, and López Portillo. In addition to leaders in the dominant party, the PRI, selected leaders of the PAN, the PPS, and other minority parties are included, as well as prominent governors of major states and mayors of major cities.

Socially significant concepts ranging from the extended

family relationships of the godfather (padrino) system to the political clique (camarilla) are covered. There are entries for the 31 states, the Federal District, and the major cities and state capitals, as well as port cities and border communities.

In addition to politics, government, economics, and the physical setting, various facets of the culture of Mexico are covered, ranging from fine arts and literature to sports.

Dynamic, modernizing Mexico demands a handy, one-volume reference which in compact but readable prose surveys both the historical and current public life of the republic. We hope this volume serves that purpose.

Donald C. Briggs
Marvin Alisky

THE DICTIONARY

ABACERO. In rural Mexico, the manager of a small general store which features groceries, especially basic foods.

ABAD Y QUEIPO, MANUEL. 1751-1825. Born in Asturias, Spain, he served as the Bishop of Michoacán. He was denounced to the Inquisition, but later exonerated. By means of sound economic ideas he attempted to prevent the loss to Spain of her American colonies. Abad y Queipo excommunicated many leaders of the independence movement of 1810, including Allende and Hidalgo.

ABANICAR. In formal speech, "abanicar" means to stir the breeze with a fan. However, in Mexican sports slang, it means to strike out as a batter in baseball.

ABARCA ALARCON, RAIMUNDO. Born on March 4, 1906, in Chilpancingo. Medical degree from the Military Medical School in Mexico City. Mayor of the city of Iguala 1949-50. Governor of the state of Guerrero 1963-69. A leader of the popular sector of the dominant Institutional Revolutionary Party (PRI). He achieved national distinction in the 1970's as an administrator of medical and surgical services for the National Railroads and for the Social Security system for government employees.

ABASOLO, MARIANO. 1783-1816. Independence figure who was born in Dolores Hidalgo in Guanajuato. He was involved in a conspiracy in 1809 to gain independence from Spain, on the invitation of Ignacio Allende, and in 1810 supported the independence effort with money from his sizeable fortune. Through him the followers of Hidalgo were given the guns and ammunition which originally belonged to the Spanish garrison at Dolores. He was captured at Acatita de Baján, along with many other revolutionaries, and was sent to a prison in Cádiz, Spain, where he died in 1816.

1

ABC HOSPITAL. The American-British-Cowdray Hospital on
    Avenida Observatorio in Mexico City. Popularly known
    as the ABC, this private hospital is maintained by Eng-
    lish-speaking residents of Mexico. Reorganized and ex-
    panded several times since the 1940's, it maintains United
    States, British, and Canadian medical standards and prac-
    tices. "Cowdray" was added to its title to honor the fam-
    ily who raised large reserve funds from charitable sources
    to insure its permanent status.

ABSENTEE LANDLORDS. Traditional agricultural production
    methods of absentee landlords owning huge estates was a
    target of reformers demanding social justice for peasants
    in the Constitution of 1917. Article 17 of the Constitution
    includes as agrarian reform the expropriation of these
    estates or haciendas, with lands which originally belonged
    to villages being returned as communal farms and other
    lands being distributed to landless peasants.

ACAPARADOR. A speculator who buys foodstuffs from small-
    scale farmers and resells them in city markets at high
    profits.

ACAPULCO. A world famous tourist resort on the Pacific
    coast of the state of Guerrero, 260 miles south of Mexico
    City. Situated on an oval bay with many beaches, it is
    backed by steep mountains. It has a mild climate all year.
    Settled by the Spaniards in 1530, Acapulco has been a
    port to the Far East since 1601. Under the guidance of
    Mexico's President Miguel Alemán 1947-1952, it attracted
    huge foreign investments in luxury hotels and affluent
    American tourists for swimming, fishing, golf, tennis,
    and nightclub entertainment. A special attraction is the
    show of divers who jump from high cliffs into the ocean.
    Its 1979 estimated population totaled 490,000.

ACCION NACIONAL see NATIONAL ACTION PARTY

ACEVES PARRA, SALVADOR. Born on April 4, 1904, in
    La Piedad, Michoacán. Medical degree from the National
    Autonomous University of Mexico (UNAM). Graduate work
    in cardiology in the United States. Professor of medicine
    at UNAM. Director of the National Institute of Cardiology
    1961-65. Assistant Minister of Health 1964-67. Minister
    of Health and Welfare in the cabinet of President Gustavo
    Díaz Ordaz, 1968-70.

ACOLHUAS. Also known as the TEXCOCANS. These Indians
lived near Lake Texcoco and were of the Nahua tribe.
They were also a part of the Aztec confederation.

ACORDADA. A tribunal set up in 1710 to eliminate banditry
in New Spain. Originally there was no appeal of its harsh
sentences. Later, the viceroy and a special committee
ruled on all sentences before they were carried out.

ACORDADA, REVOLT OF THE. Troops of the Acordada garrison in Mexico City revolted in 1828 and forced the conservative President-elect Gómez Pedraza into exile. As
a result, Vicente Guerrero, a liberal, was declared
president.

ACOSTA ROMO, FAUSTO. Born in the state of Sonora
around 1917. A tax attorney active in the Institutional
Revolutionary Party (PRI). Senator from the state of
Sonora 1952-58. He gained national prominence as a
negotiator on irrigation and labor relations problems.
Acting Governor of Sonora 1951. Assistant Attorney Gen-
eral of Mexico 1964-66. In the 1970's, a director of the
National Bank of Ejido Credit in Ciudad Obregón, Sonora.
A loser for the PRI nomination for Governor of Sonora
in 1961, 1967, 1973, and 1979.

ACUÑA. A small border city directly across the Rio Grande
from Del Rio, Texas. Acuña does not connect to the
major highways running southward except by gravel roads.

AEROMEXICO. Mexico's government-owned airline. It began
as a private company on May 15, 1934, when Antonio
Díaz Lombardo incorporated Aeronaves de México to begin
flights between Mexico City and Acapulco. In 1941 Aeronaves extended its routes to Oaxaca and Veracruz, and
in 1943 to Chiapas. In 1940, Pan American Airways
bought 40 percent of Aeronaves and in 1959 sold that
holding to the government, which at that time also purchased the remaining privately-held shares. In 1962,
Aeronaves bought Guest Airways to obtain international
air routes between Mexico and European capitals. By
1964, 90 percent of its propeller aircraft had been replaced by jet airliners. In the 1970's, Aeronaves de
México shortened its name to Aeroméxico. It flies 20
percent fewer international and 30 percent fewer domestic
passengers than Mexico's other airline, the privately
owned and operated Compañía Mexicana de Aviación.

AGIOTISTA. A Spanish term meaning "usurer" or "profiteer." Used particularly in the nineteenth century to refer to Mexican businessmen who speculated by lending money to the government for short terms, charging huge interest rates. They were very powerful during the Santa Anna period, 1829-1855.

AGRAMONT COTA, FELIX. Born in 1917 in La Paz, Baja California del Sur. Agricultural engineering degree from the National School of Agriculture in 1945. An administrator for the Ministry of Agriculture in Jalisco. Under a Rockefeller grant, he did seed production research. Assistant director of seed production for the government, he served as Governor of Baja California del Sur from 1970 to 1974. In October 1974 this territory achieved statehood.

AGRARIAN REFORM MINISTRY. The constitutional basis for this entity comes from Article 27 of the 1917 Constitution. A presidential decree in 1934 created an Agrarian Department within the Ministry of Agriculture and in 1958 it expanded into the Department of Agrarian Affairs and Colonization (DAAC), to administer land reform and to settle landless peasants on lands newly opened to farming and ranching by the government through irrigation. Since 1975 the DAAC has had the full autonomy as a separate cabinet entity, the Ministry of Agrarian Reform.

AGUASCALIENTES (CITY). The capital city of the state of the same name. Its 1976 population totaled 220,000. The city is headquarters for the state's livestock industry of cattle, sheep, and horses.

AGUASCALIENTES (STATE). A small inland state in central Mexico bounded on the south by the state of Jalisco and on the other sides by the state of Zacatecas. Its area totals 5,589 square kilometers. The name "Aguascalientes" means "hot waters," referring to the mineral springs which have given it health resorts. Mostly on a plateau of 6,200 feet above sea level, it enjoys mild climate. The census estimate in 1976 showed a state population of 430,000.

AGUASCALIENTES, CONVENTION OF. In November of 1914 Carranza, Villa and Zapata met in Aguascalientes in an effort to iron out their differences. It was unsuccessful

and the outcome was that Carranza moved his government
to Veracruz and Villa and Zapata took turns occupying the
National Palace in Mexico City.

AGUILAR, CANDIDO.   Born on February 12, 1888, in Palma,
Veracruz.   Died in 1960 in Veracruz.   Nationally known
as the vice-president of the constitutional convention in
Querétaro from November 1916 to February 1917 who
expedited the final draft of the federal Constitution of
1917.   He was Governor of Veracruz 1914-17, a Senator
in the federal Congress 1934-40.   A son-in-law of Mexican President Carranza (1915-20), he also served as
Minister of Foreign Relations during 1918.

AGUILAR, JERONIMO DE.   Spanish adventurer who survived
a shipwreck and spent eight years living among the Mayans.   Because of his knowledge of their language, he
served as an interpreter for Cortés.

AGUILAR ALVAREZ, ERNESTO.   Born on January 25, 1910,
in the Federal District.   He received his law degree from
the National Autonomous University of Mexico (UNAM) and
became a professor of law at UNAM 1938-66.   Aguilar
Alvarez was a justice of the federal Supreme Court 1966-
79.

AGUILAR TALAMANTES, RAFAEL.   Born in 1940 in Santa
Rosalía, Baja California del Sur.   Studied law and economics at the National University 1958-64.   Imprisoned
1964-70 for leading riots in Michoacán.   He was leader
of National Democratic Student Federation, a Marxist
group, and founder in 1973 of the Socialist Workers Party
(Partido Socialista de Trabajadores) as well as its secretary general.

AGUILAR Y MAYA, JOSE.   Born on July 28, 1897, in Guanajuato.   Died in 1966 in Mexico City.   Aguilar y Maya
received his law degree from the National Autonomous
University of Mexico (UNAM) and became a professor of
law at UNAM for ten years.   Governor of the state of
Guanajuato 1949-55; Attorney General of Mexico 1940-46
and 1955-58.   His writing had an influence on Mexican
public law.   He influenced the development of regulatory
law throughout the 1940's and 1950's.

AGUIRRE, MANUEL BERNARDO.   Born on August 20, 1908,

in Parral, Chihuahua. Engineering degree from the National University of Mexico. After serving as mayor of Chihuahua City, he was a Deputy in the federal Congress 1940-43 and 1961-64, and a Senator from Chihuahua 1971-74. Active in the Institutional Revolutionary Party, he was Governor of the state of Chihuahua 1974-80.

AGUSTIN I see ITURBIDE

AGUSTIN, JOSE. Born in 1944 in Acapulco. He has worked as a journalist in Mexico City while developing into a nationally known novelist, fine arts critic, and television and motion picture writer. His first novel, La tumba, published in 1964, describes wealthy Mexican youths lacking parental guidance. His 1966 novel, De perfil, analyzes the rootlessness of modern urban life. His 1969 Abolición de la propiedad, which focused on the generation gap, was a novel and a motion picture script, and in 1975 the basis for a television drama.

ALAMAN, LUCAS. 1792-1853. Born in Guanajuato, he played an active political role and worked for the independence of Mexico. After the fall of Bustamante he retired from politics until 1853, when he helped Santa Anna to become president. He hoped to persuade him to effect positive changes in Mexico's government, but Alamán's death ended all hopes for this. He is regarded as the ablest conservative statesman of Mexico and his History of Mexico (1849) is probably the best work of its kind for that period.

ALAMO, BATTLE OF THE. One of the most famous battles in the history of Texas, it is named for the old mission in San Antonio where it was fought. This battle generally marks the beginning of Texas independence from Mexico. After an early victory over the Mexicans, the Texans under General William Barrett Travis and numbering only 150, faced General Santa Anna and a Mexican force of 3,000 men in 1836. Nevertheless, for two weeks this small force held out and on March 6, to the trumpet call of the degüello, or the signal of no quarter, Santa Anna finally succeeded in overpowering the Alamo, killing all defenders. The cry, "Remember the Alamo!" became the rallying point for Texas independence, which finally became a reality after the Battle of San Jacinto on April 21, 1836.

ALANIS FUENTES, AGUSTIN.   Born on February 19, 1930,
in the Federal District.   Law degree from the National
University of Mexico (UNAM) 1953.   Professor at the
National Preparatory School 1950.   Professor of law at
UNAM 1968.   Director of Social Work for the Labor Ministry 1964-70.   Assistant Minister of Labor 1970-76.   Attorney General for the Federal District since December
1976.

ALARCON Y MENDOZA, JUAN RUIZ DE.   1580-1639.   A
Spanish playwright, although he was born in Tlacho, Mexico.   He left Mexico for Spain when he was only twenty,
and except for a brief visit back to the land of his birth,
remained there for the rest of his life.   He was a hunch-
back and because of this deformity he suffered a great
deal in society.   His most famous plays are La verdad
sospechosa (The Suspect Truth) and Las paredes oyen
(The Walls Have Ears).   His literary works are characterized by perfection of style and the tendency of his
plays to have a moral lesson.

ALCALA QUINTERO, FRANCISCO.   A Certified Public Accountant who became an administrator in 1946 at the government's National Bank of Foreign Trade and its director general 1970-80.   He formulated policies for the government's Foreign Trade Institute to increase exports
during the 1970's.

ALDAMA, IGNACIO.   1780-1811.   Hero of the Mexican independence movement.   He was a lawyer by profession, but
became wealthy through commercial ventures.   It was because of his brother, Juan Aldama, that he became active
in the independence movement, serving mainly as an advisor to Hidalgo in a non-military position as counsel and
legal advisor.   He was the first ambassador to the United
States and was captured and shot on June 20, 1811.

ALDAMA, JUAN.   A hero of Mexican independence, he was
born in San Miguel el Grande, Guanajuato.   He was one
of the inner circle which planned the independence movement of 1810 and when the plot was discovered by the
Spanish authorities it was Juan Aldama who notified Hidalgo.   He participated in many military campaigns and was
finally captured at Acatita de Baján, along with Hidalgo,
Allende and other leaders.   He was executed by a firing
squad on June 26, 1811, and his head was exhibited on

one of the four corners of the Alhondiga de Granaditas
in the city of Guanajuato.

ALDRETE, ALBERTO V. Born in 1891 in Baja California
del Norte. Died in 1959 in Mexicali. A large wheat
rancher and owner of a Mexicali flour mill. He was the
founder and owner of the Tecate brewery in Baja California which marketed beer throughout Mexico.

ALEGRE, FRANCISCO JAVIER. 1729-1788. Jesuit priest
and historian. As a youngster he already had a complete
command of Latin and by the time he was ordained he
knew Greek, Hebrew and Nahuatl, preaching to the Indians in their native language. He wrote a history of the
Jesuits in New Spain and was a true humanist, rejecting
the idea of slavery and stating that authority of one man
over others is derived from the consent of the group.
He was expelled from New Spain along with other Jesuits
and lived out his remaining years in Italy.

ALEJO, FRANCISCO JAVIER. A prominent public and business executive in the 1960's, he was Assistant Minister
of Finance during 1970-74, then Minister of National Patrimony in the cabinet of President Echeverría 1975-76,
and since December 1976 has been the director of the
government's industrial complex, Ciudad Sahagún, manufacturing railroad cars and various heavy machinery.

ALEMAN VALDES, MIGUEL. 1902- . Born in Sayula,
Veracruz, he was the President of Mexico during 1946-
1952. He was also the first popularly-elected civilian
president since the beginning of the Mexican Revolution.
His was an administration run by businessmen, the Mexican economy prospered, but his presidency was also
tainted by many charges of corruption. He did not emphasize agrarian reform, but did spend considerably on
irrigation projects, maintained a vigorous foreign policy
and took an active role in the United Nations. He advanced programs in education and science and it was during his presidency that the central campus of the University of Mexico was built.

ALHONDIGA DE GRANADITAS. A huge storage granary in
the city of Guanajuato to which the Spaniards fled during
the independence movement of 1810. The revolutionaries
eventually stormed it, massacring most of the Spaniards

inside. Today it is a national monument, but up to the 1940's served as a prison. See MARTINEZ, JUAN JOSE.

ALLENDE, IGNACIO. 1779-1811. Revolutionary insurgent and independence hero. He was born in Guanajuato in the town of San Miguel el Grande, which in his honor was later changed to San Miguel de Allende. A key figure in the independence movement of 1810, he probably should have been in charge of the armed forces, but deferred to Hidalgo. A key disagreement that Allende had with Hidalgo occurred when the latter refused to take Mexico City. Allende finally did take charge of the armed forces much later, but when it was too late to reverse the defeats already suffered. He was captured along with Hidalgo and other independence leaders at Acatita de Baján, Coahuila and was sentenced to die on August 1, 1811. His head was then sent to Guanajuato and placed on one of the corners of the Alhóndiga de Granaditas, to serve as an intimidating example of what happens to those who fight for independence from Spain.

ALMAZAN, JUAN ANDREU. A Mexican army officer who was born in Guerrero in 1891. He served with Madero and beginning in 1924 commanded the Monterrey army zone. He showed brilliance in suppressing the Escobar Rebellion of 1929. A man of conservative views, he ran for the presidency in 1940 as the candidate of the newly-organized Partido de Acción Nacional (National Action Party). He lost the election to Avila Camacho, but claimed he was the victim of fraud. Nevertheless, the results stood and Camacho was inaugurated.

ALTAMIRANO, IGNACIO M. 1834-1893. Diplomat, journalist and writer. He was a pureblood Indian from Guerrero and up to the age of fourteen spoke only his native Indian language. After attending the prestigious Colegio de Letrán in Mexico City he was caught up in the Wars of the Reform and fought on the liberal side. After the defeat of the French he took part in forming many cultural societies and taught literature. His book of poems, Rimas, is one of his most famous works and two other well-known works are Navidad en las montañas and El Zarco, published posthumously in 1901. He died in San Remo, Italy, after having served in diplomatic posts in Spain and France.

ALTOS HORNOS. The integrated steel and iron mills corporation established by the government in 1944 at Monclova, Coahuila. Altos Hornos coordinates its production with government steel mills in Michoacán, Mexico City, and Puebla, plus fifty private steel companies under a government coordinator for the Mexican steel industry.

ALVARADO Y MESIA, PEDRO DE. Ca. 1485-1541. Born in Badajoz, Spain, he was a Spanish explorer and soldier of fortune. Second in command to Cortés in the conquest of Mexico, 1519-1521. In 1523 he conquered Guatemala and El Salvador. In 1534, with 2,000 Indians and 500 Spaniards he nearly succeeded in conquering Quito, but met Pizarro and Almagro at the Bay of Caráquez and sold his expedition for 100,000 gold pesos. He was killed fighting the Indians in Jalisco, Mexico.

ALVAREZ, LUIS HECTOR. Born on October 25, 1919, in Camargo, Chihuahua. Engineering degree from Massachusetts Institute of Technology. Master's degree from the University of Texas. A leader of the conservative National Action Party (PAN) since 1956. PAN candidate for President of Mexico in 1958. A textile manufacturer in Chihuahua, he has long headed the Educational Center for Ciudad Juárez.

ALVAREZ GUERRERO, ALEJANDRO. Born on December 24, 1925, in the Federal District. Chemical engineering degree from the National Autonomous University of Mexico (UNAM). Founder of the Association of Electrical Engineers. President of the Mexican Institute of Chemical Engineers in the 1960's. President or Board member of fourteen large private corporations. Director General of Conduit of Mexico 1970-72. President of the Federation of Industrial Chambers (CONCAMIN), the national association for all Mexican industries, during 1972-73. Creator of the government's Department of Rural Industrialization for the Ministry of Industry.

ALZATE Y RAMIREZ, JOSE ANTONIO DE. 1737-1799. Priest, historian and scientist. It would be difficult to classify his work in any one category, since he was an extremely prolific writer and authority in such diverse fields as botany, history, mathematics, philology and law. He was banished from Mexico in 1767, along with the other Jesuits, but managed to return years later. He was the recipient of many international honors, being named a member of the Paris Academy of Sciences. His historic notes served to clarify the early colonial period in New Spain.

AMILPA, FERNANDO. Born May 30, 1898, in Morelos. Died in 1952 in Mexico City. Noted as longtime leader of the Union of Bus Drivers. Senator from the state of Morelos 1940-46. Secretary General of the Mexican Federation of Labor (CTM) 1946-49. For many years he represented the government on federal Conciliation and Arbitration Boards in management-labor negotiations.

AMOROS, ROBERTO. Born June 8, 1914, in Coatepec, Veracruz. Died August 14, 1973, in Veracruz. Law degree, National University of Mexico. Graduate study in economics at the University of Rome, Italy. Secretary of the office of the Presidency for President Miguel Alemán 1946-51. Director General of the National Railroads of Mexico 1952-58. He formulated many of Mexico's decentralized government agencies.

AMPARO. The writ of amparo (relief) is a federal order which can be issued on behalf of any citizen by any federal judge. It prevents any municipal or state or federal government official from action which violates constitutional or statutory laws or it compels officials to carry out such laws. The amparo is usually appealed to the federal Supreme Court. From 1917 to 1970, individual citizens or petitioning groups have won almost one-third of all such appeals to the Supreme Court. The amparo combines the concept of an injunction with the power of a writ of mandamus compelling the laws to be administered constitutionally.

ANAHUAC. The Aztec name for the central plateau of Mexico, the site of Mexico City. In Nahuátl, it literally means the "place at the center, in the midst of the circle." It also means the "place of waters."

ANAYA, PEDRO MARIA. 1795-1854. Military figure who also served as President of Mexico for a very brief time in 1847. His fame comes mainly from his heroic defense of Mexico City against the Americans. When General Twigs demanded the surrender of his men, along with their arms and ammunition, Anaya replied with his famous phrase, "Si hubiera parque, no estaría usted aquí" ("If

there were ammunition, you would not be here"). He
again occupied the presidency for a brief period after
Mexico was defeated by the United States and refused to
concede territory to the United States, resigned and lived
out his remaining years in Mexico City.

ANCONA, ELIGIO. 1835-1893. Journalist, lawyer and historian. He was born in Yucatán and was an ardent supporter of Juárez. He founded the pro-Juárez newspaper
La Píldora and a political newspaper, Yucatán. For a
time he was Governor of Yucatán and afterwards a cir-
cuit judge. He later returned to journalism. His most
famous historical work is a history of Yucatán.

ANDERSON NEVAREZ, HILDA. Born on October 10, 1938,
in Mazatlán, Sinaloa. Teacher's Certificate from the
Federal District Normal School. She also studied at St.
John's College in Maryland. A Deputy in the federal
Congress 1964-47 and 1970-73. She became a national
leader of women in politics throughout the 1960's and
1970's, serving as Secretary for Feminine Action of the
National Executive Committee of the dominant Institutional
Revolutionary Party (PRI).

ANEXO. Spanish for the word "addition." It refers to the
rural school concept developed by José Vasconcelos. See
CASA DEL PUEBLO, LA.

ANTUÑANO, ESTEBAN. Writer, industrialist and leading
economic liberal of the period 1834-1854. Believed that
the best way for Mexican industry to grow was by an increase in manufacturing. His education was British and
he adhered to the principles of the Manchester Doctrine.

APARARICIO, SEBASTIAN DE. 1502-1600. He was probably
the first road builder and wheelwright in New Spain and
among his most notable accomplishments was the opening
up of a road between Mexico City and Zacatecas for the
transport of silver. He was successful in this venture
because he was able to pacify the fierce Chichimecs with
his love and not by force of arms. Besides his earlier
exploits, he became famous as an agriculturalist and nav-
igator. He spent his last years as a brother in the Order of Saint Francis. For his extraordinary works of
charity and because of his profound humility and obedi-
ence, he was beatified by Pope Pius VII in 1789.

APATZINGAN CONGRESS. Called by the Mexican revolutionary hero José María Morelos y Pavón in the town of
Apatzingán, Michoacán in 1814. The Congress drew up
a republican constitution which called for the abolition of
slavery and equality before the law. This constitution
was short-lived, since the movement for independence
was crushed and Morelos was executed.

ARANGO, DOROTEO see VILLA, PANCHO (FRANCISCO)

ARELLANO TAPIA, ALICIA. Born in Magdalena, Sonora, in
1932. Degrees in both dentistry and in law. A leader
in Sonora in the Institutional Revolutionary Party. She
is married to Dr. Miguel Pavlovich, a surgeon and physician. After her term as a Deputy in the federal Congress 1963-64, she became the first woman ever elected
to the federal Mexican Senate, serving from 1964 to 1970.
She was mayor of Magdalena 1973-76. In 1979 she was
elected mayor of Hermosillo, the state capital, for the
1979-82 term.

ARIDJIS, HOMERO. Born in 1940 in Cutempec, Michoacán.
He studied journalism at Septién Institute in Mexico City.
A writer for various magazines, he became a leading
Mexican poet after his book of poems, La musa roja, was
published in 1958. Among his many books of poetry, the
best known are La difícil ceremonia published in 1963 and
Antes del reino published in 1963.

ARISTA, MARIANO. 1802-1855. Born in San Luis Potosí,
he had a long military career before being proclaimed
President by the Mexican Congress in 1851, a post which
he occupied until January of 1853, when he resigned. He
was the first Mexican president to be the recipient of a
peaceful transfer of power from one chief executive to
another and his administration was known for its attempts
to bring honesty to government. Unfortunately, frequent
uprisings of the military kept him from being successful
and finally lod to his resignation. He was declared a
national hero in 1856.

ARRIAGA, PONCIANO. 1811-1865. A liberal politician who
held various posts in his native San Luis Potosí and in
the federal government. He has frequently been referred
to as the Father of the Constitution of 1857 because of
the extensive work he devoted to that document. A strong

supporter of Juárez, he died before he could see the triumph of the Republic over Maximilian.

ARRIAGA RIVERA, AGUSTIN. Born in 1925 in Michoacán. Economics degree from the National Autonomous University of Mexico (UNAM). Professor of economics first at the University of Michoacán, then at the University of Tamaulipas, then at UNAM. As director general of the government's National Bank of Cinematography during 1959-62, he began the process of increasing the government's role in the film industry culminating in President Luis Echeverría's expropriation of all motion picture studios and production entities in 1975.

ASBAJE, JUANA DE see DE LA CRUZ, SOR JUANA INES

ASCENCIO, PEDRO. Revolutionary leader. Of pure Indian blood, he spoke many indigenous languages, along with Spanish. He joined forces with Vicente Guerrero and his reputation as a capable military leader continued to grow. He even defeated Iturbide, but met death in battle in June 1821.

ASIAIN, RODOLFO. Born in 1907 in Tula, Hidalgo. Died in 1963 in Mexico City. Law degree from the National University. A federal district judge. As a justice of the federal Supreme Court 1936-40, he wrote the opinion in 1938 under which the government expropriated the oil industry.

ASSEMBLY OF NOTABLES. The group of Mexican conservatives which offered the imperial crown of Mexico to Maximilian of Habsburg. This ceremony took place in French-occupied Mexico City in 1863.

ATENEO DE LA JUVENTUD (ATHENAEUM OF YOUTH) see REYES, ALFONSO

AUGUSTINIANS. Active in the propagation of the Catholic faith in Mexico, they also concentrated on building hospitals and succeeded in accumulating great wealth in Mexico.

AUTOMOBILE INDUSTRY. Automobile manufacturing began in Mexico in 1925 when the Ford Motor Company opened an assembly plant. General Motors opened a plant in

1936 and Chrysler Corporation in 1938. In 1952 the government's Diesel Nacional (DINA) truck manufacturing corporation became partners with Fiat of Italy to produce passenger cars, later shifting the DINA partnership to Renault of France. By 1964 Toyota of Japan and Volkswagen of Germany were authorized to produce in Mexico. In the 1960's and 1970's, Octaviano Campos Salas, who was Minister of Industry and Commerce 1964-70, and the Azcárrage family developed the Automex Corporation, with the Chrysler Corporation as a majority partner. The industry produces more than 400,000 trucks and cars a year and parts for the two million vehicles in use in Mexico.

AVIATION. Albert Braniff on December 8, 1910, in a Voisin biplane made the first flights into and out of Mexico City and in 1911 flew Mexican President Francisco Madero over the capital. Mexico's largest airline, Compañía Mexicana de Aviación, began in 1924 and Aeroméxico in 1934. Sixteen foreign airlines connect Mexico with most nations around the world. The Republic has 105 airports, of which 15 are large international airports.

AVILA CAMACHO, MANUEL. Born on April 24, 1897, in Teziutlán, Puebla. Died on October 13, 1955, in Mexico City. Studied accounting in Puebla. He joined the army in 1915 at the age of 18 as a lieutenant, becoming a major in 1918 and a general in 1926. A childhood friend of the leftist labor leader Vicente Lombardo Toledano, Avila became a close friend of Lázaro Cárdenas in 1920. President Cárdenas relied on Avila as Minister of Defense 1934-40, and helped him become the presidential candidate of the dominant Institutional Revolutionary Party. In his inaugural address, Avila attempted to end the Church-State controversy by proclaiming "I am a believer." In 1942 he had Mexico declare war on the Axis as one of the Allies and began rounding up German and Japanese espionage agents. In 1942, he concluded the Bracero Treaty with the United States, under which hundreds of thousands of farm workers legally migrated to the United States for two harvest seasons per year to bring in the crops at a time when U.S. farmers were in the armed forces. The bracero program was renewed as a peacetime treaty, lasting until the end of 1964. In 1943, Avila Camacho instituted the social security system in Mexico, with the Mexican Institute of Social Security

(IMSS) for workers in the private sector and the Institute of Social Security for Unions of Civil Servants (ISSSTE).

AVILA CAMACHO, MAXIMINIO.   Brother of Manuel Avila Camacho and the Mexican president from 1940 to 1946. Maximinio was appointed Minister of Communications by his brother and became wealthy by questionable means.

AYALA, PLAN OF   see   ZAPATA, EMILIANO

AYUTLA, PLAN OF.   Name given to the liberal proclamation of March 1854 issued in the town of the same name in Guerrero.   It called for a constitutional convention and led to the downfall of General José Antonio López de Santa Anna in 1855.

AZCARRAGA, EMILIO.   Born in Mexico City in the 1920's. University degree.   One of the owners of the Telesistema Corporation, which operates television Channels 2, 4, and 5, and their network of provincial affiliates throughout Mexico.   He owns majority stock in the XEW radio stations and networks and is a major stockholder in the Automex corporation which manufactures automobiles and trucks.

AZTEC.   The Indian civilization which built the largest empire in Mexico before the Spanish conquest was Aztec. The Aztecs migrated from the north into the central Valley of Mexico and founded their capital of Tenochtitlán (which is today Mexico City) in 1325 A. D. on an island of Lake Texcoco (later the lake dried out).   The Aztecs conquered most of the other Indian nations of Mexico and built an empire.   As exemplified by their huge temples, they developed an elaborate architecture to glorify their Emperor and the religion of sun worship and human sacrifice.   They developed pictograph writing and a literature of poems, philosophy, and mythology.
     The Spanish conqueror Hernán Cortés sailed from Cuba in 1519 with 500 soldiers, 16 horses, 14 cannons, and 47 muskets.   On the coast of Veracruz the Spanish troops were greeted by an envoy of Emperor Moctezuma, who gave them gold and silver ornaments, prompting the Spaniards to march to Mexico City for more wealth.   Cortés found an Indian woman named Malinche, also called Marina, who had learned Spanish from an explorer who had shipwrecked earlier.   Through her, Cortés could commu-

nicate in Nahuatl, the Aztec language. In 1521, the Spaniards easily subdued Moctezuma and his warriors, who
had never before seen horses or gunfire. The bearded
Spaniards also fit the Aztec legend of the god Quetzalcóatl, who some day was supposed to send representatives
from the sea to the east. After Moctezuma was killed in
a riot between Spaniards and Aztecs, the ranking prince
of the Aztecs, Cuauhtémoc, led an unsuccessful resistance, and was killed. The Spanish conquest of Mexico
had been completed.

AZUELA, MARIANO. 1873-1952. A doctor by training, he
gained worldwide fame as a novelist and wrote what is
probably the most famous novel of the Mexican Revolution, Los de abajo (The Underdogs), in 1916. Among
other works, he wrote Mala yerba, published in English
with the title of Marcela.

AZUELA RIVERA, MARIANO. Born March 15, 1904, in
Lagos de Moreno, Jalisco. Law degree at the National
Autonomous University of Mexico (UNAM). The son of
the famous novelist Mariano Azuela. Professor of law
at the University of San Luis Potosí, then at UNAM 1930-
58. Senator from the state of Jalisco 1958-60. Justice
of the federal Supreme Court 1951-57 and 1960-72. Author of authoritative books and articles on the writ of
amparo or injunctive relief. His legal commentaries have
become very important in Mexican legal literature involving the entire appellate system.

- B -

BAEZA, GUILLERMO. Born on June 20, 1937, in Guadalajara, Jalisco. Law degree from the University of Guadalajara. A leader in the state of Jalisco of the conservative National Action Party (PAN) since 1960, serving as
Jalisco's PAN secretary general and then state chairman.
A Deputy in the federal Congress during 1970-73 and
1976-79

BAJA CALIFORNIA DEL NORTE. One of the 31 states of
the Mexican federal republic. It has an area of 70,113
square kilometers. BCN occupies the northern half of
the Baja California peninsula which extends 1,100 miles
from the United States border. BCN divides from the

state of Baja California del Sur at the 28th Parallel, approximately 600 miles from the border. Its 1976 population totaled 1.3 million. Its capital is Mexicali. BCN was a territory until achieving the status of statehood in 1953.

BAJA CALIFORNIA DEL SUR. One of the 31 states of the Mexican federal republic. It has an area of 73,677 square kilometers. BCS occupies the southern half of the Baja California peninsula. A paved highway from Tijuana at the United States border extending 1,088 miles to Cape San Lucas at the tip of BCS opened on December 1, 1973. BCS was a territory until becoming a state on October 10, 1974. Its 1976 population totaled 182,000. Its capital is La Paz, a fishing port and resort.

BALBOA, PRAXEDES. Born in 1904 in Ciudad Victoria, Tamaulipas. Law degree from the National Autonomous University of Mexico 1925. A leader in the Institutional Revolutionary Party, he was a key formulator of federal labor and agrarian reform laws. A Deputy in the federal Congress 1930-32 and 1935-37. Governor of the state of Tamaulipas 1963-69.

BALBUENA, BERNARDO DE. 1568-1627. A priest who eventually became Bishop of Puerto Rico, he is recognized as the first Mexican poet. His most famous work is La grandeza mexicana in which he describes most eloquently Mexico City, which for him was the most beautiful city of Hispanic America.

BALDERAS, LUCAS. 1797-1847. A military figure who became famous for his savage defense of Mexico City against the Americans. He was killed at the Battle of Molino del Rey and one of the principal streets of downtown Mexico City is named in his honor.

BANCO DE COMERCIO. The largest privately-owned chain of banks in Mexico with branches in cities and towns throughout the republic. This bank's credit card is accepted by retail stores throughout Mexico displaying Bancomer card signs.

BANCO DE MEXICO. Established in 1925 as the government's central bank in charge of issuing currency, operating the mint for coins, holding the national treasury, and functioning as a federal reserve system for all other public and private banks.

BANCO NACIONAL CINEMATOGRAFICO. Established in 1941 as the government's bank for extending loans and for investing in the motion picture industry.

BANCO NACIONAL DE COMERCIO EXTERIOR. Established in 1937 as the government's bank for foreign trade, it coordinates its activities with Nacional Financiera, the government's development bank, and with the Ministries of Foreign Relations, Commerce, and Industrial Development.

BANCO NACIONAL DE CREDITO AGRICOLA. Established in 1956 as the government's bank for agricultural credit to develop the farming, livestock, fishing, forestry, and other rural sectors of the economy. It was absorbed into the Bank for Rural Credit in 1977.

BANCO NACIONAL DE CREDITO EJIDAL. Established in 1935 as the government's bank for loans to communal farms (ejidos) which belong to villages. It was absorbed into the Bank for Rural Credit in 1977.

BANCO NACIONAL DE CREDITO RURAL. Established by the government in 1977 to develop both individually-owned and communal farms and ranches, combining the functions of the former Ejido and Agricultural Credit banks of encouraging agrarian reform through loans.

BANCO NACIONAL DE DESARROLLO PESQUERO. Established June 18, 1979, by the government as the National Bank of Fishing Development, to make loans for the fishing industry cooperatives and other fishing enterprises. The former Cooperative Development loans became an agency within the Ministry of Patrimony and Industrial Development.

BANCO NACIONAL DE FOMENTO COOPERATIVO. Established in 1941 as the government's bank for developing cooperatives, it was absorbed into a new National Bank of Fishing Development in June 1979.

BANCO NACIONAL DE MEXICO. Not to be confused with the government's Banco de México, the BNM is the second largest privately-owned chain of commercial banks in Mexico, with branches in cities throughout the republic. Consumers use this bank's Banamex credit card in retail stores throughout Mexico.

BANCO NACIONAL DE OBRAS Y SERVICIOS PUBLICAS. Established by the government in 1933 as the Urban Savings and Public Works Bank, it took its present name of National Bank of Public Works and Services, popularly known as Banobras, in 1966. It makes loans to municipal and state governments for the construction, operation, or expansion of public works.

BANCO NACIONAL DEL EJERCITO Y LA ARMADA. Established by the government in 1946, this National Army and Navy Bank makes loans for home mortgages to members of the armed forces and for businesses operated by retired military personnel.

BANKERS ASSOCIATION. The Asociación de Banqueros Mexicanos (Association of Mexican Bankers) was established in August 1928 to give all commercial banks an officially recognized voice in dealing with the government and with industry. The ABM cooperates with the Employers Federation, the Federation of Industrial Chambers, and the Federation of Chambers of Commerce in presenting management's views and needs before the government and in negotiations with organized labor. In Mexico's mixed public-private economy, commercial banks and savings institutions are partners with the government banks in developing the economy, paralleling what the government's development bank, Nacional Financiera, does in terms of investments and loans.

BAÑUELOS, JUAN. Born in 1932 in Tuxtla Gutiérrez, Chiapas. He studied humanities at the National University of Mexico. During much of his writing career, he has been employed as an editor for leading book publishers in Mexico City, while writing for Revista Mexicana de Literatura and other literary journals. With the publication in 1965 of his book of poems and essays, Ocupación de la palabra, he gained national recognition as a poet, literary critic, and essayist.

BARCENA, MARIANO. 1848-1898. Scientist. He frequently worked as a harness maker, although he studied engineering, botany and the fine arts. His greatest accomplishment was in the field of astronomy and meteorology. In 1877, he inaugurated the finest accomplishment of his life, the Astronomical and Meteorological Observatory.

BARRA, FRANCISCO LEON DE LA. 1863-1939. Catholic leader and statesman. Minister of Foreign Affairs in the Porfirio Díaz regime and provisional president from May to November, 1911, after the resignation of Díaz.

BARRAGAN, JUAN. Born on August 30, 1894, in San Luis Potosí, and died there on September 28, 1974. Joined the Revolution in 1913 and became an army general in the 1920's. A Senator during 1918-20 and a federal Deputy during 1964-67 and 1970-73. He helped found the opposition Party of the Authentic Mexican Revolution (PARM) in 1954 and served as party president during 1957-74.

BARRAGAN, MIGUEL. 1789-1836. He became President of Mexico in 1835, for a period of a little over a year, but his mandate was cut short when he was stricken with typhus, a disease which ultimately caused his death. While still a general, his forces occupied the fortress of San Juan de Ulúa, thus freeing the last area of Mexican territory from the Spaniards.

BARREDA, GABINO. 1818-1881. Mexican educator who studied under Aguste Comte, the founder of positivism. He was a strong adherent of positivism and worked closely with Benito Juárez in favoring science as opposed to the humanities. In 1867 Juárez named him director of the newly created National Preparatory School and commissioned him to reorganize the country's secondary school system. His scientific and liberal influence still is evident in Mexican education.

BARRERA, JUAN DE LA. 1828-1847. One of the six Niños Héroes (Heroic Children) who died in the defense of Chapultepec Castle against the Americans. He was commissioned a lieutenant just before the American invasion of Mexico City and was put in charge of constructing fortifications in Chapultepec Park. He died in combat, while leading the defense of his country from the fortifications he himself had designed and constructed.

BARROS SIERRA, JAVIER. Born on February 25, 1915, in

the Federal District and died there on August 15, 1971. Civil engineering degree and master's degree in mathematics from the National Autonomous University of Mexico (UNAM). Dean of the UNAM School of Engineering 1955-58. Minister of Public Works in the cabinet of President Adolfo López Mateos 1958-64. President (Rector) of UNAM during 1966-70. He had the challenge of heading the National University during the extended student riots from July 26 to October 2, 1968, in which a left-led group unsuccessfully tried to force the Mexican government to postpone hosting the 1968 Olympics in Mexico City.

BASES ORGANICAS DE 1843. A conservative, centralist constitution promulgated on June 13, 1843. Its complete title was Bases de Organización Política de la República Mexicana. It permitted the election of Santa Anna in 1844, this being its main accomplishment. In 1846 it was discarded and the federalist Constitution of 1824 was re-adopted.

BASSOLS, NARCISO. Born in 1898. Mexican statesman, politician, educator and diplomat. His most important post was that of Secretary of Education in the Rodríguez administration and he carried out extensive educational reforms in 1933, extending federal control over state schools and incorporating rural school principles to the urban area. He was Secretary of Finance under Cárdenas 1935-36 and at various times was minister to Great Britain and France. He was a delegate to the League of Nations and in 1945 was ambassador to the Soviet Union. His most famous works are La ley agraria and Garantías y amparo.

BEJAR, FELICIANO. Born in 1920 in Jiquilpan, Mexico, he is a painter who also sculpts in crystal, plastic and metal. He has had little formal art education, but the artists in his village furthered the development of his talents. "Paisaje" and "Caja Tosca" are among his more famous paintings.

BENAVENTE, FRAY TORIBIO DE. Sixteenth-century missionary and historian, he adopted the name of Motolinía because it was the first indigenous word that he had heard. Like Las Casas, he constantly fought to improve the lot of the Indians, but did not believe in answering

violence with violence. He preached in many parts of
Mexico and Central America and took part in the founding
of the city of Puebla. He was a prolific writer of history, one of his most famous works being Historia de los
indios de la Nueva España. He died in 1568 and is buried
in the Monastery of San Francisco.

BERMUDEZ, ANTONIO J. Born in 1892 in Chihuahua. May-
or of Ciudad Juárez, Chihuahua, 1942-45. Director General of the government's oil industry entity, Pemex, during 1946-58. He directed the government's National Border Program of developing new industries along the border with the United States during 1961-70, encouraging
the establishment of assembly plants to create new payrolls for semi-skilled workers.

BETETA, MARIO RAMON. Born on July 7, 1925, in the
Federal District. Law degree from the National Autonomous University of Mexico (UNAM) 1948. Master's degree in economics, University of Wisconsin 1950. Professor of economics at UNAM 1951-59. A formulator of
structural changes in the Institutional Revolutionary Party
in 1972. He has been a longtime key adviser for the
Bank of Mexico. He was Assistant Minister of Finance
during 1970-74, and then became Minister of Finance and
Public Credit during 1975-76. Under President José López Portillo he has been director of the government investment corporation Sociedad Mexicana de Crédito Industrial since December 1976, which gives the government
stock holdings in newspapers, television stations, and
several manufacturing industries.

BETETA, RAMON. Born on October 7, 1901, in Mexico
City, where he died on October 15, 1965. Uncle of
Mario Ramón Beteta. Economics degree from the University of Texas. Ph.D. from the University of Mexico.
Ambassador to Italy, then to Greece. Editor of the daily
newspaper Novedades 1958-64. Minister of Finance 1946-
52.

BIEBRICH, CARLOS ARMANDO. Born on November 19,
1939, in Sahuaripa, Sonora. Law degree from the University of Sonora. Sonora chairman of the Institutional
Revolutionary Party. Assistant Minister of Governación
(Interior) under President Echeverría 1970-73. Governor
of Sonora 1973-75. He was forced to resign in October

1975 after he had state police remove land squatters and seven were killed and 14 injured. He was indicted for misusing 36 million pesos while governor, but the charges were dropped in 1977.

BONAMPAK. Archeological site in southern Mexico known for its murals. The name itself means "painted walls."

BONFIL, RAMON G. Born in 1905 in Hidalgo state. An educator, he directed the adult literacy campaign for the Ministry of Education during the 1960's and was director of teacher education for the ministry 1970-76.

BORDER PROGRAMS. The National Border Program or Programa Nacional Fronterizo was established by the government in 1961 to develop sales of Mexican-made products which compete with United States-made products in the borderlands. A separate Border Industrial Program helps develop assembly plants in Mexican cities along the U.S. border for products from U.S. electronics, musical instruments, and other firms which furnish the parts and reimport the finished products into the U.S. at reduced U.S. tariffs. These plants are located from Tijuana, B.C.N., to Matamoros, Tamaulipas.

BOULBON, RAOUSSET. A French soldier of fortune who invaded Guaymas in an unsuccessful attempt to turn the state of Sonora into an independent country. Defeated by the Mexican General José María Yáñez, he was shot by a firing squad on July 13, 1854.

BRACAMONTES, LUIS ENRIQUE. Born on June 22, 1923, in Talpalpa, Jalisco. Engineering degree from the National Autonomous University (UNAM) 1946. Master's degree. Professor of engineering at UNAM 1947-52. Director General of the National Commission of Secondary Roads 1952-64. Minister of Public Works in the Echeverría cabinet 1970-76. Mexico's leading civil engineer, he has been the consultant for the National Railroads, and for the construction of several university campuses, public and private housing projects, and leading industrial construction corporations.

BRACERO. A field worker on farms or ranches.

BRACERO PROGRAMS. From 1942 through 1964, the United

States and Mexico had a Bracero Treaty under which hundreds of thousands of farm workers were brought into the
United States for six-month periods to harvest crops or
otherwise work in agriculture. Throughout the 1970's,
millions of illegal or undocumented migrants have come
from Mexico to work in agriculture throughout the United
States. With only 7 percent of Mexico's territory under
cultivation with natural rainfall and another 7 percent with
irrigation, unemployment in rural areas in the 1970's
ranged from 20 to 40 percent. In 1979, half of the republic's five million farmers produced only 4 percent of
the total agricultural output on inefficient small holdings.
Despite the emphasis on communal farms by the institutionalized social Revolution, the larger privately-owned
farms produce most of Mexico's food. As mechanization
increases, jobs for braceros stop increasing, yet the rural work force has continued to grow, intensifying the
migrations northward and into the slums of Mexican cities.

BRAVO, LEONARDO. 1764-1812. Revolutionary leader. A
    Creole and father of the famous revolutionary leader,
    Nicolás Bravo. A follower of Morelos, he distinguished
    himself as a capable military leader and administrator,
    governing well the province of Tecpán. After being cap-
    tured by the Spaniards, Bravo was executed in 1812. He
    was declared a national hero in 1823.

BRAVO, NICOLAS. 1786-1854. Revolutionary, politician and
    President of the Republic, 1839-1844. Previous to this
    he had fought for Mexican independence during the time
    of Morelos. He fell prisoner of the Spaniards in 1817,
    but since he previously had freed 300 Spanish prisoners,
    the viceroy allowed him to go free, at which time he re-
    joined the insurgents. Bravo did spend a period of exile
    in South America and fought under Simón Bolívar. Santa
    Anna recalled him from exile in 1839. After his presi-
    dency he was responsible for the defense of Chapultepec
    against the Americans in the War of 1846-1848 and after
    being taken prisoner retired from political life. He died
    in Chilpancingo in the State of Guerrero.

BRAVO AHUJA, VICTOR. Born on February 20, 1918, in
    Tuxtepec, Oaxaca. Engineering degree from the National
    Polytechnic Institute (IPN) in 1940. Master's degree from
    the University of Michigan. Professor of engineering at

IPN, then at the Monterrey Institute of Technology
(ITESM). Director of the ITESM Summer School 1951-
55, then Dean of Engineering 1955-58, the President of
ITESM 1959-60. Governor of the state of Oaxaca 1968-
70. Minister of Public Education 1970-76. He is one
of Mexico's leading aeronautical engineers and a developer
of graduate education in engineering throughout Mexico.

BRUJA. A witch or mystic woman who practices folk magic
against evil spirits among superstitious rural and village
peasants, especially in Indian communities. If she also
practices folk medicine, she is called a "curandera."
For fees, she casts spells on enemies and feelings of
love on suitors.

BRUJO. A wizard or sorcerer often consulted in Mexican
villages. His advice, based on Indian myths, often in-
fluences the decisions peasants make in solving daily social problems.

BUCARELI, CONFERENCE OF. Conference held in 1923 in
Mexico City in which the United States agreed to recognize the government of General Alvaro Obregón, in return for which Mexico agreed not to apply the Constitution
of 1917 retroactively against the foreign oil companies.
In this manner the latter were able to continue to control
the petroleum industry in Mexico. This situation continued until 1938, when all private oil interests were nationalized.

BUCARELI Y URSUA, ANTONIO MARIA DE. 1717-1779. In
1771 he became Viceroy of New Spain and carried through
measures such as reducing the size of the army and pac-
ifying the Indians on the northern frontier of New Spain.
Under his administration the frontier of New Spain was
pushed north of what is today San Francisco, California.
He gave new impetus to the mining industry, allowing the
owners to form a more powerful organization. He was
also active in constructing hospitals and improving the lot
of the mentally ill. Free trade between Spanish America
and Spain was also established during his administration,
bringing benefits to New Spain. He is buried in Guadalajara.

BUENA VISTA, BATTLE OF. The Mexicans know it as the
Battle of La Angostura. One of the most important bat-

tles of the 1846-1848 war between Mexico and the United
States. In February 1847, Santa Anna and a force of
some 25,000 reached the site of La Angostura, near the
Hacienda of Buena Vista, in the vicinity of Saltillo. In
spite of the forced march from San Luis Potosí, considerably to the south, the Mexican soldiers fought well and
might have been victorious, but Santa Anna, after capturing two American flags, broke off the engagement and
hurried to Mexico City, where he proclaimed a decisive
victory. General Winfield Scott returned to Washington,
where he also proclaimed victory. It appears that the
overwhelming American artillery fire was decisive. Although the 5,000-man American force was outnumbered
five to one, they inflicted 3,000 casualties, themselves
suffering just a little over 700.

BULLFIGHTING. Bullfighting, known as the fiesta brava, was
brought to Mexico by Spaniards in the 16th century. Until the 1940's it remained a major public entertainment,
technically distinguished from sports as a spectacle of
life and death. Since the 1950's, bullfighting has been
as much an attraction for American tourists as for Mexicans, who much prefer soccer, basketball, baseball,
track, tennis, jai alai, and volleyball in terms of atten-
dance or participation. The Plaza de México in Mexico
City remains the largest bullring in the republic, which
on Sunday afternoons also finds approximately 20 to 30 of
the 135 rings in use each week during the season from
October into May. In terms of betting, far more money
is wagered on soccer, horseracing, or the other major
sporting events in one week than for the entire season of
bullfighting. Ranches which specialize in producing
fierce, fighting bulls for the ring have contracted their
operations since the 1960's, with the quality of the fighting animals being diminished. The bullfighters, cape
handlers, mounted picadors who handle the lances, and
the others associated with the performances are unionized
and now have pension funds, but only hundreds of youths
now apprentice as contrasted with more than a thousand
a year in the earlier decades of this century.

BULNES, FRANCISCO. 1847-1924. Mexican engineer, essayist and engineer. He was a prominent figure in the
Porfirio Díaz regime and gained favor with the latter by
belittling previous national figures, such as Benito Juárez. His best-known work is El porvenir de las naciones

hispano-americanos ante las conquistas de Europa y los Estados Unidos (The Future of the Hispanic-American Nations in the Face of the Recent Conquests of Europe and the United States). He was especially famous for articulating the científico point of view. Some of his other works are El verdadero Díaz (The Real Díaz) and La verdad completa sobre México (The Full Truth About Mexico).

BUSTAMANTE, ANASTASIO. 1780-1853. Born in Jiquilpán, Michoacán. Originally a general who fought on the Spanish side against the independence movement led by Hidalgo and Morelos, he later supported Iturbide and the Plan of Iguala in 1821. Served as vice-president under Gómez Pedraza and Vicente Guerrero. Involved in the revolt against Guerrero and became president of Mexico from January 1830 to August 1832, when he was driven out by the liberals under Santa Anna and forced into exile to England. He was later recalled during another period of conservative rule and served as president from 1837 to 1841. Generally considered honest and well-intentioned, but was frequently controlled by stronger men. He was finally overthrown in 1841 by a military coup led by Santa Anna and Paredes y Arrillaga.

BUSTAMANTE, CARLOS MARIA DE. 1774-1848. Born in Oaxaca. A liberal Mexican statesman, he was also a soldier, historian and publisher, being editor of the first daily newspaper in his country, El Diario de Méjico. He was an officer in Mexico's first war of independence and also served as secretary to Iturbide in 1821. Considered an outstanding historian of the revolutionary period in Mexico. Among his works are Cuadro histórico de la revolución de América (An Historic Picture of the Revolution in America) and Apuntes para la historia del general Santa Anna (Notes About the History of the Government of General Santa Anna).

- C -

C. T. M. see CONFEDERACION DE TRABAJADORES MEXICANOS

"EL CABALLITO" see TOLSA, MANUEL

CABEZA DE VACA see NUÑEZ CABEZA DE VACA, ALVAR

CABILDO.   A cabildo (town council) was an entity brought to
    Mexico by Spanish colonial administrators.   During the
    1810-21 struggle for independence from Spain, the Mexi-
    cans with European-style administrative experience in lim-
    ited self-government were cabildo members.   From 1822
    on, independent Mexico replaced town councils with muni-
    cipal councils.

CABRERA, LUIS.   A lawyer who furnished much of the ideo-
    logical thinking of the early days of the Mexican Revolu-
    tion.   He not only fought against Porfirio Díaz, but was
    an implacable foe of Victoriano Huerta.

CABRERA, MIGUEL.   1695-1798.   A painter born in the city
    of Oaxaca of Spanish parents.   As a boy, his talents came
    to the attention of the Archbishop of Mexico City, José
    Manuel Rubio Salina, and the latter protected and encour-
    aged the young painter.   His specialty was religious
    painting and he completed numerous works.   Among his
    more famous works are "La Vida de Santo Domingo" and
    "La Vida de San Ignacio."   He died in Mexico City.

CABRILLO, JUAN RODRIGUEZ DE.   Portuguese explorer who
    went to Mexico with Pánfilo de Narvaez in 1520 and was
    with Cortés when he conquered Tenochtitlán (Mexico City)
    in 1521.   Viceroy Antonio de Mendoza sent him to look
    for the "Strait of Anián," which purportedly crossed Mex-
    ico, but he ended up in 1542 discovering San Diego Bay.
    He died on the island of San Miguel in the Santa Barbara
    Channel on January 3, 1543.

CACAO.   The cacao tree is claimed by Mexico as one of its
    original contributions to the world.   However, most
    sources simply state that it is a New World contribution.
    The principal area where it was cultivated during colonial
    times was around the territory of Caracas, Venezuela.
    The cacao bean was used as money by the Aztecs and the
    drink made from it was a favorite of the Indians in Mex-
    ico.   Unfortunately, around the end of the 16th century
    the price had risen so sharply that the Indians could no
    longer afford to buy these beans.

CACIQUE.   A Nahuatl word from the Aztecs meaning "chief";
    a cacique in modern Mexico is a local or regional politi-
    cal boss, supporting the dominant federal officials in Mex-
    ico City in general but exerting his own local influence
    until directly challenged by the federal government.

CACIQUISMO. What Americans refer to as "boss rule,"
i. e., the wielding of power by one person through his own
political machine. Until recently, this phenomenon played
a significant part in Mexican political life and even today
cannot be totally ignored. However, the last time that
caciquismo manifested itself in an overt, violent manner
on any big scale was the unsuccessful revolt of General
Saturnino Cedillo against the government of General
Lázaro Cárdenas in 1938.

CAFE, INSTITUTO NACIONAL DEL. The National Institute
of Coffee is the government's regulatory agency for controlling coffee prices, exports, and domestic distribution
by private producers. In addition, the government has
invested in coffee production.

CAJERO. A fiscal officer in state or local government who
audits the revenues collected by the tax officials.

CAL Y MAYOR, RAFAEL. Born on September 10, 1923, in
Chiapas. With an engineering degree from the National
University and graduate study at Yale University, he directed the program of drivers training throughout Mexico
from 1964 to 1970 and has been a leading consultant on
highway construction and safety. He heads a large construction corporation. He popularized the need for formal training for both public and private drivers of automobiles and trucks throughout Mexico.

CALLEJA DEL REY, FELIX MARIA. 1753-1828. Spanish
general who was awarded the title of Conde de Calderón
because of his decisive victory over Hidalgo at the bridge
of the same name near Guadalajara in 1811. An extremely capable military man, he also had the reputation of
being very cruel, hence his nickname of "the butcher."
He defeated Morelos in 1814, thus ending for practical
purposes the initial phase of the struggle for Mexican independence. As Viceroy of New Spain, from 1813 to
1816, he successfully defended New Spain, reorganizing
and strengthening the army.

CALLES, PLUTARCO ELIAS. 1877-1945. Born in Guaymas,
Sonora, he was a teacher before taking part in the Mexican Revolution. As early as 1904 he published a newspaper attacking Porfirio Díaz, for which he was forced
to leave his native city. He later became active in the

Anti-reelectionist Party and fought on the side of Obregón
against Huerta and Villa.   He rose rapidly in power, being Governor of Sonora in 1917, Secretary of Gobernación
(a post frequently held by politicians before becoming
president) in the Obregón administration, 1920-24 and
President, 1924-28.   While president, he instituted many
reforms in public education and health.   Some of his
principal accomplishments were establishment of the Bank
of Agricultural Credit and the National Agricultural Commission.   He also set up the Bank of Mexico.   He set
off the Cristero rebellion by attempting to enforce the
provisions of the Constitution of 1917 which require the
State to register priests.   This rebellion resulted in violence and bloodshed, most churches being without priests
for three years.   Under his leadership, he united all political factions into one all-powerful group, the Partido
Nacional Revolucionario.   He appointed himself Jefe Máx-
imo de la Revolución (Supreme Leader of the Revolution)
and was the unofficial head of Mexico until Cárdenas
forced him into exile in 1936.   He returned to Mexico in
1941, but stayed out of politics.   He died in California
in 1945.

CAMARA DE COMERCIO.   Each local Chamber of Commerce
in Mexico, under a 1941 federal law, must federate with
the National Federation of Chambers of Commerce (Confederación de Cámaras Nacionales de Comercio or CON-
CANACO) as the organized voice of retail management
in negotiating with the government or with labor unions.

CAMARA DE DIPUTADOS FEDERALES.   The lower house of
the federal Congress, the Chamber of Deputies has grown
in size since its creation by the 1917 Constitution.   The
162 congressional districts, based on population, were
increased in 1964 to 178, in 1973 to 194, and in 1979 to
300.   In 1964, a system of minority-party seats in addition to the congressional district seats overwhelmingly
won by the dominant Institutional Revolutionary Party
(PRI) was created.   For 2.5 percent of the total vote, a
minority party got five Deputy seats, plus one seat for
each additional half of one percent.   In 1972 the requirements were lowered to 1.5 percent of the vote, with additional seats up to twenty-five for extra half percentages.
Under the 1979 reform, one hundred minority-party seats
based on proportional representation were created, with
six minority parties on the ballot.   Each voter gets two

ballots, one for congressional district and one for proportional representation.   Each candidate runs with a
suplente or substitute who serves if a vacancy occurs.
The chamber operates through standing committees.   Congress is dominated by the power of the federal executive
branch.   A Deputy's term runs three years and two consecutive terms are prohibited.

CAMARA DE DIPUTADOS LOCALES.   The Chamber of Local
Deputies is the State Legislature found in each of the 31
states of the republic.   Each Legislature is unicameral,
the only Senate in Mexico being the federal one.   The
size of the legislatures vary from 11 to 23 members,
with the term of office running three years.   Carrying
out the "no re-election" principle of Francisco Madero
for the Revolution, two consecutive terms are not permitted by any of the state constitutions.   After an inter-
vening term, a former Deputy can run again.   The powers of the Legislature are weak, with the Governor of
the state dominating over the Legislature, and the federal
government dominating over the Governor.   The chief
power of the state legislature is to approve or change the
budgets of each municipal government within the state.

CAMARA INDUSTRIAL.   Under a 1941 federal law, every
manufacturing or industrial corporation or wholesaler
must join the Industrial Chamber of its own industry.
Every cement producer must join the Cement Industrial
Chamber, every shoe manufacturer must join the Shoe
Industrial Chamber, every radio or television station must
join the Industrial Chamber of Broadcasters, and so on.
These industrywide chambers are federated into the National Federation of Industrial Chambers (Confederación
de Cámaras Industriales or CONCAMIN), the voice of
organized industrial management in negotiations with the
government or with labor unions.   The amount of dues
an industrial chamber pays determines its number of
votes within a CONCAMIN assembly.

CAMARILLA.   A camarilla is a political clique headed by a
successful politician who holds a government position.
His entourage can be horizontal among peers who were
classmates in school and vertical among rising administrators and their trusted assistants.   A camarilla is
based on close friendships resembling extended family
relationships.   As the leader of a camarilla rises in

government or in the Institutional Revolutionary Party
(PRI), he tries to have his camarilla associates promoted
into his higher-level office.   Eventually, a camarilla associate attains a high enough government position to lead
his own camarilla.   Thus Mexican public life is interlaced
with political cliques.

CAMINO REAL.   Camino Real (Royal Road) referred to any
major road built by the Spaniards during the colonial era
(1520-1821) to link Mexico City to provincial cities and
towns and to all ports.

CAMINOS Y PUENTES.   This federal government agency,
Federal Roads and Bridges of Connected Revenues and
Services (Caminos y Puentes Federales de Ingresos y
Servicios Conexos), serves both the Ministry of Communications and Transportation and the Ministry of Public
Works.   The agency builds, repairs, and administers all
federal highways and bridges and through intergovernmen-
tal laws, most state and local roads, including the dis-
bursement of allocated funds and the collection of toll
road revenues.

CAMPECHE (CITY).   The capital city of the state of Campeche, located on the Gulf of Mexico coast of the Yucatán
peninsula, 100 miles southwest of the city of Mérida.
Its 1976 population totaled 71,400.   Not until 1951 did the
railroad connect it to Mexico City.   Its thick walls facing
the sea were built during 1686-1704 against pirate attacks.
Since the discovery in 1974 of vast reserves of petroleum
in Campeche state, the city's retail commerce and port
activities have steadily increased.

CAMPECHE (STATE).   One of the 31 states of the republic,
its area covers 51,833 square kilometers.   Its 1976 population totaled 337,000.   Campeche lies south of the state
of Yucatán and west of the state of Quintana Roo, and
with both it shares the Yucatán peninsula in southeastern
Mexico.   Oil, shrimp, corn, and sugar cane are its chief
products.   It has year-round tropical climate and a southern interior of forests not connected to the Gulf Coast by
roads.

CAMPERO, JOSE.   An army leader from Colima in the Constitutionalist forces in 1913 who remained loyal to President Venustiano Carranza into 1920.   He became Governor

of the state of Colima in 1935, later serving as a Deputy
and then executive officer of the Senate in the federal
Congress. As a newspaper writer in Chihuahua and San
Luis Potosí from the 1930's through the 1960's, he built
support for the Institutional Revolutionary Party in northern and central Mexico.

CAMPESINO. A campesino in Mexico is a peasant-farmer.
In his name the 1910 fighting erupted for a social re-
form--the Revolution, with the slogan "Land, Bread, and
Justice." But the institutionalized Revolution has benefited the urban workers more. Campesinos constitute
one-third of the Mexican labor force and even in the
1970's used farming methods and implements lacking modern efficiency. After a half century of agrarian reforms,
campesinos in general faced subsistent living standards
and dietary, housing, and clothing standards half as ade-
quate as those of urban Mexicans. During the period
1960 through 1979, the agricultural sector of the economy
has grown an average of only 2 percent a year, one-third
to one-half the growth rate of industry during that period.
With one campesino in four unemployed since 1970, migration to cities and to the United States has increased
steadily.

CAMPESINO NATIONAL FEDERATION. The National Campesino Federation--Confederación Nacional Campesina
(CNC)--was established in 1936 by Mexican President
Lázaro Cárdenas to give peasants an organized voice for
negotiating benefits and aid from the government. The
CNC also became the core unit of the agrarian sector of
the dominant Institutional Revolutionary Party (PRI). The
CNC lobbies for agrarian reforms, bank loans and credits, government subsidies for fertilizers, and other needs
of campesinos.

CAMPILLO SAINZ, JOSE. Born on October 9, 1917, in Mexico City. Law degree from the National University.
During the 1950's and 1960's he became a leading spokesman for Mexican industrialists and business executives,
heading the National Center of Productivity and the Committee of International Activities of Private Enterprise.
After serving as director of the Mining Industry Chamber,
he headed the National Federation of Industrial Chambers.
He was Minister of Industry and Commerce in the cabinet of President Luis Echeverría 1970-76.

CAMPOS SALAS, OCTAVIANO. Born on March 22, 1916, in
San Luis Potosí. Economics degree from the National
Autonomous University of Mexico (UNAM). Graduate
study at the University of Chicago. Dean of the UNAM
School of Economics. After heading the National Teach-
ers Union, he was an administrator for the Census Bu-
reau, then manager of the Bank of Mexico. Minister of
Industry and Commerce during 1964-70. As an investor
in Automex, the Mexican corporation which manufactures
Dodge automobiles and trucks and Chrysler products, he
helped develop the automobile manufacturing industry in
Mexico.

CANACINTRA. The National Chamber of Manufacturing In-
dustries--Cámara Nacional de las Industrias de Trans-
formación (CANACINTRA or CNIT)--was established by
federal law in April 1942 as the organized voice of newer
industrialists who did not have their own chambers in the
National Federation of Industrial Chambers (CONCAMIN).
CANACINTRA has membership in CONCAMIN but also
negotiates autonomously with the government and with labor unions on behalf of industrialists.

CANALIZO, VALENTIN. 1794-1860. He was born in Monterrey and originally fought on the side of Santa Anna
against the insurgents, but eventually ended up supporting
them. He presided over the court-martial which condemned President Vicente Guerrero to death. Canalizo
was a confidant of Santa Anna.

CANDELARIA, VIRGIN OF. Among the Indians of the state
of Jalisco a special interpretation of the Virgin Mary involved a statue in a church at San Juan de Los Lagos in
1542. This Virgin of the Candelaria for centuries has
been given credit for performing miracles and remains
a part of the folk belief within the Catholic Church among
rural and village peasants. In February various Indian
and mestizo (Indian-Spanish) communities throughout Mexico hold special dances, fiestas, and prayers honoring the
Virgin of Candelaria.

CARACAS CONFERENCE. This was the Tenth Inter-American
Conference which met at Caracas, Venezuela in 1954.
The resolution which attracted the most attention was of-
ficially known as the Declaration of Solidarity for the
Preservation of the Political Integrity of the American

States against International Communist Intervention. It
amounted to a criticism of the leftist-leaning Arbenz government of Guatemala. It passed, 17-1, with Guatemala
dissenting and Argentina and Mexico abstaining.

CARBAJAL SEBASTIAN, ENRIQUE. Painter and sculptor.
It was only in 1965 that Carbajal Sebastián began to study
painting and sculpture and he already has attained considerable fame in Europe and the Western Hemisphere.

CARBALLIDO, EMILIO. Born in 1925 in Córdoba, Veracruz.
He studied drama at the National University, at universities in the United States, and in 1950 as a Rockefeller
Institute scholar studied and wrote in Europe and Asia.
With the publishing of his play Rosalba in 1950 and the
staging of his play La danza in 1955 he became a noted
Mexican playwright. His many theater plays stress middle class psychological problems. His 1958 play Medusa
brought him the most national and international fame and
prizes.

CARBALLO, EMMANUEL. Born in 1929 in Guadalajara. He
was a doctoral student at the Colegio de México graduate
school 1955-57. He co-founded with Carlos Fuentes the
Revista Mexicana de Literatura. A noted short story
writer famed for his 1965 book of stories, El cuento
mexicano del siglo XX.

CARDENAS, LAZARO. 1895-1970. Born in Jiquilpán, Michoacán. Fought in the Mexican Revolution, where he
achieved the rank of general. Steadily rose in politics,
being Governor of Michoacán, Minister of the Interior,
and Minister of War and the Navy before he became President, 1934-40. Although not possessed of a great amount
of formal education, he was regarded as honest and enjoyed the respect and confidence of workers and peasants.
Although hand-picked by Calles to be the next president,
Cárdenas succeeded in crushing his power and exiling
him. Cárdenas emphasized agrarian reform and during
his presidency approximately 40,000,000 acres of land
were expropriated and given to peasant ejidos. The opposition enjoyed freedom of speech and Cárdenas's term
marks the last time that there was true freedom of the
press in Mexico. The labor movement was organized into the Confederación de Trabajadores Mexicanos (1936)
and received favored treatment in labor disputes with

foreign and domestic management. He signed into law
the first minimum daily salary in 1935 and expropriated
the railroads in 1938. He laid the basis of Mexico's
economic independence by nationalizing the oil industry
in March of 1938. In his later years he became more
and more an advocate of revolutionary change and was
awarded the Stalin Peace Prize. He withdrew from the
Institutional Revolutionary Party in 1961 and urged greater
social change than that which was taking place. During
the Bay of Pigs invasion he expressed desires to go to
Cuba to support Fidel Castro, but was not permitted by
the government of Mexico. Although controversial, he
is regarded as one of Mexico's greatest post-revolutionary
presidents.

CARLOS IV, EQUESTRIAN STATUE OF see TOLSA, MAN-
UEL

CARNIVAL. The annual pre-Lent celebrations, culminating
in Mardi Gras dances, parades, and parties before Ash
Wednesday begins the Lent period. In Mazatlán, Acapulco, and Veracruz, ports catering to tourists, resort activities prevail. In Mexico City and major provincial cities, carnival celebrations center in private clubs. In
small-town and rural Mexico, village carnivals are most
intense in Indian communities, where folk dancers in
bright costumes and fireworks vie with special theatrical
presentations and band concerts.

CARRANZA, VENUSTIANO. 1859-1920. He was born in
Coahuila and supported Madero in the Mexican Revolution.
He claimed the presidency as early as 1914, but was disputed by Villa and Zapata. He steered a middle course
in his relations with the United States, allowing the
Pershing expedition to enter Mexico against Villa, but
remaining neutral during World War I. His hold on the
presidency was stronger from 1917 to 1920 and he made
plans to be reelected, his idea being to govern through
an obscure supporter by the name of Ignacio Bonillas and
then run for a new term of office at the end of Bonillas's
presidency. Obregón and Calles rose up in arms, and
Carranza was forced to leave Mexico City, hoping to
reach Veracruz and voluntary exile with his family and
friends. His efforts were unsuccessful and he was ambushed and murdered in May 1920.

CARRERA, MARTIN. 1806-1871. General and President of

Mexico from August 14, 1855 to September of the same year. Before occupying the highest position in the land, he had a long and distinguished career. After leaving the presidency he retired to private life, disenchanted with politics.

CARRILLO FLORES, ANTONIO. Born on June 23, 1909, in Mexico City. Law degree from the National Autonomous University (UNAM). Professor of law at UNAM 1936-52. Dean of the law school 1944-45. President of the Technological Institute of Mexico 1971-72. Founder of the National Securities Commission in 1946. He authored major banking legislation adopted by the government from the 1940's to the 1970's and several books on banking law. Director General of the government's development bank, Nacional Financiera during 1945-52, he returned to shape its policies for Mexican President López Portillo from 1977 to 1979. As Minister of Finance 1952-58 and Minister of Foreign Relations 1964-70, he formulated key financial and foreign policies. Antonio's father was the distinguished Mexican composer Julián Carillo, and his brother, Nabor, has been Mexico's leading nuclear energy expert. Antonio was elected a Deputy to the federal Congress in 1979. He has been a top advisor for the Bank of Mexico for many years.

CARRILLO FLORES, NABOR. Born on February 23, 1911, in Mexico City. Engineering degree from the National Autonomous University (UNAM). In 1942 he received the Ph.D. in science from Harvard, and became a part-time professor at UNAM. President of UNAM 1952-61. Active with the Mexican Commission of Scientific Investigation, he was liaison researcher with the United States Atomic Energy Commission and its successor Nuclear Regulatory Commission. A member of the National Commission of Nuclear Energy in Mexico since its creation, he has been since 1966 director of the Mexican Atomic Energy Center and the republic's leading authority on nuclear energy.

CARRILLO MARCOR, ALEJANDRO. Born on March 15, 1908, in Hermosillo, Sonora. Studied at Tulane University, and took a law degree at the National Autonomous University (UNAM). Professor at UNAM 1933-35. Then Dean of the National War College and Vice-President of Workers University in the 1940's. He was Deputy in the

federal Congress 1940-42 and 1964-67, a Senator from
Sonora 1970-74, and Ambassador to Saudia Arabia. He
directed all publicity for the presidential campaign of
Miguel Alemán in 1946 and was publisher of the daily
newspaper El Popular in 1943. A national leader of the
dominant Institutional Revolutionary Party (PRI), he was
publisher of the government's daily newspaper in Mexico
City, El Nacional 1968-75, then Governor of the state of
Sonora 1975-79. In 1975 he replaced the discredited Carlos Biebrich, who resigned as governor. Carrillo un-
tangled the mismanaged state government and returned
Sonora to solvency. He was a key formulator of policies
which reduced narcotics traffic into the United States.

CARVAJAL MORENO, GUSTAVO. Born in Jalapa, Veracruz,
in 1948. Degree in economics from the National Autonomous University, where he was a student of law professor José López Portillo, later to become President of
Mexico and sponsor of Carvajal as a leader within the
Institutional Revolutionary Party (PRI). A consulting economist for leading industries and governmental agencies
1970-76, Carvajal became Assistant Minister of Labor
1976-78. Having been the executive secretary for López
Portillo during the 1976 presidential campaign, Carvajal
was chosen by the president in 1978 as head of the Social
Security Institute for Civil Servants (ISSSTE) and Secretary General of the PRI. In February 1979, Carvajal became president of the PRI to help López Portillo have his
policies fully supported by the party.

CASA DEL PUEBLO, LA (The House of the People). A rural
school concept begun by José Vasconcelos when he was
Minister of Education under General Alvaro Obregón.
This type of rural school proved to be highly effective,
and besides teaching the basics (reading, writing, and
arithmetic) to all age groups, taught such varied subjects
as music, the fine arts and sanitation.

CASA MATA, PLAN OF. The pronunciamiento which led to
the abdication of Iturbide. Generals Antonio López de
Santa Anna and Guadalupe Victoria issued it in February
1823 and it called for the end of the Empire, a new congress, a new constitution and a federal form of government. Although it didn't specifically call for Iturbide's
dismissal, ten months later he abdicated.

CASAS ALEMAN, FERNANDO. Born on July 8, 1905, in

Córdoba, Veracruz, and died in Mexico City on October
30, 1968. Law degree from the National Autonomous
University. A leader in the Institutional Revolutionary
Party, he was Governor of Veracruz, then a Senator from
Veracruz. A key formulator of policy for the federal
Conciliation and Arbitration Board in the 1930's, he
served as Ambassador to Greece, to Italy, and to China.
He was Governor of the Federal District, which includes
being Mayor of Mexico City during the 1946-52 presidency
of Miguel Alemán.

CASO, ALFONSO. (1896-1970). Graduated from the National
Autonomous University (UNAM), he became a professor
of philosophy and anthropology at the University of Chicago, then Dean of graduate studies at UNAM. He gained
fame as an archaeologist who directed the excavations of
the Zapotec culture at Monte Albán in Oaxaca during
1931-43. After being archaeology director for the National Museum, he was President of UNAM. He was
Minister of National Patrimony in the cabinet of President Alemán 1946-49, and then headed the National Indigenous Institute until his passing in November 1970.

CASTAÑEDA, FELIPE. Born in 1933 in La Palma. He is
famous for his sculptured works, one of the most famous
being the "Mujer de Manto," a sculptured figure made of
polished bronze. He has held one-man exhibits in the
United States and Mexico.

CASTAÑEDA, JORGE. Born in 1929 in Mexico City. After
receiving a law degree from the National University, he
entered the foreign service and at age thirty became Ambassador to Saudi Arabia. A veteran diplomat representing Mexico at numerous United Nations, Organization of
American States, and other international conferences during the 1960's, he became his country's chief spokesman
on law of the sea and the concept of territorial waters
to 200 miles from shore. After being Mexico's chief
diplomat in Geneva at the World Health Organization and
International Labor Organization, he became Assistant
Minister of Foreign Relations. In May 1979, he became
Minister of Foreign Relations. He has taught diplomacy
at the Colegio de México graduate school since 1976 and
has authored some of Mexico's leading textbooks on international relations.

CASTELLANOS COUTIÑO, HORACIO. Born in 1929 in

Chiapas. After being Attorney General of the Federal District, a Senator for the 1976-82 term. A leading author of constitutional and administrative law.

CASTILLO LEDON, AMALIA. Born on August 18, 1902, in Tamaulipas. With her teaching certificate, she became a professor at Normal Schools in Ciudad Victoria, Tamaulipas, then in Mexico City. A pioneer woman leader in the dominant Institutional Revolutionary Party (PRI), she became the first woman on the PRI National Executive Committee. A national leader in child welfare, she became an envoy to the United Nations, then Ambassador to Finland and Sweden in 1956 and Ambassador to Austria in 1967. The first woman in a Mexican presidential cabinet, she was Assistant Minister of Public Education during 1958-64. After being President of the Inter-American Commission of Women, she was Mexico's Ambassador to the International Atomic Energy Organization during 1964-70.

CASTILLO MARTINEZ, HERBERTO. Born in August 1929 in Veracruz. Civil engineering degree from the National Autonomous University in 1954. Honorary doctorate from Central University of Venezuela. In 1972 he helped found the National Committee for Opinion Polling and Coordination. In September 1974 he founded the Mexican Workers Party (Partido de Trabajadores Mexicanos or PTM) and has continued as its Secretary General. The PTM is a socialist party with Marxist orientation.

CASTRO LEAL, ANTONIO. Born in 1896 in San Luis Potosí. Law degree and Ph.D. from the National University (UNAM), he served briefly as UNAM president. A Mexican diplomat in Chile, Cuba, France, Spain, and the United States, and Ambassador to UNESCO. Famed as the first Director General of the government's Department of Fine Arts in 1934. In the 1940's, he directed film activities for the government. He helped establish the Palace of Fine Arts as the home of symphonies and opera.

CEBALLOS, JUAN BAUTISTA. 1811-1857. After a distinguished career as a lawyer and Magistrate of the Supreme Court, he was declared President of Mexico for one month during 1853, resigning because of increasing opposition to his efforts to bring stability to his country. He was finally exiled by Santa Anna and died in Paris.

CEDILLO, MARIA MARCOS. 1900-1933. She was Mexico's first aviatrix and the niece of General Saturnino Cedillo. She met her death in a plane crash.

CEDILLO, SATURNINO. 1890-1939. Born on his father's ranch in San Luis Potosí, he supported Madero and rose to be a wealthy landowner and conservative politician. For a brief time, he was Secretary of Agriculture in the government of President Ortiz Rubio. The last caudillo to seriously challenge the authority of Mexico's central government, his private army was defeated by soldiers loyal to the Mexican president, General Lázaro Cárdenas. After fleeing to the mountains, he was killed in early 1939.

CELAYA, BATTLE OF. One of the decisive battles of the Mexican Revolution, it was fought in 1915 and pitted the forces of Obregón, who supported Carranza, against those of Pancho Villa. In the ensuing battle in which Obregón lost an arm, Villa was defeated and fled northward, leaving Carranza in control of Mexico.

CERRO GORDO, BATTLE OF. Fought in 1847, this was the decisive battle which enabled the American forces under General Winfield Scott to advance on Puebla and Mexico City. Cerro Gordo was a fortified position fifty miles northwest of Veracruz. After this victory the Americans advanced unhindered to Puebla, 85 miles from the capital. The American Army Corps of Engineers distinguished itself in this battle.

CERVANTES, VICENTE. 1755-1829. Spanish botanist who introduced new horticultural methods into New Spain. He was also a founder and director of the Botanical Gardens in Mexico.

CERVANTES DEL RIO, HUGO. Born on July 4, 1927, in Mexico City. Law degree from the National University (UNAM). Law professor part-time at UNAM for 15 years. A youth leader, then legal advisor for the Institutional Revolutionary Party (PRI). An administrator in the Ministry of the Navy 1952-56. Director General of Federal Highways 1959-65. Governor of the state of Baja California del Sur 1964-70. Minister of the Presidency 1970-76. He has been director general of the government's Federal Electricity Commission since 1976.

CFE. These initials stand for two important entities of government in Mexico, the Comisión Federal Electoral (Federal Electoral Commission) and the Comisión Federal de Electricidad (Federal Electricity Commission). See these entries.

CHAPULTEPEC, ACT OF. A measure adopted at the Chapultepec Conference of 1945, attended by all American nations except Argentina. It had two main provisions: 1) All sovereign states in the Western Hemisphere have equal status before the law. 2) An attack on one state will be considered an attack on all.

CHAPULTEPEC, BATTLE OF. It took place on September 12-13, 1847, and was the last great battle of the Mexican-American War of 1846-48. American forces under General Winfield Scott had to take Chapultepec Hill, about 200 feet high, before they could enter Mexico City. The opposing forces were about equal in number, but after an intense artillery barrage and attacks from three directions the Americans succeeded in reaching the top. The San Blas Battalion, although far outnumbered, put up the strongest resistence and the following cadets resisted to the death: Juan de la Barrera, Juan Escutia, Fernando Montes de Oca, Francisco Márquez, Vicente Suárez and Agustín Melgar. These six are remembered in Mexican history as Los Niños Héroes (The Heroic Children) and there is a huge monument dedicated to them in Chapultepec Park.

CHAPULTEPEC AQUEDUCT. In colonial times it ran along what is today Chapultepec Avenue, ending in a plaza known as el Salto del Agua. It had almost 1000 arches and was about $2\frac{1}{2}$ miles long. After it was torn down, a few arches were left as an historical monument.

CHAPULTEPEC CASTLE. Today the home of Mexico's National Museum of History, this fortress on a hill in the largest park in Mexico City was the home of Emperor Maximilian and Empress Carlotta from 1862 to 1866 durthe French occupation of Mexico. It became the home and office of dictator President Porfirio Díaz 1876-1911 and of subsequent Mexican chief executives until President Lázaro Cárdenas moved out in 1934 to the less ostentatious building of Los Pinos, the current presidential mansion.

CHAPULTEPEC CONFERENCE. Held in 1945, its official
name was the Inter-American Conference on Problems of
War and Peace. It met in Chapultepec Castle in February
and March of 1945. All Western Hemisphere states except Argentina attended and plans for hemispheric security
were discussed and carried out. The ensuing United Nations conference at San Francisco was considered, along
with an Economic Charter of the Americas. The Act of
Chapultepec was also adopted.

CHARRO. A Mexican cowboy or rancher, a charro dresses
distinctly from a working rancher or vaquero and engages
in rodeo competitions ranging from fancy riding to rope
tricks. The charro costume consists of tight trousers
covering short boots, adorned with silver thread and but-
tons and a short jacket similarly decorated. The hat with
the large brim, embroidered with gold or silver, the
famed sombrero from Jalisco, has become a folklore symbol for Mexico and is worn by folklore musicians called
mariachis. A charro wears a decorated wide leather belt
and pistol holster, a silk tie in a flowing bow, and has
a silver-adorned saddle.

CHAVEZ, CARLOS. Born in 1899, he is Mexico's outstanding
contemporary composer and conductor. He succeeded in
identifying Mexican music with the socio-cultural ideas of
the Mexican Revolution. In 1921 he wrote the ballet entitled, "The New Fire" and in 1928 organized the Mexican
Symphony Orchestra. He has written a wide variety of
works, among them operas, ballets and symphonies.
Chávez has been a guest conductor of numerous symphony
orchestras in the United States and is the author of a book
entitled, Toward a New Music.

CHAVEZ OROZCO, LUIS. Born in April 1901 in Guanajuato
and died in 1966 in Mexico City. Longtime directer of
libraries for the Ministry of Education, he served as Assistant Minister of Education, Director of Indian Affairs,
and as head of the National Teachers Union. A prolific
writer of essays, articles, and books on Mexican public
life.

CHAZARO LARA, RICARDO. Born in 1920 in Veracruz.
Graduate of Escuela Naval Militar in Veracruz. Career
navy officer since 1942 to rank of Vice Admiral. Since
1976 the Minister of the Navy.

CHIAPANECAS. One of Mexico's most popular folk dances,
the chiapanecas originated in the state of Chiapas and
spread throughout the republic. Its rhythmic handclapping
depends on a two-beat cadence to each measure for three
measures, followed by a pause and two loud handclaps.
It is played and performed for birthdays, weddings, re-
unions, or almost any happy celebration or party.

CHIAPAS. The southernmost state of Mexico, it borders
Guatemala and the Pacific Ocean to its east and south and
the states of Tabasco, Veracruz, and Oaxaca to its north
and west. Its area covers 73,887 square kilometers of
tropical jungle, rain forests, a coastal plain and highlands. Its 1976 population totaled 1,933,000. Its capital, Tuxtla Gutiérrez, had a 1976 population of 74,887.
The largest city in Chiapas, Tapachula, with a 1976 population of 85,000, lies near the Guatemalan border. One
third of its inhabitants are Indians. The chief products:
coffee and cacao. It has large archaeological ruins of
the Maya pre-Hispanic empire at Palenque and Bonampak.
In 1823 Chiapas broke away as a province of Guatemala
and became a state of the Mexican republic. Its native
musical instrument, the marimba, a wooden-type xylo-
phone, is played throughout rural Mexico and Guatemala.

CHICHEN ITZA. An archaeological site of the pre-Hispanic
capital of the Maya empire, 72 miles southeast of Mérida,
Yucatán. During 600 to 1400 A. D., the Mayas built the
pyramid of Kukulcán, the Temple of the Warriors, the
Great Ball Court, and Caracol, a 40-foot high tower 22
feet in diameter. In numerous other temples extending
over a four-square-mile area, gold masks dedicated to
the rain god Chac prevail. A pictograph writing on walls
preserves some Maya history. An underground water
system of deep wells extends over a flat, arid plain.
These were sacrificial wells in the Maya religion before
the conquest by the Spaniards in the late 1530's.

CHICHIMEC. The Chichimec Indians reached a pre-Hispanic
zenith during 950-1100 A. D., then intermingled and absorbed the Toltecs. They were conquered by the Aztecs
by 1247 A. D. In present-day Mexico, Chichimecs are
concentrated in the state of Jalisco.

CHIHUAHUA (CITY). The capital of the state of Chihuahua,
the city's 1976 population totaled 367,000. Located 200

miles south of El Paso, Texas, it is headquarters for the cattle and synthetic fibers industries of the state, in a dry, desert region.

CHIHUAHUA (STATE). The largest state in Mexico, it lies south of Texas and New Mexico, with an area of 247,000 square kilometers. Its 1976 population totaled 2,000,000, of whom 60,000 were Tarahumara Indians. It contains the prehistoric Casas Grandes ruins in the northern desert. In the south, deep gorges and forests include the vast Copper Canyon. Its most important activity remains the mining of zinc, lead, and silver, and the production of cattle. Its famous breed of dog of the same name, Chihuahua, is the world's smallest, standing 4 to 6 inches high and weighing one to 4 pounds. Chihuahua was the home state of the famed Revolutionary general and bandit, Pancho Villa, who was assassinated in 1923. This state furnished a large number of troops for the Revolutionary forces during the 1910-1920 fighting. The state's largest city, Ciudad Juárez, a twin community of El Paso, Texas, with a 1976 population of 557,000, is a major tourist and trade gateway.

CHINA POBLANA. A folklore peasant costume for women consisting of a long green skirt with a red yoke, trimmed with sequins, a white embroidered blouse, a shawl or rebozo, and red hair ribbons. Women performing the national folk dance, the Jarabe Tapatío, always wear this costume, which originated in the state of Jalisco.

CHRISTLIEB IBARROLA, ADOLFO. Born on March 12, 1919, in Mexico City and died there on December 6, 1969. Law degree from the National University (UNAM) in 1941 and UNAM law professor during 1954-57. A leader of the conservative opposition National Action Party (PAN), articulating significant criticism of the government's dominant Institutional Revolutionary Party which received nationwide attention. He was president of PAN during 1962-68, and was secretary general of PAN prior to that. A Deputy in the federal Congress 1964-67 and leader of the PAN congressional delegation. He represented PAN on the Federal Electoral Commission. As secretary of the Mexican Bar Association he became a national legal spokesman for conservatives.

CHURRIGUERESQUE. Named for the Spaniard José Benito de

Churriguera (1665-1723), it is a style of baroque architecture best described as extremely ornate and was prevalent in Colonial Mexico in the 18th century. Examples of this style are the retable of the Cathedral of Mexico and the Cathedral of Zacatecas.

CIENTIFICOS. The group of officials who surrounded President Porfirio Díaz and composed the "inner cabinet" of his government. They gained prominence beginning in 1892, when their unofficial spokesman, José Yves Limantour, became Minister of Finance. The científicos were greatly influenced by the positivist philosophy of August Comte and believed that Mexico could progress fastest by the use of scientific methods. They felt that Europe should serve as a model for Mexico, believed in white superiority, denigrated the Indian and Mestizo and equated the wealthy and powerful with the most intelligent. On the favorable side, under their management Mexico's international credit and monetary stability achieved a very favorable reputation and outwardly at least, the country appeared to be an ideal model for other under-developed countries to follow. Other científicos of note were Justo Sierra, Rosenda Pineda and Romero Rubio.

CIFUENTES, RODRIGO DE. Sixteenth-century Spanish painter from Córdoba, he was the first painter to practice his art in Mexico and probably the New World. He painted such notables as Doña Marina (La Malinche), Hernán Cortés and Viceroy Antonio de Mendoza.

CIUDAD JUAREZ. The largest city in the state of Chihuahua, it had a 1976 population totaling 550,000, and was expected to grow throughout the 1980's at the annual rate of 3 percent or more. Just across the Rio Grande border from El Paso, Texas, Ciudad Juárez is a major port of entry and exit. As with other ports of entry in Mexico, tourists and those engaged in import-export trade place additional burdens on the municipal facilities, so that the federal government maintains a Federal Betterment Board to supplement the funding of municipal facilities, ranging from road repair and maintenance to street lighting, park facilities, and supplemental sewage disposal. Board members are selected for three-year terms from among the civic, business, labor, and industrial leaders and activists in public life.

CIUDAD OBREGON. Most of the public and private buildings

have been constructed since 1925, when this relatively new city was organized within the county-wide municipality of Cajeme in the southern part of the state of Sonora. Named in honor of the Sonoran who was President of Mexico during 1920-24, Alvaro Obregón, the city had a 1976 population totaling 193, 000. It has the Technological Institute of Sonora, some of the state's major grain elevators, flour mills, cotton gins, fertilizer plants, and agricultural implement factories. It is the processing center for the cattle industry.

CLAVIJERO, FRANCISCO JAVIER.   1731-1787.   Jesuit priest and one of the most famous historians of his era. Although he will be remembered for his historical works, the most famous one being the Historia antigua de Mexico, he mastered many of the natural sciences and was an expert in classical literature. He knew many European languages, along with more than twenty languages and dialects of New Spain. He was banished from New Spain in 1767, along with other Jesuits, and lived the rest of his life in Italy. Another famous historical work of Clavijero, published posthumously in Italy in 1789, was Historia de la Antigua o Baja California. He died in Bologna.

CNOP.   The National Federation of Popular Organizations (Confederación Nacional de Organizaciones Populares), the sector of the dominant Institutional Revolutionary Party (PRI) for professionals and all those not affiliated with the agrarian or organized labor sectors of the party. CNOP was founded on February 7, 1943.

COAHUILA.   The third largest state in Mexico, it borders Texas to its north, Nuevo León to its east, Chihuahua to its west, and Durango to its south. With an area of 151, 571 square kilometers, its 1976 population totaled 1, 335, 000. The Sierra Madre Oriental divide the state into western and eastern plateaus. A desert climate prevails. At its complex of Altos Hornos plants at Monclova, Coahuila is the major coal producer of the republic and accounts for half of all the iron and steel produced. Its largest city, Torreón, had a 1976 population of 288, 000. Its state capital is Saltillo, with a 1976 population of 160, 000. Irrigation brought farming since the 1950's to the former dusty, arid Laguna region of the state's southwest, now producing cotton, corn, wheat, and grapes.

The state is Mexico's major producer of wines. From Coahuila came the first leaders of the 1910 Mexican Revolution, Francisco I. Madero and Venustiano Carranza.

CODINA, GENARO. 1852-1901. Musical composer. From Zacatecas, he showed promising ability, using the harp to compose. His most famous work is the "Marcha de Zacatecas," still widely played in Mexico. His fame was such that he toured the United States with his own orchestra, the Típica Zacateca.

COLEGIO DE MEXICO. A prestige private graduate school founded in Mexico City in 1940 by writer Alfonso Reyes and historian Daniel Cosío Villegas. Funded by the Ford, Rockefeller and other foundations, by UNESCO, and by the Mexican government. It has 200 full-time and 100 part-time students in social sciences and humanities. It has an Oriental Studies Center and can offer Asian or African linguistics depending on research. A three-year master's and a five-year doctoral program. One fifth of its students are from foreign countries. Cosío was its director until 1966 and since then economist Víctor Urquidi has been president. It publishes the quarterly Foro Internacional and numerous monographs and special studies. Colegio's alumni hold top positions in Mexican government and other universities.

COLIMA (CITY). The capital of the state of the same name. It had a 1976 population totaling 91,000. It has agricultural industries and salt corporations. It lies south of Guadalajara 200 miles via winding highway and some 30 miles from the Pacific Ocean.

COLIMA (STATE). A small state in southwestern Mexico, facing the Pacific Ocean with a 70-mile coast line and an area totaling 5,455 square kilometers. Its 1976 population totaled 317,000. Its port city, Manzanillo, has one of Mexico's natural harbors, a site for tourism. Tropical agriculture and livestock dominate its economy.

COLUMBUS, NEW MEXICO RAID see VILLA, PANCHO (FRANCISCO)

COMISION FEDERAL DE ELECTRICIDAD. The government's Federal Electricity Commission, was created in 1941 to compete with privately-owned power companies. During the period 1960 to 1962, President Adolfo López Mateos expropriated all privately-owned electric power companies in Mexico, putting them under the CFE. For the first time, uniform rates prevailed in various regions of the republic, helping with industrial growth. The CFE director general sits with the presidential cabinet and enjoys high-level autonomy.

COMISION FEDERAL ELECTORAL. The Federal Electoral Commission comes under the authority of the Minister of Gobernación or the Interior. It supervises voter registration, all elections, and vote tabulation. Its authority extends not only to presidential and congressional elections, but also to state and municipal races. It certifies political parties as meeting the legal minimum requirements as recognized parties for the ballot and administers the certifying of all candidates for public office for listing on the ballot.

COMONFORT, IGNACIO. 1812-1863. Born in Puebla. In 1833 he helped General Santa Anna overthrow President Bustamante. He was regarded as the number one candidate for the presidency of the Republic in 1855, but deferred to General Juan Alvarez. After the latter became president he named Comonfort to the cabinet post of Minister of War. Although having the reputation of a conciliator, he enraged military and church officials by signing a decree abolishing their special privileges, a move which would lead to civil war. When Alvarez was forced out, Comonfort became provisional president and served for almost two years, from December of 1855 to November of 1857. During this period he was faced with several uprisings, which he suppressed. The liberal Constitution of 1857 went into effect during his presidency, but he did not accept it enthusiastically. He was elected President in 1857, but resigned under pressure from General Félix Zuloaga. Comonfort fled to the United States and then to France. When he feared Mexican involvement in a possible war with European powers, he returned to his country and supported Juárez and the Republic. He was killed in an ambush on November 14, 1863.

COMPAÑIA MEXICANA DE AVIACION. Mexican Aviation Company or CMA is the republic's principal privately-owned airline. It began in 1921 in Tampico as the Mexican Transportation Company (CMT), flying weekly payrolls and passengers to the oilfields in Veracruz. On August 20, 1924, CMA was incorporated by Gustavo and Alberto Salinas, former military pilots, to connect Mexico City with commercial air routes to Monterrey, Saltillo, Tampico, and San Luis Potosí. By 1941 CMA served all major provincial cities plus several major cities in the United States. By 1960 CMA had converted its propeller aircraft to jet aircraft. Throughout the 1970's, CMA showed annual profits, contrasting with the annual deficits of the government-owned rival Aeroméxico airline. CMA flies 30 percent more domestic and 20 percent more international passengers than Aeroméxico.

COMPAÑIA NACIONAL DE SUBSISTENCIAS POPULARES. The government's National Company of Popular Subsistences or more accurately the Basic Commodities Corporation. CONASUPO had its origins in the government's Mexican Export-Import Company (CEIMSA), which functioned from 1949 to 1961, when CONASUPO was created. It buys corn, beans, wheat, rice, coffee, sorghum, and other major crops at subsidized prices, storing them in a government chain of warehouses. It also operates thousands of CONASUPO retail stores throughout the republic, selling food, work clothing, and a few toys and basic appliances almost at cost, to provide necessities for the poor and to encourage commercial groceries and supermarkets to hold down prices. Its stores include bakery goods, condensed milk, and some can goods sales.

CONASUPO see COMPAÑIA NACIONAL DE SUBSISTENCIAS POPULARES

CONCAMIN. The Confederación de Cámaras Industriales. See CAMARA INDUSTRIAL.

CONCANACO. The Confederación de Cámaras Nacionales de Comercio. See CAMARA DE COMERCIO.

CONCHELLO, JOSE ANGEL. Born on September 1, 1923, in Monterrey, Nuevo León. Law degree from the National University. Studied industrial development in Canadian universities. A leader of the conservative opposition National Action Party (PAN), being on its national executive committee since 1969 and party president during 1972-75. He represented Mexican employers at the International Labor Organization in Geneva in 1953. Advisor for the

National Productivity Council, for the CONCAMIN and
CONCANACO. Columnist for the newspaper El Universal, the magazine La Nación and many other periodicals.
A Deputy in the federal Congress 1967-70 and 1973-76.
PAN candidate for Governor of the state of Nuevo León
in 1979. Professor of sociology at Iberoamerican University.

CONFEDERACION DE TRABAJADORES MEXICANOS (CTM).
A confederation of Mexican labor unions organized in 1936
by Vicente Lombardo Toledano along the lines of the
American C.I.O., it filled a void left by the discredited
CROM (Confederación Regional Obrera Mexicana). In its
early years it boasted a membership of 250,000 factory
workers, 90,000 miners, 17,000 petroleum workers and
80,000 transport workers. It was Cárdenas's most powerful source of support and as a result received his backing to strike on numerous occasions. When Cárdenas
reorganized the official party into the PRM (Partido de
la Revolución Mexicana), the CTM became the official
spokesman for the labor sector, thus enjoying official
status in the government. It was the dispute between the
CTM and the foreign-owned oil companies which led to
their nationalization in 1938. It enjoyed its most militant
period during Cárdenas's term of office, but has grown
more conservative during succeeding administrations,
concentrating more on economic and social issues, rather
than on political ones. The CTM has long since been
purged of radical leftists and communists. It is made
up of 20 national unions, 31 state federations and more
than 100 local and regional federations. Estimates of its
current strength range from 500,000 to well over
1,000,000. The CTM continues to be the official spokesman for labor with the PRI (Partido Revolucionario Institucional).

CONFEDERACION NACIONAL CAMPESINA. The National
Federation of Campesinos or Peasant-Farmers was established in 1936 by Mexican President Lázaro Cárdenas
to give them an organized voice in negotiating with government or management. The CNC also functions as the
core of the agrarian sector of the majority Institutional
Revolutionary Party (PRI) which has dominated the government since 1929.

CONFEDERACION REGIONAL DE OBREROS MEXICANOS.
The Regional Federation of Mexican Workers or CROM

was founded on March 22, 1918, by labor leader Luis Morones, and by 1926 claimed a membership of two million. After the Federation of Mexican Workers or CTM was established in 1936, it eclipsed the CROM as Mexico's major federation of labor unions. The CROM became a small entity in organized labor and during the 1970's functioned as a token federation, with very limited influence in politics or government.

CONFEDERACION REVOLUCIONARIO DE OBREROS Y CAMPESINOS. The Revolutionary Federation of Workers and Peasant-Farmers was developed in 1952 and 1953 by Mexican President Adolfo Rúiz Cortines to give the dominant Federation of Mexican Workers (CTM) some competition within the Institutional Revolutionary Party (PRI) and in government and management negotiations, to strengthen the government's position through labor pluralism. By 1954, CROC had a membership of 435,000, and then began to level off. Through the 1970's CROC remained a medium-sized federation supportive of both the government and the PRI.

CONGREGA; CONGREGACION. Name given by the Spaniards during the colonial period to any Indian town. The Spaniards segregated the Indians by forcing them to live in these settlements for the following reasons: 1) to protect them from being taken unfair advantage of; 2) to assure a readily-available supply of labor; 3) to facilitate their conversion to Christianity. The greatest resettlement of Indians took place at the end of the 16th and the beginning of the 17th centuries.

CONQUISTADOR. Name given by the Spanish crown to those men who conquered the New World. The most famous conquistador of Mexico was Hernán Cortés.

CONSTITUTION OF 1917. Mexico's current federal Constitution, which replaced the 1857 Constitution of reformer Benito Juárez, was drafted by an assembly gathered in Querétaro by President Venustiano Carranza from October 1916 to February 1917. In addition to assembling political rights--freedom of speech, of press, suffrage--this charter radically broke with the past by declaring the mineral riches beneath the surface of the soil belonged to the nation and could be developed only through concessions by the government. Article 27 on land also contained the reforms pertaining to restoring communal farms to the villages from which the Porfirio Díaz dictatorship had taken them. Article 123 gave organized labor the right to strike, the eight-hour work day with extra pay for overtime, and the obligation of large employers to provide schools for offspring of workers in communities lacking them. This Constitution made elementary education secular and nationalized Catholic Church properties. Strict separation of Church and State prohibits priests, nuns, and monks from holding any governmental office.

CONSTITUTIONS. Mexico's 1824 Constitution created a federal republic. Its 1836 Constitution changed the structure to a unitary or centralized republic without states' rights. Its 1857 Constitution, inspired by reformist President Benito Juárez, nationalized properties of the Catholic Church, but this provision and others for land reform were ignored by the longtime dictatorship of Porfirio Díaz during 1876-1911.

CONSOLIDACION, LAW OF. This was a measure enforced by the Spanish crown in Mexico between 1805 and 1809 and it required the lands held by religious orders to be converted into cash and the cash transferred to the Spanish treasury. It amounted to the nationalization of the land and while it was in effect the Spanish treasury became richer by over 10,000,000 pesos.

CONTRERAS, JESUS F. 1866-1902. At an early age he demonstrated extraordinary ability in the fine arts, specializing in sculpture under the renowned master Manuel Noreña. He assisted the latter in the construction of the statue of Cuauhtémoc on the Paseo de la Reforma in Mexico City. The bronze statues in relief which form part of the "Monumento a la Raza" are perhaps his best-known work. His most impressive work is the marble statue in the Alameda Park in Mexico City, "Malgré Tout" (In Spite of All).

COQUET, BENITO. Born in 1915 in Jalapa, Veracruz. An attorney, who became a Deputy in the federal Congress, Director of the National Institute of Fine Arts, Ambassador to Cuba, then Minister of the Presidency from 1956 to 1958. As Director General of the Mexican Institute of Social Security 1958-64, he extended social security benefits to medium and small cities throughout the republic not previously covered. However, even in the

1970's, under one-fourth of the total Mexican work force was under either the private-sector or civil-servant social security programs.

CORDERO, JUAN. 1824-1884. A painter from Puebla, he studied in Rome at an early age. He gained extensive popularity in Mexico, two of his most famous works being "Moses and the Annunciation" and "The Adulterous Woman." He is regarded as one of Mexico's greatest painters.

CORONA DEL ROSAL, ALFONSO. Born in 1906 in Hidalgo state. Law degree from the National University. A reserve officer, rising through the reserve ranks from Lieutenant to Division General. A Deputy in the federal Congress 1940-43, then a Senator during 1946-52. He became Governor of the state of Hidalgo, then head of the government's Army-Navy Bank, then Minister of National Patrimony during 1964-66 and then Governor of the Federal District during 1966-70. His fame rested on his leadership within the dominant Institutional Revolutionary Party (PRI). He headed the PRI Youth, various PRI positions with the national executive committee, and was President of the PRI during 1958-64.

CORONADO see VAZQUEZ DE CORONADO Y VALDES, FRANCISCO

CORRAL, RAMON. 1854-1912. A Mexican politician whose most important political posts were those of Governor of Sonora and Vicepresident of Mexico under Porfirio Díaz. His close association with Díaz and his reputation for selling the Yaqui Indians into what amounted to economic slavery caused him to be one of the most hated men in Mexico. He died in exile in Paris.

CORREA, VICTOR MANUAL. Born on October 18, 1917, in Mérida, Yucatán. An attorney, he became the first member of the conservative opposition National Action Party (PAN) to govern a state capital since the 1929 rise to power of the Institutional Revolutionary Party. He was Mayor of Mérida during 1967-70. He helped elect two PAN members to the Municipal Council and two to the State Legislature. He was PAN candidate for Governor in 1969 and 1975. He founded the trust department for the Bank of the Southeast and popularized the trust concept throughout the state of Yucatán.

CORRO, JOSE JUSTO.   President of Mexico in 1836-1837.
He was a rather undistinguished chief executive, accom-
plishing little during his administration.   He became
president because of the death of Miguel Barragán and
governed during the difficult time when Texas broke away
from Mexico.   During his administration Mexico gave up
the federal form of government and became more centralist, abandoning the Constitution of 1824 in favor of the
Siete Leyes (Seven Laws).

CORTES, HERNAN.   1485-1547.   He was born in Extrema-
dura, Spain and was admitted to law school, but never
graduated.   He was an adventurer and it was inevitable
that the discovery of the New World would draw him there
in search of excitement.   He eventually became the secretary and confidant of Diego Velázquez, but temporarily
fell out of favor with him when he became amorously involved with a niece of Velázquez.   The latter commissioned Cortés to explore Mexico and the adjacent territories, and even though Velázquez cancelled this mission
because of intrigues directed against Cortés, he sailed
before Velázquez could stop him.
    He sailed for Mexico, traveling southwest, where he
first landed at Cozumel and Yucatán.   Hearing of a great
empire to the north, he sailed up the coast and on July
9, 1519, founded the settlement of Villa Rica de la Vera-
Cruz, known today as the city of Veracruz.   Because he
had knowledge of the dissensions existing among the Aztecs, superior technology in the form of guns and cannon,
and because of various Aztec superstitions and predictions,
he finally succeeded in conquering them and captured their
capital of Tenochtitlán on August 13, 1521.   Anyone visiting the final battle site, which is at Tlatelolco at the Palace of the Three Cultures, will see a small plaque commemorating the final battle.   It translates roughly as follows: "What happened here was not a defeat, but the
painful birth of what is today the Mexican nation."
    After his victory, Cortés was showered with honors
and awarded huge tracts of land in Mexico.   But he again
fell victim to intrigues and died in Spain, a poor and for-
gotten man stripped of his former power.

CORTES, MARTIN.   The son of Hernán Cortés and doña Marina, he is regarded as the first mestizo born from a
white-Indian union to a Spanish nobleman.   Martín Cortés
played a key role in the first general uprising led by the

González de Avila brothers to liberate New Spain from Spanish rule. The plan was to install Martín Cortés as the ruler of a new, independent monarchy, but it failed.

COSIO VILLEGAS, DANIEL. Born on July 23, 1898, in Mexico City, and died there on March 11, 1976. One of the leading writers and historians of Mexico. He studied law at the National University, then economics and history at Harvard, Cornell, Wisconsin, and London universities. Adviser to several Ministers of Foreign Relations, of Finance, and directors of the Bank of Mexico. Ambassador to the International Monetary Conference at Bretton Woods, N. H., in 1944, setting postwar agreements. Ambassador to UNESCO 1957-59 and its Secretary General in 1959. He founded the Fondo de Cultura Económica book publishing company in 1935 and directed it for many years, finally permitting the government to buy a partnership in the firm after its success as Latin America's publisher of quality books. With writer Alfonso Reyes, he helped establish the elite graduate school Colegio de México in 1940. He was the author, co-author, or editor of dozens of books, including the five-volume Historia moderna de México in 1963, La sucesión presidencial in 1975, and La sucesión: desenlace y perspectivas in 1975. As president of the Colegio until 1966, he set the standards in Mexico for doctoral-level studies in the social sciences and humanities.

CREELMAN, JAMES. American journalist who had an important interview with General Porfirio Díaz on February 17, 1908. Díaz stated that he believed Mexico was ready for an opposition party and that if he lost to it in 1910 he would peacefully turn over power to it. He did not keep his promise made at the time and had himself elected in 1910. Because of this, opposition to him grew, eventually erupting into open rebellion.

CREOLES. In Colonial Mexico, this is the term used to indicate persons of Spanish ancestry born in Mexico. As a class they were economically strong and many became quite wealthy. However, political and high church posts were denied to them and this caused increasing resentment, culminating in Mexico's independence movement. A significant factor in the organization of Creole power was the formation of the Army of New Spain in 1761, a move prompted by fear of an English invasion. Many Creoles met at Jalapa in preparation to resist this

invasion and for the first time came to realize what a
powerful class they constituted. Although accurate statistics are difficult to come by, on the eve of the Mexican revolt for independence in 1810, there were roughly
1,000,000 Creoles out of a population of slightly more
than 6,000,000.

CRISTERO REBELLION. An anti-government, anti-Calles uprising which began in 1927 and was comprised of fervent
Catholics, many of them fanatics. When Calles decided
to enforce various articles of the Constitution of 1917
directed at restricting the power of the Catholic Church,
particularly Article 130, leaders declared themselves in
rebellion. During three years no ceremonies were carried out in the churches, although some were held in
secret. There was also violence between government
forces and the Cristeros, who were particularly strong
in the states of Jalisco and Michoacán. Their slogan and
rallying cry was "¡Viva Cristo Rey!" and it was a Cristero, José de León de Toral, who assassinated Alvaro
Obregón in 1928. As the years wore on and it became
increasingly obvious that neither side was going to gain a
decisive advantage, a settlement was reached in 1930,
during the presidency of Emilio Portes Gil. The American ambassador, Dwight Morrow, played a crucial role
as intermediary in these negotiations and he had no small
part in the final compromise reached. A crucial issue
was settled when religious instruction was again permitted
in the churches. The Cristero Rebellion is significant
because it marks the end of the last major, violent controversy between Church and State in Mexico, although
there continued to be some violence in the 1930's, particularly in the state of Veracruz. Both sides came to
realize that for the good of Mexico and themselves, it
was much better to live under a peaceful truce rather
than practice intermittent violence.

CRISTEROS. Those individuals who supported the Cristero
Rebellion.

CRUICKSHANK GARCIA, JORGE. Born on July 29, 1915, in
Tehuantepec, Oaxaca. Famed for being the first
minority-party Senator in the federal Congress in this
century. Engineering degree from School of Mechanical
and Electrical Engineering. In 1938 he became secretary
of the National Socialist Youth of Mexico. In 1940 a professor at the National Polytechnic Institute (IPN). In 1943

he was elected to the Governing Council of the Workers University in Mexico City. He helped the National Union of Education Workers (Sindicato Nacional de Trabajadores de la Educación or SNTE) draft its constitution in 1943 and in 1947 became a member of the SNTE national committee. During 1948-51 he represented civil servants unions on the federal Pensions Bureau board. He helped Vicente Lombardo Toledano found the Popular Socialist Party (PPS) in 1948. Since January 1969 he has headed the PPS as Secretary General. He was the first PPS Deputy in the Oaxaca State Legislature in 1968, and a Deputy in the federal Congress during 1964-67 and 1970-73. In 1976 he was the first PPS member elected to the federal Senate for the 1976-82 term.

CUATEQUIL.   Indian name given in Colonial Mexico to the repartimiento or forced wage system.

CUAUHTEMOC.   Also known as Guatemótzin.   1502-1525. Nephew and son-in-law of Moctezuma II.   While his cousin and predecessor, Cuitláhuac was emperor, Cuauhtémoc was the head of the Aztec armies and during many months of combat successfully contained the Spanish forces under Hernán Cortés.   After Cuitláhuac's death he became emperor and was crowned on March 1, 1521.   By August of 1521 most of Tenochtitlán was in Spanish hands and on the 13th the Aztecs were finally defeated.   Cuauhtémoc and other high officials tried to flee in canoes, but were captured and imprisoned.   The tortures that this last Aztec emperor suffered, and his stoic manner of bearing them are legendary.   The Spaniards burned his feet with boiling oil, in an effort to force him to disclose the hiding place of treasures lost during the Spanish noche triste retreat.   If he did know their whereabouts he never disclosed them and these riches have come to be known as Cuauhtémoc's treasure.   Interestingly enough, when the Mexico City subway was being built, golden objects were found, objects which are believed to have been part of the Spanish booty lost during their retreat.   Accused of treachery, Cuauhtémoc was hanged on March 5, 1525, in Izancánac, in the state of Tabasco, while being taken to Honduras during one of Hernán Cortés's expeditions.   This young emperor is regarded as a national hero in Mexico.

CUERNAVACA.   The capital of the state of Morelos, Cuernavaca had a 1976 population totaling 314,000.   It contains the historic Palace of Cortés, where the Spanish conqueror of the Aztecs, Hernán Cortés, established a headquarters in the 1520's. In 1928, United States Ambassador to Mexico Dwight Morrow, as a goodwill gesture, paid famed painter Diego Rivera to decorate the corridors of that palace with murals which have become world famous, depicting Mexican history. With year-round spring climate, Cuernavaca has become a tourist resort and also the site of vacation homes for wealthy Mexicans, especially entertainment celebrities and high-level government officials. The city is only 51 miles south of Mexico City via a toll expressway which cuts through mountainous passes.

CUETO RAMIREZ, LUIS. Career officer in the army, reaching the rank of Brigadier General in 1956. Studied police administration. Put on inactive status by the army so he could serve as Chief of Police of the Federal District during 1961-69. He directed police operations during the violent student riots from July 26, to October 2, 1968, which threatened the opening of the Olympics and resulted in 200 deaths at the Plaza of the Three Cultures.

CUEVAS, MARIANO. 1879-1949. Jesuit historian. He was a university professor, but will be remembered primarily for his role as a research historian. Among his most important works are Historia de la Iglesia en México (History of the Church in Mexico), published in 1928; and Historia de la nación mexicana (History of the Mexican Nation), 1940.

CUITLAHUAC. 1476-1520. Penultimate Aztec leader who succeeded Moctezuma when he was killed. Unlike his predecessor, whose many superstitions greatly aided Cortés in his conquests, Cuitláhuac succeeded in driving the Spaniards from Tenochtitlán, killing many of them during the famous noche triste retreat of June 30, 1520. Smallpox took his life in December of 1520, less than six months after he had become Emperor.

CULIACAN. The capital of the state of Sinaloa in western Mexico, Culiacán, only 30 miles from the Pacific Ocean, has developed into a major city. With only 49,000 population in 1960, by 1976 it had 264,000 residents within its municipal limits and another 40,000 in its immediate area. Headquarters for various industries and enterprises of the state related to agriculture and fishing, the city is the major shipping site for Mexico's tomato crops, including those exported to the United States and Canada. Since the

1960's, it has been plagued with a subculture of crime, being the center for Mexico's dealers and transporters of narcotics. Most organized crime leaders in Mexico have employees or business connections in Culiacán.

CURANDERO. A kind of medical practitioner very popular in the more isolated regions of Mexico. The curandero uses many different types of herbs and is considered suspect by more orthodox medical authorities.

- D -

DANIELS, JOSEPHUS. Former United States Secretary of the Navy who was appointed ambassador to Mexico in 1934. Although the Mexican people received him initially with hostility, his genuine friendliness towards them reversed this initial feeling. He was sympathetic to Cárdenas's ideas and helped to calm foreign reactions when Mexico nationalized the oil industry in 1938.

DANZOS PALOMINO, RAMON. Born in Puebla. A leader of socialist youth groups and leftist farm groups since the 1950's. In 1963 he helped found the Independent Peasant-Farmer Federation (Confederación Campesina Independiente or CCI) to challenge the progovernment National Campesino Federation (CNC). In 1964 he established the People's Electoral Front to encourage votes for the Popular Socialist Party (PPS) instead of the dominant Institutional Revolutionary Party (PRI). Until the mid-1970's, he organized various groups of squatters who temporarily seized farm lands in northern states.

DAVILA AGUIRRE, VICENTE. (1893-1960). From Coahuila, he received an engineering degree in the United States. As a military commander from 1915 to 1920, he supported President Carranza. As Governor of San Luis Potosí, he enforced the reforms of the Revolution. He was discredited politically for supporting the unsuccessful rebellion against the government in 1923 by Adolfo de la Huerta.

DAVILA Y PADILLA, AGUSTIN. 1562-1604. An historian born in Mexico, he was a member of the Dominican Order. He was named by Philip III as "Preacher of the King" and "Chronicler of the Indies" and was commissioned by the king to write his most famous work, Historia de la Provincia de Santiago de la Nueva España del

Orden de Santo Domingo (1596). During the last four
years of his life he was Archbishop of Santo Domingo and
died in that city.

DAY OF THE DEAD. All Hallows Day, November 1, and the
day following are celebrated in Mexico in lieu of Hallow-
een. Children eat cookies and cake decorated with skulls
and crossbones. Families hold picnics at cemeteries, at
the graves of relatives. Costume parties feature masks
caricaturing celebrities.

"DECENA TRAGICA, LA." A literal translation of this
phrase would be "The Tragic Ten Days" and it refers to
the ten-day period in February 1913 when Madero's government was subjected to open anarchy and cannon fire,
culminating in the takeover by General Victoriano Huerta.

DE GANTE, PEDRO. 1486-1572. Born in what today is
Belgium. Because of the influence of Fray Bartolomé de
las Casas he became an outstanding missionary among the
Indians in New Spain. He was responsible for the establishment of many schools and churches and is well loved
in Mexico today. It was because of his influence that
Carlos V dictated the New Laws which ended what amounted to the slavery of the Indians. He is buried in the
Convent of San Francisco in Mexico City.

DEGOLLADO, SANTOS. 1811-1861. Born in Guanajuato.
Mexican reformer, politician and military figure. He
sought to limit ecclesiastical power, fought corruption in
government and led a strong effort to improve agriculture
by scientific means. One of his first important posts was
rector of the newly reopened Colegio de San Nicolás in
1847. He was Minister of War in the government of
Juárez, but was later dismissed because of recommending
foreign mediation of a dispute with English landowners.
He was known as the "Hero of Defeats" because he lost
more battles than he won. He was finally ambushed and
killed by the conservative General Leonardo Márquez in 1861.

DE LA COLINA, RAFAEL. Born in 1898 in Tulancingo, Hidalgo. Master's degree in science from the National
University. Mexican Consul in Missouri, Texas, Pennsylvania, Louisiana, Massachusetts, and California. Director of the Consular Corps. Ambassador to the United
States 1949-52, to Japan 1962-64, and to the Organization
of American States 1965-76. A key advisor on foreign
policy to Mexican presidents during the 1960's and 1970's.

DE LA CRUZ, SOR JUANA INES. 1651-95. "The Tenth Muse"; the most brilliant woman of Colonial Mexico. She became famous for her poetry and prose, but also possessed considerable knowledge of foreign languages, astronomy, painting and mathematics. Sor Juana Inés entered the Convent of St. Jerome at 18 and for the next 25 years concentrated on study and writing. Her most famous works are Liras and Sueño. While nursing ill sisters in the convent, she fell victim to one of the many epidemics and died at the age of 44.

DE LA GRANJA, JUAN. 1785-1856. He was born in Spain but became a Mexican citizen. In 1838 he founded the first Spanish-language newspaper ever to be published in New York City. However, his greatest contribution was the introduction of the telegraph in Mexico. He also founded a school to train telegraphers.

DE LA HUERTA, ADOLFO. 1881-1954. Born in Guaymas and died in Mexico City. Revolutionary figure and Provisional President from May until November of 1920. Before this time he had been Provisional Governor of Sonora and had headed the Department of the Interior. In 1920, he no longer considered himself a follower of Carranza and approved the Plan of Agua Prieta. After turning over the presidency to Alvaro Obregón in November of 1920, he was named Minister of the Treasury. At the end of 1923 he broke with Obregón and was proclaimed Provisional President by General Guadalupe Sánchez, but this rebellion failed and he was forced to live in exile in the United States until 1936, at which time he was named Inspector General of Mexican Consulates. Later, he became Director General of Civil Pensions.

DE LA MADRID, MIGUEL. Born on December 12, 1934, in Colima. Law degree from the National Autonomous University (UNAM). Master's degree in public administration from Harvard. UNAM professor of law. Assistant director of finances for the government's oil monopoly Pemex. Director of public credit for the Ministry of Finance 1972-76. Envoy of Mexico to various international conferences on economics. He also had administrative duties with the Bank of Mexico, and with the National Bank of Foreign Trade. Since May 16, 1979, he has been Minister of Planning and the Budget in the cabinet of President López Portillo.

DE LANDA, DIEGO. 1524-1579. Spanish bishop who was

responsible for the conversion of the Mayans to Roman Catholicism. His Relación de las cosas de Yucatán is the earliest description of Mayan civilization and remains a classic to this day. Unfortunately, his burning of many Mayan manuscripts destroyed much information about that Indian civilization.

DE LA PEÑA Y PEÑA, MANUEL. 1789-1850. He was a distinguished jurist and politician and was president during two separate periods during the 1840's. He signed the Treaty of Guadalupe-Hidalgo (1848) in this capacity. He also occupied many political posts. Peña y Peña was also President of the Supreme Court and belonged to various scientific organizations.

DE LAS CASAS, BARTOLOME. 1474-1566. One of the most famous religious figures of the New World, he was a wealthy encomendero who took up the cause of the Indians after observing their extreme suffering. He became a dominican priest and outstanding defender of the Indian. His work, Brevísima relación de la destrucción de las Indias (A Very Brief Account of the Destruction of the Indies) formed the base of the British-inspired Black Legend. Although he spent relatively little time in Mexico, he was appointed Bishop of Chiapas and served in what would later be that southern Mexican state from 1544 to 1547.

DE LA VEGA DOMINGUEZ, JORGE. Born on March 14, 1931, in Chiapas. Economics degree from the National University. Professor of finance at the National Polytechnic Institute (IPN). Dean of the IPN School of Economics 1962-64. Director of economic, political, and social studies for the Institutional Revolutionary Party (PRI) 1968-70. He was an economist for the Ministry of Industry and Commerce, the Small Business Bank, and assistant director of the government's Diesel Nacional truck and automobile manufacturing. After directing sales, he became during 1970-76 Director General of the government's Basic Commodities Corporation (CONASUPO), then Governor of Chiapas, then Commerce Minister.

DE LA VERA CRUZ, FRAY ALONSO. 1504-1584. Augustinian priest and educator. He was born near Toledo and received his doctorate in scholastic philosophy and theology from the University of Salamanca. He arrived in New Spain and Mexico City in 1536 and in 1540 he began a long career as educator in Michoacán. When the Uni-

versidad Real y Pontificia de México was founded in 1553
Fray Alonso occupied various chairs of learning there,
becoming one of the most respected educators of his
time.   He wrote numerous books and was learned in many
fields.   His writings about the geography of California
proved highly valuable for Father Kino, who explored so
much of that region.

DEL RIO, ANDRES.   1765-1849.   Teacher and mineralogist.
He was born in Spain and studied mineralogy in several
European countries.   He studied under Humboldt and when
he was almost 30 accepted a chair at what is today the
School of Engineers.   He discovered vanadium and was a
member of several international scientific societies.   At
the same time he identified closely with Mexico, becoming a Mexican citizen and dying in Mexico City.

DEL ROSAL, MARTA.   Born in Hidalgo in 1920.   Diploma
from the National School for Teachers in Mexico City.
Studied at Claremont College in California.   A pioneer
woman political leader in the dominant Institutional Revolutionary Party (PRI), she organized the PRI's National
Women's Committee in 1951 and joined the PRI's National
Executive Committee in 1952.   A Deputy in the federal
Congress 1958-61 and 1964-67.   She organized nursery
schools and the Nursery Department for the Ministry of
Public Education throughout the 1940's and 1950's, becoming the Republic's foremost consultant on preschool
education.

DE OLID, CRISTOBAL.   1490-1524.   Spanish conquistador
who arrived in the New World in 1518 and played an important role in the conquest of Mexico under Hernán
Cortés.   After the conquest of the Aztecs, Cortés sent
de Olid south to conquer what is today Honduras.   After
being successful, he was assassinated by two other Spaniards who had been his prisoner, Francisco de las Casas
and Gil Gonzáles de Avila.

DIAZ, FELIX.   1868-1945.   Nephew of the Mexican dictator,
Porfirio Díaz.   He led an unsuccessful rebellion against
Madero in 1912, after which he was imprisoned.   Was to
succeed Huerta as president, but the latter sent him on
a diplomatic post to Japan instead.   He again was involved in political intrigue after returning to Mexico,
leading an unsuccessful revolt against Carranza.   For
this he was exiled in 1919 and not allowed to return to

his native land until 1937.   He finally died in the city of
Veracruz in 1945.

DIAZ, PORFIRIO.   1830-1915.   Mexican general and president.   He was born in Oaxaca and studied under Benito
Juárez at the Institute of Oaxaca.   He worked as a li-
brarian and also studied law.   He took up arms during
the Revolución de Ayutla in 1855, beginning his military
career in this manner.   Díaz fought with the liberals in
the Wars of the Reform and was one of Mexico's most
distinguished generals in the struggle against Maximilian,
capturing Mexico City in 1867.   Several times he was an
unsuccessful candidate for the presidency and finally over-
threw Lerdo de Tejada, being named Provisional President in 1876.   In all, he was elected president seven
times.   A controversial figure, he did bring stability to
Mexico, a stability which it had not known since the start
of the independence movement in 1810.   The countryside
was pacified by his favored group of guardias rurales, a
kind of highway patrol.   Many of these individuals were
common criminals, but people could now boast of being
able to leave their doors unlocked at night, for it was
widely known that anyone breaking the law would be dealt
with in an extremely harsh manner.   Díaz disregarded
the masses and always felt that Mexico's future lay with
the white man, that the Indian was good for little more
than heavy, physical labor.

His inner group of advisers, known as the científicos
and led by José Yves Limantour, believed strongly in
this philosophy and were guided by the positivist belief
that Mexican life could be improved by purely scientific
means, devoid of religious and metaphysical ideas.   Díaz's policy was known as "Pan o Palo (Bread or the
Club)."   One was rewarded for his cooperation and punished for his failure to demonstrate it.   He was a master
at manipulating the groups which supported him: the
Church, army, politicians, great landholders and foreign
business interests.   He kept the army large and was
careful to placate potential opponents with favors.   He
encouraged railroad building, particularly lines connecting
with the United States, encouraged foreign investment and
increased the power of the Church.   Furthermore, he
allowed huge tracts of Indian lands to fall into the pos-
session of native and foreign interests.   Many world figures praised Mexico and regarded Díaz as a truly pro-
gressive figure.   On a visit just three years before the
outbreak of the Mexican Revolution and Díaz's downfall,

Elihu Root regarded him as "one of the greatest men to be held up for the hero worship of mankind."

It was very easy to mistake oppression for tranquility during the porfiriato. In 1894 the budget was balanced for the first time and in 1896 the onerous alcabala, a carry-over sales tax from colonial times, was finally abolished. Millions of pesos were spent and many foreign dignitaries attended the hundredth anniversary of Mexico's independence in 1910. No expense was spared to make Mexico City a showcase for Díaz's regime. However, his ever-increasing oppression of the great majority in Mexico led to his downfall in 1910, when he was forced into exile and died in Paris, where his body remains to this day. Perhaps his most often repeated quotation, a reflexion of the way many Latin Americans feel about the close proximity of their countries to the powerful United States, is the following: "¡Pobre México, tan lejos de Dios y tan cerca de los Estados Unidos (Poor Mexico, so far from God and so close to the United States)!"

DIAZ BALLESTEROS, ENRIQUE. Born in Morelia, Michoacán. Law degree. Administrator with the National Railroads. Since 1961 with the Basic Commodities Corporation (CONASUPO), and its Director General since May 1979.

DIAZ COVARRUBIAS, FRANCISCO. 1833-1889. Teacher, geographer and astronomer. From Veracruz, he taught at the Colegio de Minería, the Escuela de Minas and finally at the Escuela Nacional de Ingenieros. He made original contributions in astrophysics and correctly predicted the eclipse of the sun in 1857. After the triumph of Juárez he worked in his government and headed a Mexican commission to Japan in 1874 to study the planet Venus.

DIAZ DE LA VEGA, ROMULO. 1800-1877. General and supporter of Iturbide. At various times he fought against the Texans, French and Americans. He was President of Mexico in 1855 for a little less than a month. Forced into exile, he returned when the conservatives gained power and he fought against Juárez. He was captured, but because of his long history of fighting Mexico's foreign enemies he was set free, lived a secluded life and died in Puebla.

DIAZ DEL CASTILLO, BERNAL. c.1495-1581. Soldier and

historian, he wrote the best account of the Spanish conquest of Mexico entitled, Verdadera historia de la conquista de la Nueva España (True History of the Conquest
of New Spain). He had accompanied Hernán Cortés during
his conquest of the Aztecs and after the conquest of
Tenochtitlán he accompanied Cortés south to Honduras
and witnessed the killing of Cuauhtémoc at the hands of
the Spaniards. His history was written more than 40
years after the events as an answer to apocryphal accounts of the Conquest which had been circulated. Although not written in a scholarly manner, its detailed
description of events makes it the best account ever written of the destruction of the Aztec nation. It was published originally in 1632 in Madrid, but a 1904-5 edition
in two volumes by the Mexican historian Genaro García
gives probably a more faithful rendition of the events.

DIAZ INFANTE, LUIS. Born in 1896 in León, Guanajuato.
An attorney who served as a Deputy in the federal Congress, and as acting Governor of Guanjuato, he became a
federal judge and ultimately a Justice of the federal Supreme Court 1950-58. Although a member of the Institutional Revolutionary Party (PRI), he caused a furor in
Mexico by joining the far-right Sinarquista movement
which supports opposition conservatives against the PRI.

DIAZ ORDAZ, GUSTAVO. Born on March 11, 1911, in San
Andrés, Puebla. Law degree from the University of
Puebla. Professor of law and then vice-president of the
University of Puebla. A Deputy in the federal Congress
1943-46 and then a Senator 1946-52. Prosecuting Attorney
in Puebla, then a justice of the State Supreme Court of
Puebla. Minister of Gobernación (Interior) under President López Mateos during 1958-64. President of Mexico
during 1964-70, having the republic host the Olympics in
October 1968. His administration faced the most serious
challenge to public order since the Revolutionary fighting
of 1910-20 during student riots organized by the far left
during July-October 1968, culminating in the death of 200
at the Plaza of Three Cultures on October 2. His administration stressed the construction of public housing and
the expansion of the petrochemical industry through government investments. In December 1976 he became Mexico's Ambassador to Spain, but in August 1977 resigned
in disagreement with President López Portillo's policies
towards Spain. He returned to law practice in Mexico
City. He died on July 15, 1979, in Mexico City.

DIAZ SERRANO, JORGE. Born in Nogales, Sonora, on February 6, 1921. Mechanical engineering degree from the National Polytechnic Institution (IPN) in 1941. Graduate study, University of Maryland. From 1946 to 1958 he was a key executive with Fairbanks Morse machinery corporation in Mexico, as well as private electrical, maritime transportation, and petroleum equipment companies. In December 1976 he became director general of the government's Petróleos Mexicanos or Pemex, the agency operating the entire petroleum industry. He rejected the incomplete geological surveys kept since 1938 showing Mexico with eleven billion barrels of proven reserves. He put into the field full-time the largest team of geological surveyors ever assembled in Latin America and found that Mexico had 40 billion barrels of proven oil reserves and a probable total in excess of 60 billion barrels. He devised a production schedule of 2.5 million barrels of oil a day for the 1980's, converting Mexico into one of the world's major producers and exporters of petroleum.

DIDAPP, JUAN PEDRO. Born in Durango. Diplomat and journalist. Wrote articles in the early 1900's condemning one-man rule and advocating political parties. Executed by Huerta's agents after being accused of spying for Carranza. Although they did not have an immediate effect, his writings helped stir greater interest in politics in Mexico.

DIEZMO. An ecclesiastical tax of 10 percent collected in colonial times to defray the costs of church administration; it amounted to a tithe. All Spaniards and mestizos were obliged to pay it. However, all church property and clergymen's wages were exempted from this tax. The Indians were largely exempt from it, paying 10 percent in goods only over the value of crops introduced from Europe, mostly cattle, wheat and silk. However, collection from the Indians appeared to be lax and many of them did not pay the tax. It has been calculated that at the end of the colonial period in New Spain, the diezmo collection amounted to $1,800,000 pesos annually.

DISTRITO FEDERAL. The Republic's Federal District containing Mexico City and numerous suburban communities. The DF has a Governor appointed by the President. The Governor also functions as a de facto Mexico City mayor. His DF Department heads parallel the key administrators in a state and in a municipal government. The DF elects two Senators plus Deputies to the federal Congress. The DF has its own system of federal courts. For geographic administration, the DF is subdivided into Delegations, which are groups of communities.

DIVISION DEL NORTE see VILLA, PANCHO (FRANCISCO)

DOMINGUEZ, BELISARIO. A physician who followed Francisco Madero into the 1910 Revolution, and became a Senator. In 1913, when Domínguez publicly denounced General Victoriano Huerta for killing Madero, Domínguez himself was murdered. His death so enraged Congress that Huerta dissolved it and appointed a new, docile Congress in 1914.

DOMINGUEZ, MIGUEL. 1756-1830. Independence figure. He was a lawyer who actively worked for independence from Spain as early as 1808, when Ferdinand VII became the prisoner of Napoleon. He was eventually arrested by the Spanish authorities and stripped of his position of Mayor of Querétaro. After independence he served on the provisional governing committee of Mexico and later as President of the Supreme Court. He died in Mexico City.

DON JUAN TENORIO. A play about an adventurer and famed lover, imported in colonial times from Spain. In this version, Don Juan repents his sins and goes to Heaven. This play is performed at fiestas of villages celebrating their annual patron Saint's Day, and during various religious holidays.

DOÑA MARINA see MALINCHE, LA

DONIS, ROBERTO. Born in 1934 in San Luis Potosí, he studied painting at the famous school of painting and sculpture, La Esmeralda in Mexico City. He has taken part in more than 50 group exhibitions, both in the Americas and in Europe. Representative of his work is "Corte transversal de un pensamiento."

DOVALI JAIME, ANTONIO. Born on October 3, 1905, in Zacatecas. Engineering degree from the National University (UNAM). Dean of the UNAM Engineering School 1959-66. Director of construction for the National Railroads. Director for the building of the Chihuahua-Pacific

Railroad linking Chihuahua state and its Copper Canyon with the Pacific Coast of Sinaloa 1952-61. He headed the National Institute of Petroleum 1966-70, which founded many petroleum reserves uncharted and unreported. As Director General of the government's Pemex 1970-76, he increased oil production enough to convert Mexico into a petroleum exporting nation.

DUCOING, LUIS HUMBERTO. Born May 15, 1937, in Guanajuato. Law degree from the University of Guanajuato. A national leader of the National Federation of Campesinos (CNC) since 1964. As a Deputy in the federal Congress, he pushed agrarian legislation. Governor of the state of Guanajuato 1973-79.

DUPRE CENICEROS, ENRIQUE. Born in 1913 in Durango. Engineering degree from the National University. As a Deputy in the federal Congress and then as a Senator, a key formulator of legislation on irrigation and on water usage 1952-62. Governor of Durange state 1962-66. A leader of the National Campesino Federation (CNC), and longtime pólicy advisor for the Department of Agrarian Affairs and its successor, the Ministry of Agrarian Reform.

DURAN, DIEGO. (1538-1588). A mestizo priest and historian who translated Aztec literature and culture from Nahuatl into Spanish for Spanish colonial officials in the 16th century.

DURANGO CITY. Ciudad Durango or Durango City is the capital of the state of Durango. It had a 1976 population totaling 210,000. This city is located 500 miles northwest of Mexico City, at an elevation of 6,300 feet above sea level. It is the largest city in the state, and its economy stresses lumber and mineral processing industries, with founderies, textile mills, and tobacco factories. It serves as an important railroad and highway link between El Paso, Texas, and Mexico City.

DURANGO (STATE). A state in northwestern Mexico, Durango is the fourth largest state in the republic, with an area of 119,648 square kilometers. Its western region is dominated by the Sierra Madre Occidental, with pine and oak forests. The northern region of the state is desert, except for the irrigated farmlands in the Laguna district, formed by hydroelectric projects on the Nazas River.

Mining, ranching, corn, and cotton are mainstays of the economy. Durango produces silver, gold, lead, copper, and iron ore.

DZIB CARDOZCO, JOSE. Born on January 12, 1921, in Campeche. An attorney and oceanographer who as a professor of oceanography at the University of Campeche since the 1950's has nationally influenced legislation about fishing in Mexican territorial waters as well as the administration of laws pertaining to fishing and to all major research relating to the seas. As president of the University of Campeche, in 1961 he encouraged state universities facing the Gulf of Mexico or the Pacific Ocean to organize or expand their degree programs involving the fishing industry. He also promoted practical fishing schools for skilled tradesmen.

- E -

ECHAVE IBIA, BALTASAR. Born in Mexico around 1580, he was the son of Echave "El Viejo" (The Old One). His works represent a transition from the Renaissance to the Baroque style and what few paintings remain are housed in the Escuela de Artes Plásticas. He died in 1660.

ECHAVE ORIO, BALTASAR. 1548-1630. Born in Guipúzcoa, Spain, he is known as "El Viejo" (The Old One), to distinguish him from his son. Arrived in Mexico around 1580 and was married there. An excellent painter of this period, his works "La Visitación" and "La Anunciación" can be seen at the Escuela de Artes Plásticas. Several of his works can also be seen in the National Cathedral in Mexico City.

ECHEVERRIA, FRANCISCO JAVIER. 1797-1852. Born in Jalapa in the state of Veracruz, he occupied various political posts until being named president of Mexico for a very brief period in 1841. After leaving the presidency he continued to occupy various governmental and cultural posts. He died in Mexico City.

ECHEVERRIA ALVAREZ, LUIS. Born on January 17, 1922, in Mexico City. Law degree from the National University (UNAM) 1945. Graduate study in Santiago, Chile. Professor of law at UNAM 1947-49. Executive secretary to the president of the Institutional Revolutionary Party

(PRI), then director of publicity for the PRI, member of the PRI national executive committee, then PRI executive officer. In government, he began in 1952 as director of accounts for the Ministry of the Navy, then executive officer for the Ministry of Education. As senior cabinet member under President Díaz Ordaz during 1964-70, he was Minister of Gobernación (Interior). As President of Mexico, 1970-76, he took a position of Third World nations in foreign policy, vigorously supporting the Communist, Socialist, and Arab blocs in the United Nations in an unsuccessful bid to become UN Secretary General. He expropriated the tobacco production industry in 1972 and the motion picture production industry in 1975. In 1976 he pushed extensive expropriations of medium-size farms in Sonora, Sinaloa, and other northern states, engendering a controversy over the constitutionality of his actions. During his administration, the lucrative tourist industry severely contracted. In September 1976 he devalued the peso from 12.50 to 23 to the dollar, ending 22 years of stability for the Mexican currency. He became Ambassador to UNESCO in 1977 and Ambassador to Australia in 1978. In 1974 and 1975 he was personally attacked by students while speaking at UNAM, an unheard of occurrence in modern Mexico since the institutionalizing of the Revolution in 1920.

ECHEVERRIA ALVAREZ, RODOLFO. Born in Mexico City. Brother of Mexican President Luis Echeverría (1970-76). Deputy in the federal Congress 1952-55 and 1961-64, and a Senator 1964-70. For years a motion picture and theater actor under the name "Rodolfo Landa." A key formulator of government policy for the motion picture industry since 1964 and especially during periods when he headed the Mexican Actors Union. Director General of the government's National Cinema Bank 1970-76.

ECHEVERRIA RUIZ, RODOLFO. Born in Mexico City. Nephew of former Mexican President Luis Echeverría and son of Rodolfo senior, former head of the Cinema Bank. Attorney who served as a Deputy in Congress. Director of Youth for the Institutional Revolutionary Party (PRI), he became PRI executive officer from 1970 to 1976. Since 1976 he has been Assistant Minister of Labor in the López Portillo cabinet.

ECONOMY. The economy of Mexico during the colonial era and through the 19th century depended upon mining and

agriculture. With the institutionalizing of the social Revolution in the 1920's and 1930's, the economy began to
diversify. Since the 1940's, industrialization has been
a budget and policy priority of the federal government.
In recent decades, the government has increased its investments, making it the senior partner, and the private
sector the junior partner, in many major sectors of the
economy. The government controls 88 percent of the 30
largest industries in a public-private mixed economy.
Economically, 5 percent of all Mexicans are classified
as wealthy, 30 percent as middle class, and 65 percent
as working class.

EDUCATION.   Educational reform has been a major promise
of the ongoing social revolution. The government maintains a national university and 39 state and technical universities and institutes of higher learning, vocational and
teachers colleges, and preparatory schools. The federal
and state governments both maintain primary and secondary schools. Yet with the population explosion of the
1970's, one school-age Mexican in three could not find
classroom space. The 1978 drop-out rate at the sixth
grade reached 70 percent. The 1970 census found the
average formal education for the total population was the
fourth grade and the 1980 census projection figure was
the fifth grade. The official literacy rate is 76 percent
but a lower percentage of the population is fully func-
tionally literate.

EJIDITARIO.   An ejiditario is a farmer on an ejido, i.e., a
communal farmer. Any member of the community owning
the farm who is eighteen years of age or older can qualify as an ejiditario where he or she actually engages in
farming, based on permanent residence and family relationships.

EJIDO.   An ejido is a Mexican communal farm belonging to
an Indian or mestizo (hybrid Spanish-Indian) village or community. Villages owned ejidos at the time the Spaniards
conquered Mexico in 1520. During the 1876-1911 dictatorship of Porfirio Díaz these farms were taken from the villages and given to favored government administrators or
sold by the government to large landowners. A principal
goal of the social Revolution proclaimed in 1910 and le-
galized in the 1917 Constitution was restitution of ejidos
to their community owners. Inefficient farming methods
have plagued these farms with low production yields.

Each ejido with a general assembly elects its own Commission president, secretary, and treasurer to run the farm and a grievance committee to check on that administration.

ELECTORAL LAW. From 1946 to 1978, the Electoral Law required a political party to have 75,000 members registered in at least two-thirds of the states to qualify for the ballot. The 1978 Electoral Law gives temporary registration to parties in existence since 1973. To retain its legal status and qualify for the ballot a party must now in its first election for the federal Congress win at least 1.5 percent of the total national vote.

ELHUYAR, FAUSTO DE. 1755-1833. Born in Spain and studied in various parts of Europe. In 1785 he was named Director General of the School of Mines in New Spain, a post which he held until the latter months of 1821, when he resigned and returned to Spain. He discovered the element tungsten and is regarded as one of the key men responsible for the establishment of science study in New Spain.

ELIZONDO. Soldier who betrayed Hidalgo, Allende and other leaders of the independence movement at Acatita de Baján in Coahuila, causing them to be executed.

ELIZONDO, SALVADOR. Born in 1932 in Mexico City. Studied at Mexican and European universities. A Fellow at the Mexican Writers Center, his short stories for years have been published in magazines such as Siempre and Universidad de México. In 1965 he wrote and directed the film "Apocalipsis 1900." His 1965 novel, Farabeuf, won Mexican and foreign awards. It is a study of loneliness and violence.

ELIZONDO LOZANO, EDUARDO ANGEL. Born in 1922 in Monterrey, Nuevo León. Law degree. President of the University of Nuevo León 1965-67. Governor of the state of Nuevo León 1967-70. After major student riots, he resigned his governorship mid-way in his six-year term. In the 1970's he was a judge of a state district court.

EMPLOYERS FEDERATION. The Confederación Patronal de la República de México (COPARMEX) or Employers Federation of the Republic of Mexico, founded in 1929, is a voluntary association of employers from retail commerce, manufacturing industries, wholesalers, and other private-sector management. COPARMEX lobbies and negotiates with government and labor unions.

ENCINAS JOHNSON, LUIS. Born on October 23, 1912, in Hermosillo, Sonora. Law degree from the National University. He became nationally known for overcoming his physical afflictions to lead a vigorous, successful public life. As a young adult, he caught leprosy and was cured. With impaired vision, he had to wear dark glasses and be read to, yet he went on to be Attorney General of Sonora, State Supreme Court justice, President of the University of Sonora 1956-61, then Governor of the state of Sonora 1961-67, then Director General of the National Bank of Agricultural Credit 1970-73, then into law practice.

ENCOMIENDA. An area in colonial Mexico which contained substantial numbers of Indians. In each encomienda, also called a repartimiento, Indians were required by the Viceroy to pay tribute to the Spanish conquerors and to work free for them.

ENRIQUEZ COYRO, ERNESTO. Born in 1901 in Mexico City. Degree from the University of Barcelona, Spain, then a law degree from the National University of Mexico (UNAM). In 1951 he was the founder and first Dean of the UNAM School of Political and Social Sciences. Assistant Minister of Education 1958-64. He reorganized the Ministry of National Patrimony in 1951.

ESCOCESES. Term used when referring to the Scottish Rite Masons. See WARD, H. G.

ESCUTIA, JUAN. 1827-1847. Niño Héroe (Heroic Child). Juan Escutia was from Nayarit and had just started to attend the Escuela Militar in Chapultepec Park when he found himself defending the Escuela Militar against the Americans. Rather than allow the Mexican flag to fall into the hands of the invaders, it is popularly believed that he wrapped himself in it and jumped to his death from a cliff. His remains are interred in the "Monumento a los Niños Héroes" in Chapultepec Park.

ESPINOSA DE LOS MONTEROS, ANTONIO. (1903-1959). Master's degree from Harvard University. Economist and Ambassador to the United States 1945-48, he was one of the founders of the School of Economics at the National

University (UNAM).   Director General of the government's
development bank, Nacional Financiera, 1935-45.

ESTRADA REYNOSO, ROQUE.   Born in August 1883 in Zacatecas, where he died in 1966.   Law degree from the University of Guadalajara in 1906.   He became a Brigadier
General during the 1913-15 battles of the Revolution.   After being secretary to President Francisco Madero, he
was executive secretary to President Venustiano Carranza
1914-15.   He was the major opposition candidate for president of Mexico against winner Alvaro Obregón in 1920.
He was a justice of the federal Supreme Court 1941-52.
After he joined the unsuccessful rebellion of Adolfo de la
Huerta in 1923, he was exiled to the United States, but
allowed to return and later became a leader in the dominant Institutional Revolutionary Party, being co-opted into
the pro-government establishment.

EXCELSIOR.   The leading daily newspaper of Mexico, Excelsior was founded in 1916 by Félix Palavicini (1881-1952)
as the first modern news-oriented daily in Mexico, with
news reports instead of editorial views on the front page.
It became cooperatively owned by key employees.   In July
1976 a purge directed by followers of Mexican President
Echeverría, sensitive to severe criticism, ousted longtime
executive publisher Julio Scherer García, and his top editors.   The paper has recovered its ability to run stories
critical of government administrators but takes a pro-
establishment position in general.   Its circulation of
300,000 Sundays and 250,000 weekdays reaches important
government officials and business and civic leaders
throughout Mexico.

- F -

FABELA, ISIDRO.   Born on June 28, 1882, in the state of
Mexico.   Died August 12, 1964, in Mexico City.   An attorney who served as Minister of Foreign Relations under
Mexican President Victoriano Huerta during 1913-15, then
served President Carranza as Ambassador to Italy and
Spain, then to Brazil, Chile, and Uruguay, then to Argentina during 1915-20.   Mexico's envoy to the League of
Nations International Labor Office 1937-40.   A judge of
the International Court of Justice at The Hague 1946-52.

FABREGAS, MANOLO.   Born on July 15, 1921, in Mexico

City as Manuel Sánchez Navarro Jr., the son of theater
actor Manuel Sánchez Navarro of one of Mexico's prestige
families tracing back to colonial-era aristocracy, and film
actress Fanny Schiller. He graduated from Texas Military Institute in 1938 and took the stage name "Manolo
Fábregas" in honor of his famous grandmother, theater
actress Virginia Fábregas. After acting in the theater,
films, radio, and television, he became a theater
producer-director-actor in the late 1940's, adapting
Broadway hits into Spanish, such as "Life with Father."
By 1959, his "My Fair Lady" made him Mexico's leading
producer-director as well as the star in the Professor
Higgins role. His 1970 theater production of "Fiddler on
the Roof" broke Mexican box office records, as did his
1971 film "Mecánica Nacional," which played for two
years. He also hosted a "Tonight" and a "Weekend" talk
show on television until the late 1970's. He operates his
own Teatro San Rafael and Teatro Manolo Fábregas, Mexico's leading live-drama theaters. He has produced, directed, or starred in Broadway hits ranging from "Bare-
foot in the Park" to "Man of La Mancha" plus Mexican
plays from "Tenorio" to "Death of Juárez" and "Juan
Derecho."

FAESLER, JULIO. Born in 1930 in Chihuahua. An attorney
who became an economics and finance professor at the
National Polytechnic Institute (IPN), and then the director
of the IPN doctoral program in foreign trade. He was
director of the government's Institute of Foreign Trade
1970-76, and has been a longtime advisor on Mexico's
import and export policies.

FAMILY EXTENDED RELATIONS. In Mexico family extended
relations take on social and political significance shaping
public and private life. A godfather (padrino) and a godmother (madrina) after a child's christening become the
lifelong compadre and comadre or co-father and co-mother
for the child and his or her parents. These relationships
form social circles and are basic units in political parties,
lobbying groups, and for political cliques essential in obtaining appointments to non-routine governmental positions.

FAMILY PLANNING. Not until April 1972 did any Mexican
government publicly advocate family planning, even though
the steadily decreasing death rate and the high birth rate
in the 1950's and 1960's had brought an annual population
increase of 3.6 percent. Public health disease controls

have increased Mexico's longevity from 48 years in 1940 to 64 years in 1979. Decades of Church-State political conflicts had nullified the impact of the papal encyclical against birth control. But the social psychology of ma-chismo or male virility emphasizes that a man beget children with his wife and with any consenting female.

The government opened its first Family Planning Centers in 1973 to begin its program to reduce the annual population increment and thereby reduce the severe pressures on its resources, services, and economy. Even with the migration of millions northward into the United States in the 1970's, more than 800,000 new jobs a year would have had to be created to absorb the excess in the job market and the economy could not grow to that extent. By 1979, 6,000 centers throughout the republic were dispensing free contraceptive pills and birth control literature. However, only 26 percent of fertile-age women were using the centers and fewer than 10 percent of their husbands were. The government has sponsored radio soap operas and talk shows, television programs, comic books, and advertising campaigns stressing "responsible parenthood." Social Security and Public Health Ministry clinics distribute pamphlets and free contraceptives. In the early 1980's the government hopes its vigorous campaign for family planning will have begun to reduce the annual population increment to under 3 percent.

FARIAS, LUIS M. Born on June 7, 1920, in Monterrey, Nuevo León. Law degree at National University (UNAM). Professor of philosophy at UNAM. President of the National Federation of University Students. Television and radio commentator for the XEW and XEW-TV networks 1946-58. Founder and first director of the National Association of Broadcast Announcers 1951. Head of the XEW Union of Artists 1946-64. Executive officer for the Department (Ministry) of Tourism 1964-67. Director of Information for the Ministry of Gobernación (Interior) 1958-64. Governor of the state of Nuevo León 1970-73. A Deputy in the federal Congress 1955-58 and 1979-82 and a Senator 1970. Since 1975 he has been publisher of the Mexico City daily newspaper El Nacional, owned by the government.

FARRELL CUBILLAS, ARSENIO. Born on June 30, 1921, in Mexico City. Law degree from the National University (UNAM) and law professor at UNAM for 25 years. Legal consultant for the Aviation Pilots Union, the Cinema

Production Workers Union, and for the Society of Authors and Composers. Former president of the National Chamber of Alcohol and Sugar Industries. Director General of the government's Federal Electricity Commission 1973-76. Director of the government's Mexican Institute of Social Security for the 1976-82 period.

FASCISM see SINARQUISMO

FEDERALISM. It has never been a powerful force in Mexico, even though on paper it has had a federalist type of constitution and government organization most of the time since 1824. The story of federalism in Mexico is reflected in the constant rivalry between liberals, who have generally identified themselves with the federalist concept of government decentralization and the conservatives, who have generally advocated a strong central government. In 1836 the conservatives succeeded in gaining control and replaced the federalist constitution, the conservative constitution lasting until 1846, when the liberals replaced it with another federalist constitution. This document was later incorporated into the Constitution of 1857 and in 1917 the present constitution was proclaimed, one which resembles its predecessors in many ways. Nevertheless, Mexico continues to be governed by a strong central government, a true federal government remaining an idea rather than a reality.

FEDERATION OF CIVIL SERVANTS UNIONS. The Federación de Sindicatos de los Trabajadores en Servicio del Estado or the Federation of Unions of Civil Servants (Workers in the Service of the State) unites all unions of federal employees. State government and municipal government employees unions have a similar federation. The FSTSE was organized in 1938. In disputes with the government, the FSTSE appeals to the federal Tribunal of Arbitration. The FSTSE maintains its own social security system or institute (ISSSTE) autonomously from the private-sector's employees social security system.

FELIX SERNA, FAUSTINO. Born in May 1913 in Pitiquito, Sonora. Teacher's diploma from the Sonora Normal College. Municipal Councilman, then Mayor of Ciudad Obregón, Sonora. Organized the Caborca Cotton Company, a Sonora trucking service, and founded Sonora Truckers Union. A Deputy in the federal Congress. Governor of the state of Sonora 1967-73.

FERNANDEZ DE LIZARDI, JOAQUIN. A journalist who used the 1812 period of press freedom in Mexico City to propagandize for independence from Spain with pamphlets and his newspaper El Pensador Mexicano. He was one of the precursors of independence.

FERNANDEZ MACGREGOR, GENARO. (1883-1959). An attorney who was founder and publisher until the 1950's of the Mexican Journal of International Law. Assistant Minister of Foreign Relations 1911-14, he was a key legal adviser for the Ministry of Foreign Relations 1917-24 and helped Mexico gain diplomatic recognition from the United States. He was a judge of the International Tribunal of Arbitration at The Hague in the 1940's.

FERNANDEZ MANERO, VICTOR. Born in 1898 in Villahermosa, Tabasco. Medical degree. A physician who served as a Deputy in the federal Congress, then as Governor of Tabasco during 1936-39. In 1940 he joined the presidential cabinet and by 1943 had expanded the Department of Health into a full Ministry of Health and Welfare. He later served as Ambassador to France, then to Yugoslavia.

FERNANDEZ ROMO, EMILIO. Born on March 26, 1904, in Sabinas, Coahuila. After training as an actor and film technician, he became Mexico's leading motion picture director. As an actor, he has been billed as "El Indio," his Indian features being emphasized. In 1938 he apprenticed at various studios in Hollywood and remained in Hollywood to observe the editing of Sergeil Eisenstein's classic film "Viva México." By 1979 he had directed 39 motion pictures in Mexico, beginning with "La isla de la pasión" in 1941. His "María Candelareria" in 1943 established him as a leading director. Next his film "Enamorada" brought stardom to actors Pedro Armendáriz and María Félix. In 1943 he directed and produced "Flor Silvestre," which was the first Mexican film starring Dolores del Río, although she had been a Hollywood star since 1931. His film "Islas Marías" about the harsh penal colony brought prison reform to Mexico. His movie "Un día de vida" in 1950 became one of the most acclaimed and successful films in Latin America. Among his other artistic and financial successes were "Salón México," "La Red," "La Choca," "Soy puro mexicano," and "La bien amada."

FIDEICOMISOS. These are government development lending
agencies for cooperatives, such as Fideicomiso Pesquero
for fishing cooperatives, and others for small businessmen, skilled workers in industries related to tobacco and
sugar, and small-scale artisans such as silversmiths.

FINANCE MINISTRY. Originally the Ministry of the Treasury
in 1821, it became the Ministry of Finance in 1917 and
the Ministry of Finance and Public Credit in 1958 (Secretaría de Hacienda y Crédito Público). It operates federal tax collections, and other government income, dis-
burses federal expenditures, and administers credit and
investments extended by the government through decentralized government agencies and banks.

FINE ARTS NATIONAL INSTITUTE. The federal government's National Institute of Fine Arts, semi-autonomous
under the Ministry of Public Education, was created by
a law enacted in December 1946. The director of the
Instituto Nacional de Bellas Artes administers a symphonic orchestra, a classical ballet company, a folklore ballet
company, a music conservatory, art museums and gal-
leries, the National Anthropology Museum, federally-
funded libraries, and various artistic activities throughout
the republic.

FINE ARTS PALACE. The Palacio de Bellas Artes on
Juárez Avenue in the center of Mexico City was constructed in 1934 by a team of architects from Italy, adapting
features of classical theaters of Europe into a composite.
The muraled glass curtain was built by Tiffany's jewelry
company of New York. This building is the theater for
the National Symphony, the National Folklore Ballet, and
the major opera and symphonic concerts in Mexico.

FISHING, DEPARTMENT OF. A federal agency created in
December 1976 by President José López Portillo, the
autonomous Department of Fishing coordinates its work
with the Ministry of Agriculture and Hydraulic Resources.
Fernando Rafful, a career public administrator, has directed it since the agency's inception. It deals with all
commercial fishing activities and the marine resources
in territorial ocean waters and rivers and lakes. By
law, all shrimp fishing fleets in Mexico must be cooperatives working with government coordinators. This department works jointly with the Ministry of the Navy in
maintaining the republic's fish hatcheries and keeping
inventories of marine resources.

FLORES, EDMUNDO. Born in 1918 in Mexico City. An
economist and public administrator whose articles and
essays in the 1950's and 1960's influenced Mexico's policies and exports and imports. He was a visiting professor at the Woodrow Wilson School of International Affairs from 1972 to 1974, then Mexico's Ambassador to
Cuba from 1974 to 1975. He directed the Institute of
Political, Economic, and Social Studies (IEPES) of the
Institutional Revolutionary Party, 1975-76, and since 1976
has been director of the government's National Council
of Science and Technology (Consejo Nacional de Ciencia
y Tecnología).

FLORES MAGON, ENRIQUE. 1887-1954. The youngest of
three brothers, he is regarded as a precursor of the
Mexican Revolution, although he played a much less active
role than his more famous brothers. He died in Mexico
City.

FLORES MAGON, JESUS. The oldest of the three Flores
Magón brothers, he was born in Oaxaca in 1872. With
his brother Ricardo he founded an anti-Díaz newspaper,
El Demócrata, which Díaz promptly closed. This marked
the height of his revolutionary fervor, for he gave up all
pretense of being a revolutionary and withdrew from participation.

FLORES MAGON, RICARDO. 1873-1922. Revolutionary
leader and the most famous of the three Flores Magón
brothers. He was a lawyer by profession and is generally regarded as the intellectual precursor of the Mexican
Revolution. Along with his brother Jesús, he founded the
newspaper La Regeneración, which promptly caused his
encarceration. He later published the newspaper from
his exile in San Antonio, Texas and continued to attack
the government of Porfirio Díaz. In 1906 he founded the
Mexican Liberal Party and in 1911 led a rebellion in Baja
California. Ricardo Flores Magón never joined forces
with Madero, refusing to have anything to do with what
he termed a "bourgeois revolution." For writing seditious
literature, he was sentenced in 1918 to the federal penitentiary at Ft. Leavenworth for 20 years and died in
1922.

FLORES SANCHEZ, OSCAR. Born in Chihuahua. Law degree. Senator from Chihuahua 1952-58. Governor of
the state of Chihuahua 1968-74. Since 1976, he has been

Mexico's federal Attorney General in the López Portillo cabinet. He has conducted the most vigorous campaign against drug smuggling within Mexico and into the United States in modern times.

FLORES TAPIA, OSCAR. Born in 1914 in Saltillo, Coahuila. Teacher's diploma from Normal College. A Senator from Coahuila 1970-76. Within the Institutional Revolutionary Party (PRI), he has been director of editorial activities, on the PRI national executive committee, the PRI secretary for popular action, and head of the National Federation of Popular Organizations (CNOP).

FONATUR. The National Fund for Tourism or Fondo Nacional de Turismo (FONATUR) was created by the government in 1972 to handle government investments in hotels and resorts facilities throughout the republic. FONATUR funded and built most of the facilities at the resort of Cancún on the Yucatán coast.

FONDO. In 1965 Mexican President Gustavo Díaz Ordaz created twelve new development agencies called fondos (funds). These are major government lending outlets for different types of activity in the Mexican economy, such as tourism, the fishing industry, the sugar industry, and the housing industry.

FONDO DE CULTURA ECONOMICA. The Fund of Economic Culture is a prestigious book publisher founded in 1935 by historian Daniel Cosío Villegas. Later the government became a senior partner in the company, expanding it to the largest publisher of quality books in Latin America.

FONDO DE PROMOCION DE INFRAESTRUCTURA TURISTICA. The government's Fund for Promotion of Tourism Infrastructure (INFRATUR) builds various facilities helping develop tourist resorts.

FONDO NACIONAL DE LA VIVIENDA PARA LOS TRABAJA-DORES. The government's Institute of the National Fund for Workers Housing (INFONAVIT), was created in 1971 to construct low-cost housing for workers throughout the republic.

FONDO NACIONAL DEL CONSUMO DE LOS TRABAJADORES. The government's National Fund for Consumption by Workers (FONACOT) helps upgrade workers' consumption and subsidizes a few basic commodities which are necessities for the working class.

FOREIGN CLUB. A very profitable casino controlled by Plutarco Elías Calles which catered mainly to middle and lower income Mexicans. Cárdenas closed it down, thereby incurring the wrath of the man who had so much to do with putting him in power.

FOREIGN RELATIONS MINISTRY. The Secretaría de Relaciones Exteriores or Ministry of Foreign Relations maintains Mexico's diplomatic corps abroad and handles all binational and multinational affairs of Mexico.

FRAGA, GABINO. Born in 1899 in Morelia, Michoacán. An attorney who was head of the National Banking Commission, Assistant Minister of Foreign Relations, and a justice of the federal Supreme Court, who was best known as a founder of the Institute of Public Administration, and promoted the concept of higher education for the careers in public administration in the 1950's.

FRAIRE, ISABEL. Born in 1934 in Mexico City. A writer for literary magazines, she became nationally known in the 1970's for translating and publishing the poetry of Ezra Pound and T. S. Eliot. Her own volume of poems, Solo esta luz, in 1969 brought her international recognition.

FRANCO SODI, CARLOS. (1904-1961). An attorney from Oaxaca, he was federal Attorney General during 1952-56, then a justice of the federal Supreme Court during 1956-61. He had also been director of the Mexico City federal penitentiary and his many articles and commentaries on criminal law helped modernize Mexican penal law from the 1940's to the 1960's.

FREEMASONRY. The Masonic York Rite and Scottish Rite lodges became active in Mexico in 1822 and promoted the concepts of anti-clerical politics aimed at separation of Church and State. A leader in the struggle for Mexico's independence from Spain, Vicente Guerrero, became grand master of the York Rite in 1824. In the 1850's, as a leader of Freemasonry, Mexican President Benito Juárez got the 1857 Constitution to separate Church and State and nationalize cemeteries. Most of the Mexican presidents since 1920 have been 32-degree Masons as a gesture

showing their support of the legal separation of Church
and State and the curtailment of religious-based partisan
politics.

FREMONT, JOHN.   American explorer and soldier of fortune.
His occupation of California in 1846 led to a revolt in
Mexico City, resulting in the liberals defeating the cen-
tralists and returning to power.

FUENTES, CARLOS.   Born in 1928 in Mexico City.   He received a law degree from the National University, then
studied in European and United States universities.
Fuentes has become the most influential writer in Mexico
since the 1950's.   He edited the magazine El Espectador
and was one of the founders in 1955 of the Revista Mexicana de Literatura.   In 1954, publication of his volume
of short stories, Los días enmascarados, brought him
national recognition.   His 1958 novel, La región mas
transparente, examines the social structure of Mexico
City by focusing on the financial ruin of a former Revolution leader.   His 1959 novel, Las buenas conciencias,
portrays provincial life.   His 1962 Aura deals with Mexican beliefs in ghosts.   His 1962 novel, La muerte de
Artemio Cruz, reviews the life of a dying ex-leader of
the Revolution, with the protagonist symbolizing Mexican
history since 1910 and emerging modernization of the
republic.
    In 1967 he published his best-known novel, Cambio
de piel (Change of Skin) which made him well known
throughout Latin America and Europe, and has been translated into English, French, Russian, Czech, Portuguese,
German, Japanese, and other languages.   It won the prestigious Spanish Premio Biblioteca Breve.   The story is
narrated by an aging nihilist who with other travelers
must spend the night in the Aztec city of Cholula.   Through
flashbacks, he probes the decline of modern society.
    Fuentes also has written plays, such as Todos los
gatos in 1970, and six motion picture scripts including
the 1966 "Tiempo de morir."   His essays on politics and
economics, giving a socialist view, total in the hundreds
in Mexican magazines, plus his articles in Saturday Review, the New York Times, London Times, and several
European magazines.   The Mexican magazine Siempre has
published the largest number of his essays.

FUENTES, MARIO.   Born in 1934 in Cruillas, he studied
painting and sculpture at the National University in Mexico

City. Some of his most representative works are the paintings "Familia" and "Mujer" and the sculpture "Cristo," the latter located at San Nicolás de las Garzas.

FUEROS. Special privileges enjoyed by the clergy, particularly the custom of priests and clergy being tried in special Church courts.

- G -

GACHUPIN. Term used in Mexico to refer to the Spaniards and used mostly in a derogatory manner. In colonial times this was the way that the Creoles, who were seldom granted real political power, derisively referred to the peninsular Spaniards. It literally means "man who wears spurs" and is probably Aztec in origin.

GADSDEN, JAMES. (1788-1858). The United States Minister to Mexico who concluded the 1854 U.S.-Mexico treaty for the purchase of some Mexican territory. See GADSDEN PURCHASE.

GADSDEN PURCHASE. In 1854 the United States Minister to Mexico, James Gadsden, signed a treaty with Mexican President Antonio López de Santa Anna whereby the U.S. purchased 29,670 square miles (76,845 square kilometers) of territory in northernmost Sonora and Chihuahua, the Mesilla Valley, this area becoming the southernmost parts of Arizona and New Mexico. The price was $10 million in gold, which General Santa Anna spent rather than remit to the Mexican treasury. This sale was partly responsible for Santa Anna's overthrow in 1855. U.S. President Franklin Pierce directed the negotiating of the treaty so that the Southern Pacific railroad could be constructed from Texas to California through low mountain passes, avoiding the higher elevations to the north, above the border which had been set in 1848, after the U.S.-Mexican War.

GALEANA, HERMENEGILDO. 1762-1814. Revolutionary leader, he was a follower of Morelos and saved the latter's life during the battle for Cuatla. His actions during the siege of Acapulco in 1813 were decisive in the taking of that port by the insurgents. Because of his extraordinary leadership qualities, he was nicknamed "Tata Gildo" (Uncle Gildo) by his followers. He was killed in an

ambush, and when independence finally came to Mexico
he was declared a national hero.

GALEANA, JUAN PABLO.   1760-1814.   Revolutionary leader.
He was born in Guerrero of an English father and a Mexican mother, becoming a follower of Morelos along with
his brothers Hermenegildo and José.   Juan Pablo, along
with his brothers, played a key role in the siege of
Cuatla and in the surrender of Acapulco to Morelos.   He
was probably killed in 1814, ambushed along with his
brother Hermenegildo, but his body has never been found.

GALINDO, SERGIO.   Born in 1926 in Jalapa, Veracruz.   He
was director of publications at the University of Veracruz
for ten years.   His 1959 novel, La justicia de enero,
prompted changes in the immigration service.   His 1960
novel, El bordo, popularized the psychological probing of
the reforms of the Revolution.

GALVAN LOPEZ, FELIX.   Born in 1913 in Guanajuato.
Graduated from the Military College in 1930 and rose
through the officer ranks to Division General.   As Inspector General of the Army in the 1960's, he modernized all enlisted personnel's technical training.   He
brought the computer into daily operations of the armed
forces.   Since 1976 he has been Minister of Defense.

GALVAN RIVERA, MARIANO.   1782-1876.   Editor and book
publisher.   He founded the book publishing industry in
Mexico and was responsible for many published authors
in his country.   Among his most famous publications was
El periquillo sarniento, by Fernández de Lizardi.   Because of his conservative ideas he became a member of
the Junta de Notables, which backed Maximilian and the
reestablishment of the monarchy in Mexico.   After the
downfall of Maximilian he served time in prison, was
eventually released and died in Mexico City.

GALVEZ, JOSE DE.   1729-1787.   A Spaniard, he was sent
by Charles III to New Spain, where he served from 1765
to 1772, being the last visitor-general sent to New Spain.
His principal mission was to install the intendency system
and during his first year succeeded in having the viceroy
recalled.   After this move he injected an efficiency into
New Spain never before experienced, thus helping to establish Charles III as one of the greatest of Spanish
kings.   He supervised the expulsion of the Jesuits in 1767

and countered Russian territorial threats by extending the
limits of New Spain as far north as San Francisco Bay.
He sent Fray Junípero Serra to California and established
garrisons and missions at San Diego and Monterey. In
his general report of 1771 he recommended numerous reforms, many of which related to mining and tax reforms.
Understandably, he is regarded as the greatest visitor-
general ever to be assigned to New Spain.

GAMBLING. Since 1934 Mexico has prohibited casino gaming
but for a century has permitted betting on horse races
and jai alai. The government operates a National Lottery
twice a week, with the proceeds helping to support hospital care for the poor. Each agent selling lottery tickets
must be licensed by the government.

GAMBOA, FEDERICO. 1864-1939. A novelist, playwright
and diplomat, he was born in Mexico City. Occupied
various diplomatic posts and in 1913 was Secretary of
Foreign Relations in the Huerta government. After the
latter's downfall Gamboa went into exile until 1923, when
he returned to his native country and supported himself
by teaching and writing. He also became President of
the Mexican Academy of the Spanish Language. Gamboa
is known primarily as a novelist, having a mainly modernistic style. His most famous play is La venganza de
la gleba and his most famous novel is Santa, which was
eventually made into a movie.

GAMIO, MANUEL. 1883-1960. Indianist, anthropologist and
archaeologist born in Mexico City. Considered one of the
outstanding experts in the world on Indian civilizations in
Mexico, he made a detailed study of Teotihuacán, discovering the Temple of Quetzalcóatl, known as La Ciu-
dadela (The Citadel). He is also famous for a study of
the population of the Valley of Teotihuacán. Gamio was
Subsecretary of Education in 1925 and Director of the
Interamerican Institute of Indigenous Studies from its
founding in 1942 until his death. Among his many works
are Investigaciones arqueológicas en México, El Templo
de Quetzalcóatl and La población del Valle de Mexico.

GANDARA, CESAR. Born in Sonora from a family tracing
its aristocratic roots back to the Spanish colonial era of
the 16th century. Owner of the largest hotels and motels
in the state of Sonora since the 1950's. Former president of the National Association of Hotels of Mexico.

Mayor of Hermosillo during 1958-61. Secretary of State
for Sonora during 1967-73. In Mexico, there are no
lieutenant governors, and the Secretary of State performs
that function as well as being the executive officer for a
state just below the governor.

GARCIA, GENARO. 1867-1920. Mexican historian who edited
the most complete and faithful edition of Bernal Díaz del
Castillo's Verdadera historia de la conquista de la Nueva
España (True History of the Conquest of New Spain).
This edition was published in 1904-5 in 2 volumes and is
based on the original manuscript kept in Guatemala City.

GARCIA, JESUS. 1881-1907. He was a locomotive fireman
in Sonora and saved the town of Nacozari from catastrophe
by single-handedly driving a dynamite-laden train out of
town. The train was already burning when he took over
the operation of it and it blew up at a safe distance from
Nacozari, killing García. He is known as the Hero of
Nacozari.

GARCIA BARRAGAN, MARCELINO. Born in 1895 in Jalisco.
An army general who became a political reformer, he
was director of the Military College, then Governor of
Jalisco. In 1950 he helped General Henríquez Guzmán
organize the Federation of People's Parties (Federación
de Partidos del Pueblo de México or FPPM), among
dissidents from the dominant Institutional Revolutionary
Party (PRI). Although the FPPM registered 100,000 voters in two-thirds of the states, Henríquez drew 580,000
votes in the 1952 presidential election. García Barragán,
as FPPM president and campaign director during 1950-
54, stressed the anti-crony platform. In 1954 the Federal Electoral Commission cancelled the FPPM's status as
a registered party over technicalities in registering voters. García was Minister of Defense 1964-70, having
rejoined the PRI.

GARCIA CONDE, PEDRO. 1806-1851. Politician, cartogra-
pher and military figure. From a very young age he was
attracted to the military and at the age of 34 he was already a general. At the same time he was active politically, serving in various posts in his native Sonora. Because of his cartographic skill he was responsible for
fixing the new boundaries of Mexico and the United States
after the War of 1846-1848.

GARCIA CRUZ, MIGUEL. (1909-1969). An engineer from
Oaxaca who became a leading demographer and pioneer
in population studies in Mexican universities in the
1950's. He served as the second highest administrator,
Secretary General, of the Mexican Institute of Social
Security (IMSS), for private-sector workers, from the
inception of the social security system in 1943 through
1958, for 15 years. He headed the Social Welfare Commission.

GARCIA CUBAS, ANTONIO. 1832-1912. Engineer and geographer. He graduated from the Colegio de Ingenieros
with honors, specializing in geography. He managed to
stay free of political difficulties, being well-regarded by
both Maximilian and Juárez. He was made a member of
the Order of Guadalupe by Maximilian and occupied a high
position in the Secretariat of Development in the Juárez
government. Among his works are Curso de geografía
elemental and El libro de mis recuerdos.

GARCIA GONZALEZ, ALFONSO. 1909-1961. An attorney
who was Governor of Baja California del Norte 1947-52,
then Ambassador to Colombia 1952-58, then Director
General of Tourism 1959-61. As a university student,
he was heavyweight boxing champion of Mexico and promoted Mexican boxing teams at Central American and
Pan American Games and the Olympics in the 1950's and
helped develop Mexican professional boxers in lighter
weights rated world challengers and champions throughout
the 1950's. He headed the Mexican Sports Federation.

GARCIA GRANADOS, FRANCISCO. 1786-1841. Politician
and military figure. He helped to write the Constitution
of 1824 and was named as Minister of Public Finance in
the government of Guadalupe Victoria. He occupied numerous political positions afterwards, among them being
Governor of Zacatecas. Because he was responsible for
so many improvements in Zacatecas, he was affectionately
referred to as "Tata Pachito" (Father Pachito). He fought
against Santa Anna, was defeated by him and retired from
public life, dying in the city of Zacatecas.

GARCIA ICAZBALCETA, JOAQUIN. 1825-1894. He is regarded as one of the most capable historians of his era
and was praised for his erudite abilities by the famous
Spanish scholar Ramón Menéndez Pelayo. He translated
and published Prescott's Historia de la conquista del

Perú, but probably his greatest work is the Bibliografía mexicana del siglo XVI. He died in Mexico City.

GARCIA PUJOU, LEON. (1898-1972). An agrarian leader from San Luis Potosí. A Deputy in the federal Congress 1928-30, 1937-40, and a Senator 1940-46. One of the founders of the National Campesino Federation (CNC) in 1936.

GARCIA RAMIREZ, SERGIO. Born in 1938 in Guadalajara, Jalisco. An attorney who as a federal judge in the 1960's pioneered to bring modern rehabilitation of delinquent children to Mexico. Assistant Minister of National Patrimony, then Assistant Minister of Gobernación (Interior) 1972-76. Founder of the first prison without bars in Mexico. Leading authority on penal laws.

GARCIA SAINZ, RICARDO. Born on June 8, 1930, in Mexico City. An attorney who became head of the Income Tax Department of the Ministry of Finance 1956-58 and assistant director of Social Security 1966-76. Minister of Programming and the Budget in the López Portillo cabinet from November 1977 to May 1979. He was best known for his vigorous leadership of the National Association of Importers and Exporters in the 1960's.

GARRIDO CANABAL, TOMAS. Minister of Agriculture in the Cárdenas administration and a supporter of Calles.

GARRIDO DIAZ, LUIS. (1898-1973). Professor of law at the University of Michoacán, then its president 1924-28. A co-founder of the Mexican Association of Universities and Institutions of Higher Education. President of the National Autonomous University (UNAM) 1948-52. A federal judge, and assistant publisher of the Mexico City daily El Nacional. Executive Secretary of the government's National Savings Bonds program during the 1950's and 1960's.

GARRO, ELENA. Born in 1920 in Mexico City. She became one of the few Mexican women to win fame as a playwright and screen writer. She is best known for her 1959 play La señora en su balcón and the 1964 play La dama boba.

GASCON MERCADO, ALEJANDRO. Born in 1932 in Nayarit. President of the Youth Division of the Popular Socialist Party (PPS) 1953-56. Member of PPS national commit-

tee, PPS secretary of press and publicity, PPS director
of economic studies, then executive officer of this opposition minority party. A Deputy in the federal Congress
1970-73. He was president of the National Federation of
Boarding Schools for Workers' Children. His brother,
Julián Gascón Mercado, was Governor of Nayarit 1964-70.

GASCON MERCADO, JULIAN. Born on January 28, 1925, in
Tepic, Nayarit. Medical degree from the National University. A physician and surgeon who, although the candidate of the dominant Institutional Revolutionary Party
(PRI), also received the nomination of the Popular Socialist Party (PPS) to be elected Governor of the state of
Nayarit in 1964, through the efforts of his brother, Alejandro, a PPS leader. Julián's term as Governor was
from 1964 to 1970.

GAXIOLA, FRANCISCO JAVIER. Born in 1898 in Toluca,
Mexico. The attorney who founded the Mexican Bar As-
sociation in 1923. He was also president of the National
College of Lawyers from 1957 to 1972. He had been
Governor of the state of Baja California del Norte 1929-
32 and Minister of Industry and Commerce 1940-44.

GIL PRECIADO, JUAN. Born in 1909 in Jalisco. Professor
of mathematics, then Dean of the Polytechnical School of
the University of Guadalajara. Mayor of Guadalajara
1956-58. Governor of Jalisco 1959-64. Minister of Agriculture 1964-70. He made the United States-Mexican
Hoof and Mouth Disease Commission effective.

GINER DURAN, PRAXEDES. Born in 1893 in Camargo, Chihuahua. A Deputy in the federal Congress, then a Senator, during the 1928-34 period. Governor of the state
of Chihuahua 1962-68. A young officer under General
Pancho Villa 1911-18, he later became a Division General. In 1929 he helped former Mexican President Plutarco
Calles in organizing the founding of the dominant Institutional Revolutionary Party (PRI), then known as the National Revolutionary Party (PNR).

GODFATHER SYSTEM see FAMILY EXTENDED RELATIONS

"GOLONDRINAS, LAS." A traditional Mexican folk song,
"Las Golondrinas" or "The Swallows" is played at engagement parties, at retirement banquets, and other special
festivities.

GOLPE DEL ESTADO. A sudden change in government by
force, or a coup d'état. Mexico suffered some golpes
in the 19th century but has been free of them in this
century, in contrast to many other Latin American republics. During the full-scale warfare of the Revolution
from 1910 to 1920, the murder of President Madero in
1913 and the challenges to President Carranza from 1915
to 1920, seemed like golpes, but sustained fighting followed.

GOMEZ ARIAS, ALEJANDRO. Born in Oaxaca in 1900. An
attorney who helped found the Popular Socialist Party
(PPS) and was its vice-president in 1948.

GOMEZ FARIAS, VALENTIN. 1781-1858. A physician and
politician born in Guadalajara. Outstanding liberal leader
who held many political positions, for many years he was
Vice President under Santa Anna. As early as 1833 he
held the presidency for two brief periods, while Santa
Anna was away on military missions. He urged congress
to pass many liberal measures, such as abolishment of
compulsory tithes and reduction of the size of the army,
whereupon Santa Anna forced him into exile, a pattern
which was to play a significant part in his life. After a
brief, unsuccessful liberal uprising in 1840, he was once
again forced into exile. He suffered the same fate later,
when he attempted to reduce the power of the clergy.
All his life he fought for liberal ideas, such as freedom
of the press, freedom of expression and significant curtailment of Church power. He was President of Mexico
from 1846 to 1847, taking over while Santa Anna fought
the Americans. He opposed the Treaty of Guadalupe Hidalgo, which ended the war with the United States. His
running battle with the Church again forced him into exile. Nevertheless, in 1850 he was nominated for president, but failed to gain that office. After the Revolution
of Ayutla he lived to see his life long ambition accomplished, the adoption of his ideas in the form of the Constitution of 1857. Among his notable achievements was
a law establishing the National Library and the creation
of a national agency to foster secular education.

GOMEZ GOMEZ, RODRIGO. (1897-1970). An accountant and
banker who in 1960 led the movement that had Mexico
join the Latin American Free Trade Association. Director General of the Bank of Mexico from 1952 to 1970.

GOMEZ MORIN, MANUEL. Born on February 27, 1897, in Chihuahua, and died on April 19, 1972, in Mexico City. The founder of the conservative opposition National Action Party (PAN). Law degree from the National Autonomous University (UNAM) in 1918. UNAM law professor 1919-72. Law school dean 1922-24. President of UNAM 1933-34. Assistant Minister of Finance 1919-21. In September 1939, Gómez Morín, with the help of Efraín González Luna, founded the PAN and presided over its first assembly. He was elected PAN president and retained that post to 1949. Every three years beginning in 1940, he had PAN field candidates for federal Deputy and Senator in increasing numbers and Panistas in the Chamber of Deputies since 1946. In 1946, 1952, 1958, 1964, and 1970, he helped the PAN national assembly choose a presidential candidate. He helped PAN get proportional-representation minority-party seats in 1964, a system enlarged with the 1979 elections.

GOMEZ MORIN TORRES, JUAN. Born in 1924 in Mexico City. An attorney and son of the founder of the National Action Party (PAN). A Deputy in the federal Congress, he was PAN secretary general during 1969-72 and has long been on its national executive committee.

GOMEZ PEDRAZA, MANUEL. 1790-1851. Born in Querétaro. Military figure and President of Mexico in 1833. He fought against the revolutionaries on the side of Spain, but when independence was won he became a supporter of Iturbide. Was declared president in 1828, but Santa Anna deposed him and Gómez Pedraza went into exile in France. He finally occupied the presidency for a brief period in 1833, the most notable event of his administration being the expulsion from Mexico of the Spaniards. Forced to resign the presidency, he occupied various high political positions and died in Mexico City.

GOMEZ SEGURA, MARTE. (1896-1973). An agricultural engineer from Tamaulipas. A federal Deputy and then a Senator. Governor of Tamaulipas. Minister of Agriculture 1928-30 and 1940-46. As president of the National School of Agriculture, in 1923-24 he modernized it into a university and technical institute.

GOMEZ VELASCO, ANTONIO. Born on September 3, 1897, in Sayula, Jalisco. A longtime leader of the moderately-conservative opposition Party of the Authentic Mexican

Revolution (PARM), which in 1954 he helped establish as
a legally-registered party, along with Generals Juan Barragán and Jacinto B. Treviño.   An army captain in 1913,
he rose through the ranks to Division General.   Served
as Assistant Minister of Defense.   He introduced modern
physical education in army training.   For World War Two
service, he received the French Legion of Honor.   Since
1977 he has been president of the PARM.

GOMEZ ZEPEDA, LUIS.   Born in 1905 in Aguascalientes.
A Senator during 1964-70 and a member of the national
executive committee of the Institutional Revolutionary
Party (PRI).   Secretary General of the Union of Railroad
Workers 1962-68.   He helped found that union in 1933.
An administrator of the government's National Railroads
since 1937.   Director General of National Railroads under
President Echeverría 1972-76, he was reappointed by
President López Portillo in 1976 until 1982.

GONZALEZ, EPIGMENIO.   1778-1858.   He was a merchant
who took an active role in the uprising of September 16,
1810, and was with Hidalgo when the decision was made
to begin the independence struggle.   He used his house
as an arms depot and factory.   After being discovered
by the Spaniards, he was imprisoned and later banished
to the Philippines, but returned eventually to Guadalajara
and died there.

GONZALEZ, MANUEL.   1833-1893.   Born in Matamoros, he
originally fought against the liberals, but with the advent
of Maximilian and the French intervention (1862-1867) he
supported Juárez and became a close confidant and friend
of Porfirio Díaz, who was highly instrumental in González
serving as president from 1880 to 1884.   There was rap-
id economic progress during his administration, although
charges of corruption were made.   Notable achievements
were the total implementation of the metric system and
the inauguration of railroad service between Mexico City
and El Paso, Texas.   Also during this time, Mexico
achieved the ability to communicate with all parts of the
world by an underwater cable connecting Veracruz and
Tampico with Brownsville, Texas.   In spite of a law
restricting freedom of the press, he never persecuted it,
even though at times the press attacked him vigorously.
He died while serving a third term as governor of Guanajuato.

GONZALEZ APARICIO, LUIS. (1907-1969). An architect from Veracruz, he directed the reconstruction of the state government building in Hermosillo, Sonora, then the government's housing projects in the state of Morelos. He headed the Papaloapan River Commission 1950-52. He instituted the government's modern market construction program in the 1950's and 1960's.

GONZALEZ AZCUAGA, PEDRO. Born November 11, 1945, in Campeche. An administrator and member of the national executive committee of the Party of the Authentic Mexican Revolution (PARM). He was PARM president from January 1973 through 1975.

GONZALEZ BLANCO, SALOMON. Born on April 22, 1902, in Playa, Chiapas. Law degree from the National Autonomous University (UNAM). Law professor at UNAM part-time for 15 years. Judge of Supreme State Court, then of Federal District Court in Villahermosa, Tabasco. Assistant director of accounting for the Ministry of Finance. Director of Conciliation for the Ministry of Labor, then the ministry's executive officer. Governor of the state of Chiapas 1978. Minister of Labor 1958-64. His numerous works helped shape modern labor law in Mexico.

GONZALEZ BOCANEGRA, FRANCISCO. 1824-1861. Composer of the verse of the National Anthem. Ironically, he was expelled from Mexico, along with his parents, because of his Spanish background. Years later, however, he returned to his native San Luis Potosí. In 1853 he was declared the winner of a contest held to write the verse for the National Anthem. He died of typhus in Mexico City.

GONZALEZ CASANOVA, PABLO. Born on February 11, 1922, in Toluca, Mexico. The republic's best known political scientist. Ph.D. in political sociology from the University of Paris. Author of the most widely used textbook on Mexican government, Democracia en México, published in 1965. Dean of the School of Social and Political Sciences of the National Autonomous University (UNAM) and UNAM's Institute of Social Investigations 1964-70. President of UNAM 1970-72. In December 1972 he was forced to resign after failing to end numerous strikes at the UNAM.

GONZALEZ COSIO, MANUEL. Born in 1915 in Querétaro.
An engineer who served as a federal Deputy, then a Senator, and as Governor of Querétaro 1961-67. He developed and directed water and conservation policies for
the government during the 1950's for desert zones and
for forest areas.

GONZALEZ DE AVILA, ALONSO and GIL. They both died
in 1566. Two brothers who were among the very early
advocates of independence from Spain and were put to
death for this reason. They were actively involved in
an attempt to become independent by means of creating
a separate Mexican throne and placing the son of Hernán
Cortés on it.

GONZALEZ DE AVILA, GIL. Spanish conquistador who died
in 1543. He explored Central America extensively and
played a key role in the assassination of Cristóbal de
Olid. It was by this move that González de Avila and
Francisco de las Casas won their freedom, as they had
been taken prisoner by Olid. González de Avila eventually was sent back to Spain and never returned to the
New World.

GONZALEZ DE LA VEGA, FRANCISCO. Born in 1901 in
Durango. Law degree from the National Autonomous
University (UNAM). Founder of the University of Du-
rango in 1957. Attorney General of Mexico 1946-52.
President of the Mexican Academy of Penal Sciences.
As a UNAM law professor, his students included four
Presidents of Mexico: Miguel Alemán, Adolfo López
Mateos, Gustavo Díaz Ordaz, and Luis Echeverría.
Through them, he shaped penal law from the 1940's
through the 1970's.

GONZALEZ HINOJOSA, MANUEL. Born in 1912 in San Luis
Potosí. An attorney and law professor at Ibero-American
University who was one of the founding members of the
National Action Party (PAN) in 1939. President of PAN
during 1969-72 and 1975-78. A Deputy in Congress dur-
ing 1967-70 and 1973-76.

GONZALEZ LUGO, HUGO P. Born in Nuevo Laredo, Tamaulipas. An attorney, federal Deputy, then Governor of
Tamaulipas 1945-47. He was removed as governor by
President Alemán after he freed the police chief of Ciudad Victoria, who had murdered the editor of the daily

newspaper in Victoria, El Mundo, chief critic of his administration. He was manager of the federal government's National Bonded Warehouses 1949-52, and Ambassador to Bolivia 1970.

GONZALEZ LUNA, EFRAIN. Born October 18, 1898, in
Autlán, Jalisco, and died on September 10, 1964, in Mexico City. Famed as an opposition presidential candidate
and the father of a presidential candidate. Law degree
from the University of Guadalajara. Leader of the Catholic Association for Mexican Youth in 1921. A founder,
along with Manuel Gómez Morín, of the conservative National Action Party (PAN) in 1939. PAN presidential
candidate in 1952. His son, Efraín González Morfín, was
the PAN presidential candidate in 1970. He helped increase Catholic influence in Mexican public life.

GONZALEZ MORFIN, EFRAIN. Born on June 5, 1929, in
Guadalajara, Jalisco. Studied philosophy and economics
at the University of Innsbruck, Austria, and at the Sorbonne, Paris. Leader of the National Action Party (PAN)
youth group. Member of the PAN national executive committee since 1960. A Deputy in the federal Congress
1967-70. PAN presidential candidate in 1970, receiving
2 million votes to 11.9 million for Luis Echeverría of
the Institutional Revolutionary Party (PRI), or the largest
vote ever received by a PAN candidate. His father had
been the PAN presidential candidate in 1952.

GONZALEZ ORTEGA, JESUS. 1824-1881. General and politician. A strong supporter of the liberals and Benito
Juárez, in 1858 he was designated Governor of Zacatecas
and defeated the conservative forces in this state during
the following year. His continued successes against the
conservatives caused his prestige to increase to such a
degree that his supporters approached Juárez and asked
that he step down in favor of their man, who by virtue
of being President of the Supreme Court was Vice President of Mexico. Juárez refused and González later fell
into disfavor because of his inability to defeat the conservative General Mejía. Later, after being put in charge
of the Battle of Puebla because of Zaragoza's death, he
was forced to surrender and taken prisoner by the French,
but escaped and went into exile in New York City. Later, he attempted to claim the presidency of Mexico, but
was unsuccessful. He died in Saltillo.

GONZALEZ TORRES, JOSE. Born on September 16, 1919, in Michoacán. An attorney who was secretary general of the National Action Party (PAN) 1959-62 and PAN candidate for President of Mexico in the 1964 election won by Gustavo Díaz Ordaz.

GOROSTIZA, JOSE. (1901-1973). From Tabasco, a Mexican diplomat who served in Britain, Italy, Cuba, Norway, Guatemala, and the United Nations in New York. Director General of the Mexican diplomatic service 1946-49. Mexico's ambassador to the Inter-American Treaty of Reciprocal Assistance in Rio in 1947 and the chartering of the Organization of American States in Bogotá in 1948. He was then Ambassador to Greece. Minister of Foreign Relations during 1964. He headed the National Commission of Nuclear Energy during 1965-70 and developed Mexico's basic policies on nuclear energy.

GRIJALVA, JUAN DE. Ca. 1489-1527. Spanish explorer from Segovia and nephew of Diego Velázquez, the first governor of Cuba. Sent by Velázquez to explore the Mexican coast around Yucatán, he discovered Cozumel Island and heard reports of the Aztec kingdom to the north. The first man to use the term New Spain. His explorations led to the Cortés expedition of 1519 and ultimately to the conquest of all of present-day Mexico and Central America by Spain.

"GRITO DE DOLORES." Spanish phrase meaning "Cry of Dolores" and it refers to the revolutionary speech given by Father Miguel Hidalgo y Costilla outside his parish church in the village of Dolores, near Querétaro on the morning of September 16, 1810. Hidalgo condemned those Spaniards who supported the French in their occupation of the Iberian Peninsula, professed allegiance to Ferdinand VII and upheld his belief in the Catholic faith. At this time, he still maintained that some ties with Spain were desirable. However, as time went on, the Cry of Dolores came to mean the desire for absolute independence from Spain.

GUADALAJARA. The second largest city in Mexico and the capital of the state of Jalisco. Located 300 miles west-northwest of Mexico City, at an elevation of 5,200 feet above sea level. Its 1976 Census Bureau estimate showed a total population of 1.7 million for the municipality but

its greater metropolitan area exceeded 2 million. With
a year-round temperate climate and many parks, foun-
tains, and broad avenues, it is known as the "Pearl of
the West." Clustered downtown are several historical
buildings dating from colonial times or from the 19th-
century struggles against Spain, and against the French
occupation in the 1860's. The cathedral with Byzantine
architecture was built in 1618. The Degollado Theater
was built in 1856 to resemble the La Scala Opera House
of Milan, Italy. A noted painter of the Revolution, José
Clemente Orozco (1883-1949) decorated many public buildings with his famous murals of Mexican history. The
state's University of Guadalajara was founded in 1792 and
is rivaled and excelled academically by the private Autonomous University of Guadalajara, founded in 1935.
Guadalajara's medical school, with 2,000 students from
the United States, has more foreign students than any
other medical school in the Western World. The city is
the agricultural and wholesale distributing center of western Mexico and second only to Mexico City as a retail
trade center. Industries range from chemicals and cement to textiles and lumber. The suburb of Tlaquepaque
is famous for ceramics. Guadalajara ranks third in Mexico behind Mexico City and Monterrey as an industrial
center.

GUADALUPE, ORDER OF. An honorary organization formed
by Agustín de Iturbide, who reigned for less than a year
(1822-23) as Agustín I. Never a really popular organization, it went out of existence when Iturbide was deposed,
but enjoyed a brief rebirth during the latter years of
Santa Anna (1853-55). Maximilian was the last to res-
urrect it, 1864-66, after which it went out of existence
permanently.

GUADALUPE, VIRGIN OF. In 1531 an Indian, Juan Diego,
claimed to have seen an apparition of the Virgin Mary
with the face of an Indian on Tepeyac Hill, now the suburb north of Mexico City called Villa de Guadalupe Hidalgo. The Catholic Church declared the Virgin of Guadalupe patroness of New Spain in 1754. The cult exalting
Mexico's patron saint is especially strong among women,
and venerates motherhood. The shrine, built in 1709,
became a basilica in 1908. The 1848 peace treaty between Mexico and the United States was signed at this
shrine.

GUADALUPE-HIDALGO, TREATY OF. This was the treaty that ended the war between the United States and Mexico and was signed on February 2, 1848. Mexico lost California, Nevada, Arizona, New Mexico, Utah and part of California. It was also forced to recognize Texas as United States territory as far south as the Rio Grande. For the loss of about half of its territory Mexico received an indemnization of $15,000,000 dollars and the United States agreed to assume its citizens' claims against Mexico, which amounted to over $3,000,000 dollars.

GUANAJUATO (CITY). The capital of the state of Guanajuato, founded in 1554 as a mining center, and the major silver producing district until the 1840's. Its pottery and toy factories and historic buildings of the 1810-21 independence struggle draw tourists. Its 1976 population totaled 61,000.

GUANAJUATO (STATE). A state in central Mexico with an area of 30,567 square kilometers. It has the Bajío plain drained by the Lerma River, with irrigation projects. The Bajío is a major breadbasket of the republic, its largest producer of potatoes and sweet potatoes. It is also a major producer of corn, peanuts, alfalfa, garlic, onions, strawberries, and livestock. Its 1976 population totaled 2.8 million. The state's native son, Father Miguel Hidalgo, declared Mexico's revolution against Spain, on September 16, 1810, at the town of Dolores, Guanajuato.

GUARDIAS RURALES see RURALES

GUATEMOTZIN see CUAUHTEMOC

GUAYABERA. A man's combination shirt-jacket worn in tropical regions over an undershirt in place of a coat. Made of white cotton, it has lapels and four large pockets and is worn outside the trousers, the hem being hip-length.

GUAYMAS. A leading port of northwestern Mexico on the Gulf of California in the state of Sonora, 80 miles south of Hermosillo. Its economy rests on commercial fishing, processing of marine products, headquarters for shrimp fleets, shipping of cotton and other exports from all over northwestern Mexico, and as a resort for sport fishermen.

It is connected to La Paz, Baja California del Sur, by
daily ferry service, and is a major highway, railroad,
and air link to Mexico City. Named for the Guaymas
Indians, the pre-Hispanic ancestors of today's Seris who
still live in coastal Sonora. Guaymas became a military
post and port in 1767. A railroad connecting it to Nogales at the United States border was completed in 1882.
Its 1976 population totaled 104,000.

GUERRA OLIVARES, ALFONSO. (1897-1967). A diplomat
from Nayarit who served as a Senator and Assistant Minister of Foreign Relations. An Ambassador to West Germany 1953-64, he helped expand Mexico's trade with the
European Common Market.

GUERRERO, PRAXEDIS. 1882-1910. He was a revolutionary
figure who was born in Guanajuato and supported Francisco Madero. He launched raids into Mexico from exile
in the United States even before the start of the Mexican
Revolution in 1910. He was killed at the end of December 1910, leading his men into combat near the town of
Janos in Chihuahua.

GUERRERO, VICENTE. 1782-1831. Soldier and politician
during the first years of Mexico's independence. He
fought alongside of Morelos, and when the latter was
executed in 1815 his band of guerrillas was one of the
principal sources of resistance to the Spaniards, however
weak and sporadic this resistance was. He later joined
forces with Iturbide and his Plan of Iguala, playing a
major role in Mexico's final bid for independence. In
April 1829 he resorted to arms to attain the presidency,
having lost the election to Gómez Pedraza. Santa Anna
gave him valuable assistance in this successful bid. In
December, 1829 Santa Anna unseated Guerrero and placed
General Anastasio Bustamante in the presidency. Guerrero was at a serious disadvantage because he tended to
be too trusting and forgiving of his enemies. José Antonio Facio, a minister in Bustamante's administration
who was acting on the latter's orders, had him shot.
The fact that Lucas Alamán was an official in Bustamante's government and refused to resign, even after the
sordid execution of Guerrero, is probably the biggest blot
on his integrity. Guerrero is regarded as a genuine hero
in Mexico, and a state is named in his honor.

GUERRERO (STATE). A state in southern Mexico, with a

Pacific Ocean coastline. Its area totals 63,794 square kilometers. The Sierra Madre del Sur separates its coastal region from the remainder of the state. Fertile valleys ring the Balsas River. With a tropical climate, it has heavy summer rains but a series of dams built in the 1950's brought flood control, irrigated farming, and substantial electric power and light industries. Its economy relies on fishing, corn, sesame, coconuts, forestry, and mining. Its largest city, Acapulco, with a 1979 population of 490,000, is a world famous resort and a major port. Its capital, Chilpancingo, had a 1976 population of 90,000. The city of Taxco has been preserved as a colonial town famous for its silversmith artisans. Created as a state in 1849, it was named after a martyred Mexican President, Vicente Guerrero (1782-1831).

GUITARRON. A Mexican oversized guitar which uses the strings of a bass viol and serves as a string bass in an orchestra.

GULF OF CALIFORNIA. Also known as the Sea of Cortés. The territorial waters of the Pacific between the Baja California peninsula and mainland Mexico's coastline as far south as Mazatlán. Some 600 miles in length and averaging 80 miles in width, it boasts the best salt water sport fishing in the world, plus extensive commercial shrimp and other fishing.

GULF OF MEXICO. The extension of the Atlantic Ocean and the Caribbean encompassed by the United States coastline from Florida to Texas and the Mexican coastline from Matamoros to the Yucatán peninsula.

GUTIERREZ NAJERA, MANUEL. 1859-1895. Born in Mexico City, he was a literary figure who excelled particularly as a poet. Although considered a Romantic, he was the forerunner of the Modernist movement in Mexico and is regarded as the inspiration of Amado Nervo and Enrique González Martínez. His complete mastery of poetic form is shown in "Odas breves," probably his best poem. His poems "Tristissima Nox" and "Serenata de Schubert" are also among his most famous. He also wrote extensive prose, having written for about 40 newspapers and literary magazines under more than 20 pen names. Description of reality is what predominates in his prose.

GUTIERREZ RINCON, EFRAIN. Born in 1897 in Chiapas.

Engineering degree from the National Autonomous University. He fought in the Revolution under General Emiliano Zapata as a captain from 1915 to 1916 as a key staff officer. Governor of the state of Chiapas 1937-40, then Secretary General of Agrarian Affairs, then Director General of the National Agricultural Credit Bank.

GUTIERREZ ROLDAN, PASCUAL. Born in 1903 in Mazatlán, Sinaloa. Degrees in agronomy and economics, and a Ph. D. in economics. He directed all of the government's steel plants 1952-58, then headed the government's Petróleos Mexicanos 1958-64.

GUTIERREZ RUIZ, DAVID GUSTAVO. Born in 1940 in Tabasco. Economist with graduate studies in Paris. He represented Mexico before the European Common Market in 1963. Governor of Quintana Roo 1971-75. Since 1976 he has been director of the government agency for fertilizers, Guanos y Fertilizantes.

GUZMAN, MARTIN LUIS. Born in Chihuahua in 1887. A novelist and journalist who fought under Villa and Carranza. His experiences in the Mexican Revolution caused him to concentrate on native themes, creating a genuine Latin American novel. His most famous work is El águila y la serpiente, translated into English in 1930 as The Eagle and the Serpent. Founder of the magazine Tiempo, also known as Hispano Americano, in 1942 and remained its publisher until 1974.

GUZMAN, NUÑO BELTRAN DE. He was born in Guadalajara, Spain and died around 1545, being a Spanish conquistador who also held colonial administrative posts. Guzmán personified the worst qualities of the Spanish conquerors and was the type of person who could give credence to the infamous "black legend." While governor of Pánuco from 1526-1528, he confiscated many encomiendas, giving them to his friends, sold many Indians into slavery and forced the caciques to pay heavy tribute. He and his audiencia were excommunicated in 1529, and fearing imprisonment for his actions he went north, exploring as far as Sinaloa. Eventually, he settled in Jalisco. Guzmán founded many cities, among them Guadalajara and Culiacán. Among his many crimes in this area he encouraged the Indians to rebel, so that he could sell them into slavery. Guzmán pompously referred to this area as Greater Spain, but after his arrest it was renamed Nueva Galicia.

After the authorities became aware of his many excesses
he was recalled to Mexico City, tried and spent two years
in prison there. He finally was sent back to Spain, remaining in prison until his death.

GUZMAN NEYRA, ALFONSO.   Born in 1906 in Veracruz.
An Attorney who was a justice of the federal Supreme
Court 1952-76 and was Chief Justice 1959-64. A leader
in the Institutional Revolutionary Party (PRI), he was a
key campaign adviser for President Avila Camacho in
1940 and President Alemán in 1946.

GUZMAN WILLIS, MANUEL.   (1900-1973). A rancher who
headed and developed the Association of Cebu Cattle
Ranchers. He was Mayor of Tampico, then a Senator
from Tamaulipas 1952-58.

- H -

HACENDADO.   Owner of a large estate prior to the 1910
Revolution. These large estates included both farms and
ranches and their workers, or peones, who usually were
born on the estates and spent their entire lives working
there in debt. Hacendados were prime targets of those
fighting the Revolution.

HACIENDA.   The huge estates which came into existence after
the Conquest, evolving from the encomiendas. They have
been a constant problem over the years because of several reasons. Up until recently, most Mexicans lived in
the country and were farmers, but these huge estates did
not allow for widespread ownership of the soil. It has
been estimated that at the close of Spanish rule less than
5000 haciendas controlled the best acreage in Mexico.
They were often owned by absentee landowners and administered by trusted confidants, the owners living in fashionable houses in Mexico City or Europe.
Up to President Lázaro Cárdenas's time land reform,
which refers to the breaking up of these large estates,
was a neglected problem. In spite of the early efforts
of the Mexican Revolution and especially Emiliano Zapata,
not much was done initially in the way of land reform.
President Alvaro Obregón, who governed from 1920 to
1924, distributed a token 2.8 million acres of land, fearing that any meaningful effort would cause too much of a
repercussion in the national economy. However, Presi-

dent Lázaro Cárdenas, who believed very strongly in the
program, had 45 million acres distributed during his administration (1934-1940). Adolfo López Mateos (1958-
1964) also emphasized it, 25 million acres being distributed during his administration. By the late 1960's it was
officially declared that all agricultural land had been distributed. Nevertheless, new lands are occasionally "discovered." All in all, land reform has probably been
more successful in Mexico than in any other Latin American country.

HACIENDA MINISTRY. The Secretaría de Hacienda y Crédito
Público (Ministry of Finance and Public Credit) is the
modern successor to the old Ministry of the Treasury,
created in 1821. This ministry has authority over treasury reserves and deposits, the banking federal reserve
system, the coinage mint, currency, rates of interest,
and government credit, as well as collection and dis-
bursement of federal taxes and all over federal income
and revenue and authorized expenditures.

HALCONES. A group of protesters and street demonstrators,
the Halcones (Falcons) were organized by the federal government in 1968 and used to counterbalance anti-government
rioters in 1971, 1974, 1975, and to a lesser extent since
1976. These pro-government groups unofficially help police contain Communist-led and other far-leftist groups
engaged in acts of violence, especially at schools and universities. Both groups tend to range in age from teen-
agers to those in their late twenties, and most are students or former students.

HANK GONZALEZ, CARLOS. Born on August 28, 1927, in
Galeana, México. Teacher's Diploma. Professor of primary, then secondary schools 1941-51. Mayor of Toluca
1955-57. Member of the national executive committee of
the Institutional Revolutionary Party (PRI). Deputy in the
federal Congress. As Director General of the government's
Basic Commodities Corporation (CONASUPO) 1964-70, he
expanded CONASUPO retail stores for the poor all over
the republic, selling food and consumer essentials almost
at cost. He was Governor of the state of México 1970-
76 and since 1976 has been Governor of the Federal District for a term ending in 1982. As DF chief and de
facto Mexico City Mayor, he has created 34 new, broad
thoroughfares to unclog traffic, after extensive slum
clearance and street widening.

HAY, EDUARDO. 1877-1941. Engineering degree from the
University of Notre Dame. As a Revolutionary general,
he was Chief of Staff for President Francisco Madero in
1911, then a top adviser to President Carranza 1915-20
and President Obregón 1920-24. Under President Cárdenas, he was Minister of Foreign Relations 1935-40.

HENESTROSA, ANDRES. Born in 1906 in Oaxaca. A widely
syndicated newspaper columnist and also Mexico's leading
historian about the press, publishing, and mass media.
A Deputy in the federal Congress 1958-61 and 1964-67.
Director of literature for the National Institute of Fine
Arts 1952-58. Publisher of the magazines El Libro y
el Pueblo and Letras Patrias. Well-known author of
hundreds of short stories and essays from the 1940's
through the 1970's.

HENRIQUEZ GUZMAN, MIGUEL. Born on August 4, 1896,
in Piedras Negras, Coahuila, and died on August 29,
1972, in Mexico City. A career army general who
bucked the dominant Institutional Revolutionary Party
(PRI) trying to be President. He joined the Revolutionary
in 1912 as a cadet guarding President Madero. In 1950
when he challenged the inner-circle system of selecting
presidential candidates, he was expelled from the PRI
and began his Federation of People's Parties of Mexico
(FPPM), and was its presidential candidate in 1952, winning 580,000 votes, to 2.7 million for Adolfo Rúiz Cortines of the PRI, 286,000 votes for the National Action
Party candidate, and 73,000 for the Popular Socialist
candidate.

HERMOSILLO. The capital of the northwestern state of
Sonora, this city is 180 miles south of the Arizona border. Its 1976 population totaled 267,000. In 1942 the
University of Sonora was founded there, and a modern
state library built nearby. The city has textile mills,
cotton gins, and is the trade and financial center for a
large part of northwestern Mexico. Although four Mexican Presidents who were Governors of Sonora--Plutarco
Calles, Alvaro Obregón, Adolfo de la Huerta, and Abelardo L. Rodríguez--were closely associated with the Revolutionary leadership which spawned the dominant Institutional Revolutionary Party, Hermosillo became the first
state capital to elect an opposition National Action Party
(PAN) Mayor for 1967-70, Jorge Valdez Muñoz. In 1953,
Hermosillo was among the first Mexican cities to create

Civic Betterment Boards to help the municipal government
finance parks, street lighting, and other local public
services.

HERNANDEZ, LUISA JOSEFINA.   Born in 1928 in Mexico
City.   After receiving her degree in drama at the National Autonomous University (UNAM), she did graduate
work at Columbia University as a Rockefeller scholar,
then became the first woman to be professor of drama
at UNAM.   Her 1951 play, Aguardiente, won many prizes.
Her other plays from 1957 to 1964 stress social satire.

HERNANDEZ CORZO, RODOLFO.   Born in 1909 in Chiapas.
Chemistry degree from the National Polytechnic Institute
(IPN).   Ph. D. from Stanford University.   Dean of the
IPN School of Biological Sciences; IPN President until
1958.   Mexico's leading educator and research scientist
in biochemistry.   Director for the government's wildlife
conservation programs during the 1960's and 1970's.

HERNANDEZ DE CORDOBA, FRANCISCO.   1475-1518.   A
Spanish explorer, he arrived in Cuba in 1511 and was
sent by Diego Velázquez to explore the Caribbean and
what today is Mexico.   After severe attacks on them by
the Indians, in which many Spaniards were killed or
wounded, Hernández de Córdoba himself suffering serious
injuries, he returned to Cuba with the other survivors
and died there.

HERNANDEZ DELGADO, JOSE.   Born in 1904 in Guanajuato.
An attorney who was Director General of the government's
development bank, Nacional Financiera, from 1952 through
1970 under three presidents: Ruiz Cortines, López Mateos, and Díaz Ordaz.

HERNANDEZ HERNANDEZ, FRANCISCO.   Born in 1908 in
Tlaxcala.   A former Deputy and Senator who from the
1940's through the 1960's alternately served as director
of the Congressional Library and publisher of the Diario
Oficial, the federal journal in which all federal laws are
promulgated.

HERRERA, ENRIQUE.   Born in 1938 in Mexico City.   A social sciences professor, Assistant Minister of Communications 1970-76, he founded the Mexican News and Information Agency (NOTIMEX) in 1968.

HERRERA, JOSE JOAQUIN.   1792-1854.   Born in Jalapa,

Veracruz. Politician and military figure. Initially, he
fought on the side of the Spaniards against the Mexicans
in the independence war, but eventually joined forces with
Iturbide and supported him in the final struggle for independence, attaining the rank of brigadier general. While
acting president in 1844-1845, he wanted to negotiate the
Texas independence dispute with President Polk, but was
overthrown by the more militant forces led by General
Mariano Paredes y Arrillaga. Herrera opposed war with
the United States, but he served as the next man in line
to Santa Anna. An honest, mild mannered individual, he
was elected president and served from 1848 to 1851. He
died in Mexico City.

HIDALGO, ERNESTO. 1896-1955. A journalist with Excelsior who was Governor of his native state of Guanajuato
from September 1943 to January 1946, when President
Avila Camacho removed him from office after rioters
broke down law and order and killed dozens. The rioters
were protesting fraudulent elections administered by the
Institutional Revolutionary Party (PRI), and prompted
electoral commission reforms in the state.

HIDALGO (STATE). A state in central Mexico with northern
tropical lowlands and the Sierra Madre Oriental elsewhere.
Its plateau is drained by the Moctezuma River and many
hot springs. Its area totals 13,040 square kilometers.
Its 1976 population was 1.4 million. Its economy depends
on corn, beans, barley, and maguey, and silver, gold,
lead, and zinc mines, which were famous in past centuries. In the state capital, Pachuca, are cement and
manganese production. At Tulancingo, truck and railroad
boxcar manufacturing. The state has an archaeological
site at Tula, ancient capital of the Toltec Indians in pre-
Aztec times.

HIDALGO Y COSTILLA, MIGUEL. 1753-1811. Known as the
Father of his Country because he initiated the armed insurrection which culminated in the independence of Mexico from Spain in 1821. A Creole, he was born on a
hacienda in the state of Guanajuato, where his father was
the administrator. He studied at the prestigious Colegio
de San Nicolás in Morelia, known as the city of Valladolid
at that time, later becoming rector. He was ordained in
1778. Possessing a keen mind, he got into trouble with
the Inquisition and among his crimes were the reading of
the French revolutionary writers and the translation of

their works into Spanish. A true intellectual, he established the first insurgent newspaper, <u>El Despertador Americano</u>, and on December 6, 1810, signed a proclamation outlawing slavery, Mexico being the first hispanic-american country to do this. Even though he escaped conviction by the Inquisition, nevertheless he was banished to the village of Dolores, where he associated himself closely with the Indians. He had a sincere interest in the welfare of the people, engaging in such activities as the raising of silk worms and the growing of grapes for wine, both activities prohibited by the Spanish Crown. It is not certain when he developed a strong allegiance for the independence movement, but it is known that he was lukewarm to the idea at first. That his feelings had become much stronger was evident in September of 1810, when word reached him that a plot had been discovered and that it would be well to move before his probable arrest.

In the early morning of September 16, 1810, Hidalgo gathered the villagers together, distributed arms and told them that this was the start of a new era, which would mean independence from Spain, although officially he did not go that far, since he still maintained a pretense of supporting Ferdinand VII, a prisoner of Napoleon in France. After inciting them to action, he set out to capture Guanajuato. When he passed through Atotonilco, he came across an image of Our Lady of Guadalupe and used it as a rallying standard. When he reached Guanajuato his mob numbered close to 100,000 and the relatively few Spanish soldiers and their dependents sought refuge in the government granary, the Alhóndiga de Granaditas. When this building was finally broken into, a blood bath ensued from which there were no survivors among the soldiers, Hidalgo's followers going on a rampage indicative of an undisciplined mob. At times, this revolutionary leader must have had serious doubts about his followers, since he was forced to fire on them, this being the only way he could control them.

By November first he was at the gates of Mexico City, occupying what today is the Colonia del Valle neighborhood of Mexico City proper. But he hesitated and lost at least half of his army through desertion. Then he turned northward toward Querétaro and then back to Morelia. In Guadalajara he received one of his warmest welcomes, where the people bestowed upon him the title of Serene Highness. That Hidalgo had the weakness of basking in false glory is indicative of the title he bestowed upon himself--Captain-General of America. Nevertheless, he was a true patriot who cared for those who had no power to fight injustice by themselves. From this point on Hidalgo's fortunes changed dramatically for the worse. He was pursued by Spanish forces and captured in March 1811 at Acatita del Baján. He was shot by a firing squad in Chihuahua on July 30, 1811, less than a year after he had led the opening battle in the independence movement against Spain. To intimidate those who would dare to question Spanish rule, his head was placed in a small cage on the highest part of one of the corners of the Alhóndiga de Granaditas in Guanajuato, the scene of the bloodiest triumph of the insurgent forces. There it remained until the final triumph over the Spaniards in 1821. In 1824 his body was taken to Mexico City and buried with full honors.

As a revolutionary, Hidalgo must be regarded as a failure, but to the Mexican people he symbolizes a union between Creole and Indian, between influential and poor classes, which would not come about for at least another hundred years, if then. Hidalgo made a sincere effort to help the poor, raise their standard of living and create a united, prosperous Mexico. This is probably why he is so highly revered in Mexico.

HINOJOSA, COSME R. (1879-1965). Director General of the Postal Service in the 1920's and 1930's. He was the longtime head of the council for the government's National Pawnshop, which lends more money than private pawnshops. He formulated the law which prevents pawned national relics from being resold if museums have claims on them for historical value to the nation.

HIRSCHFIELD ALMADA, JULIO. Born in 1917 in Mexico City. An engineer, he was Director General of Airports 1970-73, then Minister of Tourism 1973-76. He was kidnapped in September 1971 by the Marxist-led guerrillas of the Zapatista Urban Front, and released after a three-million peso ransom was paid. He has been vice-president of the H. Steel Company, manufacturer and retailer of office furniture and watches throughout the republic. His kidnapping brought into the open the far-left guerrilla violence President Luis Echeverría tried to keep out of the news during 1970-76.

HOLY OFFICE see INQUISITION

HOUSTON, SAM see SAN JACINTO, BATTLE OF

HUAPANGO.   Folk music which originated in the state of
    Veracruz.   A huapango shifts back and forth from a rapid
    beat to slower rhythms similar to Spanish flamenco danc-
    ing.

HUARACHES.   Indian sandals, which continue to be very pop-
    ular in Mexico.

HUASTECA.   The Huasteca Indians are a tribe concentrated
    in the states of Veracruz and San Luis Potosí, noted for
    their folk dances and huapango music.   Along with the
    Totonaca Indians, they perform the Flying Pole Dance in
    which they descend a high pole suspended by a whirling
    rope tied to one ankle.

HUERTA, VICTORIANO.   1845-1916.   Born in Jalisco.   Gen-
    eral and president.   Before joining the revolutionary
    forces, he was an officer under Porfirio Díaz, attaining
    the rank of brigadier general in 1902.   After Madero's
    rise to power, he crushed the troops of Pascual Orozco
    under his orders, but all indications are that he made
    off with millions of pesos, for which Madero relieved him
    of his command, only to use him to crush a revolt by
    Félix Díaz, the brother of the ousted dictator.   He main-
    tained close ties with the American ambassador, Henry
    Lane Wilson, and plotted the overthrow of Madero, being
    responsible for his death and that of his vice-president,
    Pino Suárez.   He assumed the presidency in 1913, al-
    though he was at a definite disadvantage since the United
    States never recognized him.   This was not a happy peri-
    od for Mexico, since Huerta, a heavy drinker, proved to
    be extremely cruel and inept.
        Rebellion in the north, principally by Pancho Villa,
    and general disorder throughout the country marked the
    beginning of his downfall.   An incident in Tampico speeded
    up the process.   Some American sailors disembarked in
    Tampico from the Dolphin and were immediately jailed
    for having entered a forbidden war zone.   When the Mex-
    ican commander refused to authorize a 21-gun salute to
    the American flag in apology, American marines occupied
    Veracruz.   This turn of events, along with serious mili-
    tary reverses to Villa, Carranza and Zapata, caused
    Huerta to resign and flee the country, eventually ending
    up in the United States, where he was arrested in New-
    man, New Mexico on charges of conspiracy.   He suc-
    cumbed to cirrhosis of the liver while in American cus-
    tody.

HUICHOL. The Huichol Indians were among the last to come under Spanish rule. Their tribe concentrates in the state of Jalisco. Their religion is essentially pagan, technically Catholic. They consider the deer a sacred animal and use the hallucinogenic plant peyote to communicate with spirits and pagan gods.

HUIPIL. A straight, shapeless, sleeveless blouse worn by Indian women and mestizo peasant women.

HUITZILOPOCHTLI. The principal deity of the Aztecs, he was known as the "Hummingbird God," "Lord of the Universe," and frequently was synonymous with the sun. It was believed that as he made his journey across the sky, a journey fraught with grave danger, he needed human blood to sustain him. For this reason the custom of human sacrifice became so important to the Aztecs. The Temple of Huitzilopochtli was the largest one in Tenochtitlán and was built on the same site occupied at the present time by the Cathedral of Mexico City.

Legend has it that Huitzilopochtli told his followers to begin a pilgrimage south, a journey which would end on the site where they would see an eagle perched on a cactus with a snake in its mouth. He assured his followers that they would have his constant protection and guidance. The Aztecs came across this sight on what today is Mexico City and built their own city there, calling it Tenochtitlán.

HUIZAR, CANDELARIO. A Mexican composer who wrote **Pueblerinas** (1931).

HUMAN SETTLEMENTS MINISTRY. The Secretaría de Asentamientos Humanos y Obras Públicas was created in December 1976. It combined the Ministry of Public Works and the Department of Human Settlements into the Ministry of Human Settlements and Public Works. The Human Settlements agency had been created in 1971 to help the government cope with the staggering problem of slum clearance and the high rate of migration of rural Mexicans into the cities. From 1891 to 1935 and from 1939 to 1959 the Ministry of Communications and Public Works was a cabinet entity, and in 1959 the Ministry of Communications and Transportation was created as was the autonomous Ministry of Public Works. In December 1976, Pedro Ramírez Vázquez, architect and founder and former president of the Metropolitan Autonomous University, was appointed by the President of Mexico as the first Minister of the SAHOP.

HUMBOLDT, ALEXANDER VON. 1769-1859. German scientist, naturalist, world traveler and author. Visited Latin America between 1799-1804, journeying to Mexico and co-authoring Voyage aux régions équinoxiales du Nouveau Continent, a 30-volume work published between 1807 and 1834. He arrived in Acapulco on March 22, 1803, and Mexico City on April 11, conducting scientific experiments along the way. He visited such places as Cuernavaca, Guanajuato, Pachuca and Querétaro. Humboldt made phenomenal use of his time in Mexico, exploring silver mines, mountain peaks and canals. He even carried out astronomical observations in the Aztec teocalli of Cholula, on his way to Veracruz. Humboldt left Veracruz for Havana on March 7, 1804, having been in Mexico for almost a year.

- I -

IBARRA, FRANCISCO DE. 1539-1575. Spanish Governor and Captain General of Nueva Vizcaya. He founded Durango and successfully opened many mines in Zacatecas.

IBARRA IBARRA, GUILLERMO. Born in 1911 in Alamos, Sonora. An attorney who was president of the National University Student Federation in 1933, became a judge of the Federal Tax Court, then head of the Federal Conciliation and Arbitration Board, then publisher of the government's daily newspaper in Mexico City, El Nacional, 1948-56. He was a Senator during 1958-64, and helped bring proportional representation minority-party seats to Congress, though himself a leader of the dominant Institutional Revolutionary Party (PRI).

IBARRA MUÑOZ, DAVID. Born in 1930 in Mexico City. An economist and a Certified Public Accountant. He became known throughout Latin America for his many articles and books on economic development. He was director of planning for the Ministry of Public Works. Then he was director for Mexico for the UN's Economic Commission for Latin America (CEPAL) 1967-69. He was Assistant Director General 1970-76 for the government's development bank, Nacional Financiera (NAFIN), and was NAFIN

Director General 1976-77.   Since 1977 he has been Minister of Finance and Public Credit in the cabinet of President López Portillo.

IGUALA.   A city in southwestern Mexico in the state of Guerrero, 80 miles south of Mexico City, whose population in 1976 totaled 88,000.   It is notable as the site of the proclamation on February 24, 1821, of the Plan of Iguala, the basis for Mexico's independence from Spain.

IGUALA, PLAN OF.   Drawn up by the Mexican leader Iturbide in 1821.   It dealt with Mexican independence and its three main points were equality under the law for Creoles and Spaniards, Roman Catholicism as the only acceptable religion and the establishment of an independent empire under Ferdinand VII or another member of European royalty acceptable to Mexico.   It was generally supported by Mexican independence leaders.

IGUANA.   A large lizard native to the subtropical and tropical zones of Mexico.   A full grown iguana can reach five feet in length, and has a scaled body and a long tail.   Non-poisonous, it is considered edible by Indians.

IMPORTERS AND EXPORTERS ASSOCIATION.   The National Association of Importers and Exporters of the Mexican Republic (Asociación Nacional de Importadores y Exportadores de la República Mexicana or ANIERM) was created in 1940 to promote foreign trade.

IMSS.   The Instituto Mexicano del Seguro Social (Mexican Institute of Social Security) was created in 1943 to provide retirement pensions and medical care for workers in the private sector of the economy.   Each worker covered contributes 8 percent of his salary and his employer contributes 8 percent into the worker's IMSS fund.

INCOME DISTRIBUTION.   In order to improve income distribution in Mexico, the ongoing Revolution has enacted many reforms.   Before 1920, 2 percent of the families got half of the national income.   By 1965, 1.8 percent of the high-income families received 15 percent of the national income.   In 1962, the government enacted the Profit-Sharing Law, which created a National Commission for Profit-Sharing (Comité Nacional de Reparto de Utilidades or CNRU).   After deducting for taxes, profits on invested capital, and funds for expansion, repairs, and modernization, each private corporation through a local CNRU calculates a percentage of profits for distribution to the firm's full-time employees. Each worker's share is based on his lowest and highest wage for the year and the number of days of work.

INFONAVIT. The Instituto del Fondo Nacional de la Vivienda para los Trabajadores (Institute of the National Fund for Workers' Housing) since 1971 has been financing low-cost home mortgages, low-rent public apartments, and slum clearance. This government program funds and constructs housing which the private sector cannot underwrite.

INQUISITION. The Inquisition was formally established in Mexico in 1569 and lasted until the country gained its independence. Also known as the Holy Office, it was much less harsh in Mexico than in Spain, while serving primarily as an instrument to maintain political and religious orthodoxy. It is ironic that although the Inquisition in Mexico did not prosecute Indians after 1575, the first person to be tried was an Indian, Marcos of Acolhuacán. It is doubtful if more than 60 people were put to death in Mexico by the Inquisition during the entire colonial period.

INSTITUTE OF SOCIAL SECURITY FOR GOVERNMENT WORKERS see ISSSTE

INSTITUTO MEXICANO DEL CAFE. The government agency, Mexican Institute of Coffee, which buys coffee crops at subsidized prices to help producers maintain a minimum income.

INSTITUTO MEXICANO DEL PETROLEO. The government's Mexican Institute of Petroleum is a research entity for the government's agency operating the entire petroleum industry, Petróleos Mexicanos.

INSTITUTO MEXICANO DEL SEGURO SOCIAL   see   IMSS

INSTITUTO POLITECNICO NACIONAL. The government's National Polytechnic Institute (IPN), in Mexico City, is the national institution of higher learning second only to the National Autonomous University of Mexico (UNAM). Begun in 1937, it stresses engineering, medicine, dentistry, the physical sciences, and most major technolog-

ical specialties. Like other Mexican universities, it
maintains its own preparatory schools of the tenth through
twelfth grades, which combine high school and community-
college level courses as preparation for entrance to the
IPN.

INSURANCE ASSOCIATION. The Asociación Mexicana de Instituciones de Seguros (AMIS) or Mexican Association of
Insurance Institutions, created in 1946, unites all private
insurance companies as a lobbying group before the government, unions, and the public and as the organized
voice of the insurance profession.

INTENDENCY. Administrative unit introduced into New Spain
in 1786, the Viceroyalty being divided into 12 intenden-
cies. The man who governed this unit was the intendent
and his principal functions had to do with justice, finance,
war and industry. The viceroys feared this new political
unit and eventually they were relegated to almost figure-
head status. The intendency system was designed to increase efficiency and honesty in government, but it was
never really given a fair opportunity to prove itself, sus-
picion and the eruption of the independence movement in
New Spain in 1810 preventing it.

INTER-AMERICAN CONFERENCE ON PROBLEMS OF WAR
    AND PEACE see CHAPULTEPEC CONFERENCE

INTERIOR MINISTRY. The Secretaría de Gobernación or
Ministry of the Interior perhaps should be translated as
Internal Affairs. Gobernación is the most important cabinet post and its head ranks right behind the President
of the Republic in power. A 1958 law created the Ministry of the Presidency which Presidents López Mateos and
Díaz Ordaz tried to build up to balance the power of
Gobernación, but during the Echeverría administration of
1970-76 this ministry relinquished more and more authority back to Gobernación, and President López Portillo,
after taking office in December 1976, abolished the Ministry of the Presidency, assigning some of its functions
to a new Ministry of Planning and the Budget. Gobernación was created by the 1917 Constitution as liaison
between the federal executive branch and the governments
of the states and municipalities. The Gobernación Minister is the President's chief executive in dealing with all
other entities of the executive branch and with the legislative and judicial branches. Gobernación directs the

Federal Electoral Commission, the national registry of voters, and has authority over granting legal status to political parties and the conduct of campaigns and elections. Gobernación is the final executive authority on immigration, emigration, prisons, broadcasting, films, crime prevention, federal police, criminal justice, and other sensitive aspects of public life which may be also under other cabinet ministries and semi-autonomous entities.

IRON AND STEEL INDUSTRY. The iron and steel industry began in 1903, when the first steel plant went into operation. Mexico possesses sizable iron ore fields, but most of them are located in relatively inaccessible regions of northern Mexico. However, the country lacks sufficient coal deposits. The industry is located chiefly in the northern part of the country, with principal plants being in Monterrey, Monclova and Mexico City. Even though Mexico's steel production is second only to that of Brazil in Latin America, it still does not produce enough for its own needs. Steel production in 1971 was 3,780,000 tons.

ISLAS BRAVO, ANTONIO. (1885-1949). An attorney from Puebla who was a justice of the federal Supreme Court 1940-49. His 1928 book Presidential Succession reinforced popular sentiment against a second presidential term for Alvaro Obregón, who had tried to violate the Revolution's basic principle of "No re-election" before Obregón's assassination in 1928.

ISSSTE. The Instituto de Seguridad y Servicios Sociales de los Trabajadores del Estado or Institute of Social Security for Government Workers, organized in its present form in 1957, is a system distinct from that (IMSS) for workers in the private sector. ISSSTE benefits have consistently been better than those provided by IMSS, insuring the government a large group of loyal supporters. In addition to retirement pensions and medical service, ISSSTE provides some cultural and recreational activities.

ISTHMUS OF TEHUANTEPEC. The shortest nationwide distance across the republic, running 120 miles across southern Mexico from the Gulf of Mexico south-southwest to the Pacific Ocean through the states of Veracruz and Oaxaca. The highway and railroad which connect the port of Coatzacoalcos on the Gulf with Salina Cruz on the Pacific run more in a north-south direction than east-west.

This tropical area is noted for its marimba folk music
and dances. The people of the region take their name,
Tehuanas, from the town of Tehuantepec. Tehuana women
carry huge baskets of fruit, flowers, vegetables, or other
goods balanced on their heads. Tehuana men and women
combine the cultures of Zapotec, Mixtec, and other Indian groups of the region with mestizo innovations.

ITURBE, RAMON F. 1889-1970. An army general from
Sinaloa second in command to General Alvaro Obregón
during the 1912-14 Revolutionary battles in the north. He
was expelled from the dominant Institutional Revolutionary
Party (PRI), then called the Mexican Revolutionary Party,
in 1940 for supporting the presidential candidacy of Juan
Almazán against Víctor Avila Camacho.

ITURBIDE, AGUSTIN. 1783-1824. Politician and military
figure. Born in Valladolid, now present-day Morelia, he
fought originally on the Spanish side against the independence movement, but switched sides in 1820 and supported
Mexican independence. An unscrupulous leader, he had
himself proclaimed Emperor Agustín I shortly after Mexican independence, but was overthrown and forced into
exile in Europe. In a conciliatory move he was provided
with a pension but told never to set foot on Mexican soil
again. Nevertheless, he attempted to regain his throne
and landed near Tampico, at Soto la Marina. Shortly
afterwards he was captured and shot.

ITZCOATL. Ruler between 1427 and 1440, he is considered
to be the founder of the Aztec Empire, responsible for
bringing some 24 settlements under Aztec rule and making
Tenochtitlán the most important center in the Valley of
Mexico.

IXTAPAN DE LA SAL. A famous resort spa of hot springs
near Cuernavaca, on the highway from Mexico City to
Acapulco.

IXTLACCIHUATL. Mexico's most famous volcano. "Ixtlac-
cíhuatl" is the Aztec word for "white woman," which the
mountain peak's outline resembles. It has an elevation
of 17,342 feet above sea level, on the eastern rim of the
central Valley of Mexico which surrounds Mexico City.
Nearby on the same eastern rim is its twin volcano,
Popocatépetl, at an elevation of 17,887 feet. The legend
of Ixtla was a folk story of the volcano in pre-Hispanic

times. The beautiful daughter of a powerful Aztec emperor was offered in marriage to whichever warrior would save his throne from enemies waging war. The bravest warrior, Popo, defeated the enemy but his rivals sent back the false news that he had been killed. The princess became ill and died. The conquest by the Spaniards reinforced the legend and the two volcanoes became symbols of the conquest as well as fertility symbols.

- J -

JACOBIN SOCIETY. The informal name for the York Rite Masonic Lodge active in Mexico City and national politics from 1824 until 1835. Its leader was Miguel Ramos Arizpe, a leader of the federalist movement who had insured that the new republic adopt a federal form of government. The society originally had been helped by Joel Poinsett, the United States Minister (lower-ranking ambassador for non-major powers) to Mexico.

JAGUAR. A large, ferocious, spotted feline native to the Mexican mountainous jungles. The jaguar was a major symbol in the religion, literature, and culture of the Aztec and Maya empires in pre-Hispanic times.

JALAPA. The capital but only the third largest city of the state of Veracruz, and the site of the state university. Jalapa is on the slopes of the Sierra Madre Oriental, forty miles from the Gulf of Mexico. It is at an elevation of 4,500 feet above sea level. Its 1976 population totaled 185,000. This modern city has preserved an old section or colonial-era neighborhoods with cobblestone streets. Jalapa is a traditional road and railroad link from the port of Veracruz City to Mexico City.

JALAPEÑA. A type of cheese which originated in the Jalapa region of Veracruz but now can be found in stores and on meal tables throughout Mexico. Jalapeña cheese contains peppers and is very spicy, lending itself to many types of tropical dinners.

JALISCO. A state in southwestern Mexico bordering the Pacific Ocean, with the state of Nayarit to its north and Michoacán to its east and south. Its area covers 80,157 square kilometers. The northern sector of Jalisco is part of the central Mexican plateau, with the remainder a

mountainous basin with a narrow coastal lowland. Lake
Chapala is partly in Jalisco and partly in the state of
Michoacán. Much of Jalisco is drained by the Lerma
River system. Jalisco is the prototype of Mexican symbolic folklore, and the place of origin of mariachi folk
music, the fancy charro costumes including the broad-
brimmed sombrero, the brightly-colored striped shawl
or sarape, and tequila, a strong liquor made from fermented cactus and named after a local town in Jalisco.
The state is a leading producer in the republic of cattle,
horses, corn, dairy herds, and milk. Its capital, Guadalajara, is the second largest city in Mexico, with its
metropolitan area having 2 million residents. The state
in 1976 had a population totaling 4.2 million.

JARA RODRIGUEZ, HERIBERTO. 1884-1968. A general in
the Revolutionary battles of 1910-1919, often in his native
Veracruz. In 1914 he commanded the naval cadets
against United States forces which temporarily occupied
Veracruz City. He was a member of the 1916-17 constituent assembly at Querétaro which drafted the federal
Constitution. He was a Senator in Congress, then Governor of Veracruz during 1926-30. He was Minister of the
Navy in the cabinet of President Avila Camacho 1940-46
and caused widespread criticism from naval officers and
newspapers that a general, rather than an admiral, held
that position. In Querétaro, he was a leader of the radicals who got the most basic land, labor, and other social reforms written into the 1917 Constitution.

JARABE TAPATIO. The jarabe tapatío is the national folk
dance of Mexico, originating in the state of Jalisco. A
man in a charro or cowboy suit and a woman in a china
poblana dress dance with vigorous stomping, circling a
large sombrero. It is known as the Mexican hat dance.

JARAMILLO, JUAN. Spanish captain who married Malintzín
(La Malinche) on the urging of Cortés. He took her to
Spain where both spent the remaining years of their lives.
See also MALINCHE, LA.

JARAMILLO, RUBEN. Born in 1900 in Morelos and assassinated on May 23, 1962, in Xochicalco, Morelos. As a
teen-ager, Jaramillo joined the troops under General
Emiliano Zapata and fought in Revolutionary battles of
1913-18. He became an organizer for landless peasants
in the 1930's, and from 1940 to 1962 led numerous groups

of land-squatters, protesting the slowness of the government's distribution of nationalized farm lands. His headquarters remained in Tlaquiltenango, Morelos, but his
efforts ranged from Baja California to Chiapas. In 1958
he became loosely allied with Jacinto López, leader of
the General Union of Workers and Campesinos of Mexico
(Unión General de Obreros y Campesinos de México or
UGOCM), organizing temporary land seizures in northern
states. The UGOCM had been established by Marxists
from the Popular Socialist Party. After the far-left
Movement of National Liberation (MLN) was founded in
1961, Jaramillo received some MLN assistance. By
then, Jaramillo had become the best-known symbol of
peasant alienation in the republic and the most effective
rural critic of the government's land reform program.
Early in 1962 Jaramillo's squatters began to occupy farms
throughout central Morelos, including properties belonging
to the state's chief executive, Governor Norberto López
Avelar. Federal troops were called in to end chaos the
state government could not handle. In a gunfight on May
23, an army captain kidnapped Jaramillo and his wife and
later killed them as military rebels although neither was
armed nor leading any guerrillas. In subsequent land
seizures through 1979, no other squatters group had
achieved the public impact of the Jaramillo groups during
the 1958-62 period.

JAROCHO. A nickname for residents of the state of Veracruz, and often specially applied to folklore dancers and
musical groups consisting of a harp, violin, and small
guitars, played by men in white cotton trousers and jackets with peaked straw hats.

JECKER LOAN OF 1859. A Swiss by the name of Jecker negotiated a $15,000,000 dollar loan to conservative ele-
ments in Mexico at a highly usurious rate. When the
Juárez government defaulted, Jecker, who had become a
French citizen, asked his government for help in securing
repayment. This was the official reason for Napoleon's
invasion of Mexico in 1862.

JEFE MAXIMO DE LA REVOLUCION. Name given to Plutarco
Elías Calles. A free translation would be, "Maximum
Leader of the Revolution."

JIMENEZ, JOSE MARIANO. 1781-1811. Independence leader
and a mining engineer by profession, he was born in the

city of San Luis Potosí. He attained the rank of lieutenant general, and one of his main contributions was super-
vision of the manufacture of large numbers of cannon for
the revolutionaries. After Hidalgo was driven from
Guanajuato, Allende ordered Jiménez to begin insurrec-
tions in the north. His forces enjoyed success, taking
Saltillo and what today is San Antonio, Texas. He was
captured at Acatita de Baján in Coahuila and executed by
a firing squad on July 26, 1811.

JIMENEZ, MIGUEL BERNAL. 1910-1956. Composer of the
symphonic suite Michoacán (1940) and Noche en Morelia
(1941). He also composed the historical opera Tata
Vasco (1941), based on the life of Vasco de Quiroga.

JIMENEZ CANTU, JORGE. Born in 1914 in Mexico City.
A medical degree from the National Autonomous University (UNAM). Governor of the state of México 1975-81.
Head of the National Commission for School Construction
during the 1950's. As general manager of the Basic
Commodities Corporation (CONASUPO), he directed numerous government programs for rural improvements in
crop marketing 1964-69. As Minister of Health and Welfare, 1970-76, he promoted family planning in provincial
cities and towns.

JIQUILPÁN. A tiny village in western Michoacán and the birth
place of General Lázaro Cárdenas.

JOHN PAUL II. Pope John Paul II became the first head of
the Catholic Church ever to visit Mexico, for six days
during January 26-31, 1979. He opened the third Latin
America Conference of Bishops in Puebla. The Polish
cardinal who became Pope in 1978 challenged decades of
anti-clerical tradition to ameliorate Church-State relations.
Cross and crown had been entwined in the colonial era
and the hierarchy had been foes of social reform before
the Revolution started in 1910. The Pope visited the
shrine of the Virgin of Guadalupe, Mexico's patron saint,
and Mexico City, Monterrey, Guadalajara, and Oaxaca
City.

JONGUITUD, CARLOS. A leader in the Institutional Revolutionary Party (PRI) since the 1960's, a former Senator
from the state of México, who since 1976 has been in the
presidential cabinet as director of the Institute of Social
Security for Government Workers (ISSSTE).

JOURNALISM. After Spanish printer Juan Pablos installed
the first printing press in Mexico in 1534, books, pamphlets, and journals licensed by the government were
published. Weekly newspapers helped engender Mexico's
fight for independence from Spain in 1810. In 1805 appeared the first daily newspaper, El Diario de México,
edited and published by Carlos de Bustamante. In 1978,
the republic had 240 daily newspapers. But provincial
papers have grown slowly because Mexico City dailies
circulate nationally among government and civic leaders.
The three largest metropolitan areas surrounding Mexico
City, Guadalajara, and Monterrey have 60 percent of the
total daily newspaper circulation. The remainder of Mexico, with 80 percent of the population, has 40 percent of
the circulation. Daily radio broadcasting in Mexico began
in July 1923 at a station later called XEB. On August
31, 1950, Channel 4 or station XHTV began Latin America's first daily television broadcasting. Today privately-
owned and government-owned radio and television stations
and networks blanket the republic. Whereas less than one
fifth of Mexico's adults buy or read daily newspapers,
better than 95 percent of all Mexicans obtain their daily
news from radio.

JUAREZ, BENITO PABLO. 1806-1872. Born in San Pablo
Guelatao, Oaxaca, he was a pure-blooded Zapotec Indian
and is regarded by many as Mexico's greatest statesman
and politician. He lost both of his parents when he was
three and for many years afterwards he was cared for by
his uncle. At the age of 12 he was still illiterate and
had yet to learn Spanish, but due to the efforts of a kind-
ly Franciscan he showed outstanding scholastic aptitude
and quickly made up for past deficiencies. For a while
he planned to enter the priesthood, but finally decided
against it, becoming a lawyer and entering public life.
     He had a long and distinguished career, culminating
in the Laws of the Reform and the presidency of Mexico
in 1858. Juárez was forced to leave Mexico City by Maximilian and the invasion of French-led forces. After his
victory over Maximilian he was again elected president
in 1867, a position he held until his death in 1872.
Among his many reforms was the establishment of a civil
registry, a drastic limiting of the power of the Roman
Catholic Church, nationalization of cemeteries and the
changing of marriage into a civil contract. His fondest
ideal was that people should be governed by laws and not
by the whims of men. The most famous phrase attributed

to him is the following: "El respeto al derecho ajeno es la paz y la democracia es primero" ("Respect for the rights of others is the basis of peace, and democracy is foremost"). He practiced honesty in government and always insisted on it in others, but his respect for the democratic process sometimes took on an exaggerated form, considering the evolutionary state of democracy in Mexico at that time. There were times when he would allow the legislature long periods of debate over issues which he should have insisted be resolved in much less time. Mexico holds him in the highest esteem and has bestowed upon him the very prestigious title of "Benemérito de las Américas (Hero of the Americas)."

JUZGADO GENERAL DE INDIOS. A special court established in 1573 and designed to aid Indians. The latter could appear before the court and denounce abuses committed against them by Spaniards and others in authority. The Juzgado is a good example of sincere efforts on the part of the Spanish Crown to eliminate exploitation of its Indian subjects.

- K -

K. This letter is not in the Spanish alphabet but is employed in transliterations or transcriptions of Maya, Aztec, and other Indian words and in foreign words and foreign proper names. Usually words beginning with a "K" sound can be found in Spanish under the letter "Q" as in "que" and "qui" prefixes.

KINO, EUSEBIO. A Jesuit from Spain, Father Kino founded settlements, churches, and missions in the state of Sonora from 1687 until 1700. He also founded the Mission San Xavier del Bac south of Tucson in 1700, then part of Sonora in colonial Mexico. He is buried at the principal church in the city of Magdalena in northern Sonora.

KINSHIP. Among Indian groups and rural and small-town mestizo societies, kinship plays a vital social and political role in Mexico. Elaborate distinctions are made for first, second, and more remote cousins and for paternal and maternal in-laws. Godparents at christenings become unofficial members of the children's families and lifelong associates of the parents. The institution of godparenthood, the padrino system, functions among all social

classes, both urban and rural, extending from baptism to
confirmation to weddings, ceremonies for a new home or
business, funerals, birthdays, and most other social
events.

KUKULCAN. The Maya name Kukulcán is the same as the
Aztec Quetzalcóatl, meaning serpent god with feathers of
the quetzal bird. Both Mayas and Aztecs believed him
to be the god of the morning and evening stars.

- L -

LA ANGOSTURA, BATTLE OF see BUENA VISTA, BATTLE
OF

LA MALINCHE see MALINCHE, LA

LABASTIDA, JAIME. Born in 1939 in Los Mochis, Sinaloa.
He studied philosophy at the National University, then be-
came a writer for the Revista Mexicana de Literatura,
Revolución, and most other leading Mexican magazines.
In addition to being a leading short story writer and es-
sayist, he is a noted poet since the 1960 publication of
La espiga amontinada, a volume of his poems.

LABOR MINISTRY. The Secretaría de Trabajo y Previsión
Social or Ministry of Labor and Social Needs had its beginning as the Department of Labor within the Ministry
of Development and Industry of the first Revolutionary
government in 1911. Not until 1932 did it gain its autonomy and not until 1940 did it adopt its current name. It
enforces the federal labor code, all federal, state, and
local labor laws, and overseas labor-management relations. It administers Federal Conciliation and Arbitration
Boards, the National Commission for Minimum Wages,
and the National Profit-Sharing Commission.

LABOR UNION PLURALISM. In México, the hundreds of
unions federate within a pluralistic system. There is a
federation for federal government workers unions and one
for state and municipal government workers unions. In
the private sector, a majority of the labor unions belong
to the Mexican Federation of Labor (CTM), but some belong to the Revolutionary Workers Federation (CROC),
some to the Regional Federation (CROM), and some are
autonomous, as the National Federation of Sugar Cane

Workers. In 1958 the CTM joined some autonomous unions, such as railroad and electrical workers into a Workers Unity Bloc. In the rival Mexican Workers Bloc in 1960 grouped most electrical workers unions, the CROC, and the Sugar Cane Unions Federation. Since 1965 the two blocs loosely coexist as the Congress of Labor in an annual conference.

LABRA, WENCESLAO. Born in 1895 in Zumpango, México. He served five 3-year terms as a Deputy in Congress, and was a Senator during 1934-37, and Governor of the state of México 1937-41. He was a longtime member of the central executive committee of the Institutional Revolutionary Party (PRI) and its secretary for organization and statistics. In 1936 he was one of the founders of the National Campesino Federation (CNC).

LACANDON. The Lacandon Indians live in the Usumarinta River Valley of the southernmost state of Chiapas and descend from the ancient Mayas. They have remained relatively isolated from Mexican culture and therefore speak a traditional Mayan dialect. They are short in stature and wear their hair long and loose, and engage in hunting and basic cultivation. In 1978, only 500 of them remained unassimilated. In the Chiapas city of San Cristóbal de las Casas a private museum preserves their history from pre-Hispanic to modern times.

LAND LAW OF 1883. A law which favored the large landowners in its original form, in 1894 it was strengthened even more in their favor. Surveying companies were chartered which were empowered to survey all lands for which written titles were either suspect or nonexistent. They were given one third of all land surveyed and were also allowed to seize any suspect lands. These companies in turn sold the land in large blocks to the hacienda owners.

LAND REFORM see HACIENDA

LANZ DURET, FERNANDO. Born in 1916 in Campeche. An attorney and writer for the Mexico City daily El Universal who became Mexico's leading war correspondent 1942-45, chronicling Mexico's activities as one of the Allies in World War Two. In the 1950's he was a Deputy in Congress and then a Senator 1958-64.

LATIFUNDIA. Very large estates or plantation-ranches which were targets of land reform under the Revolution beginning in 1910.

LAVALLE URBINA, MARIA. Born in 1908 in Campeche. An attorney, she became the first woman in Mexico appointed a federal judge, presiding over the Federal District Superior Tribunal 1947-52. She then directed social welfare for the Ministry of Gobernación (Interior) until 1963 and was a Senator 1964-70.

LAZO BARREIRO, CARLOS. (1914-1955). An architect who was in charge of design for the building of the campus of the National Autonomous University of Mexico (UNAM) during 1949-52, eleven miles from downtown Mexico City. He was a professor of architecture at UNAM 1943-55.

LEON. An industrial city of central Mexico in the state of Guanajuato, 250 miles northwest of Mexico City, at an elevation of 5,800 feet above sea level. Founded in 1576, it is a center for marketing cattle and hides and leather production and the largest shoe manufacturing center in the republic and in Latin America. In 1978 more than 600 tanneries and shoe factories mass produced 200,000 pairs of shoes per day. Its 1976 population totaled 600,000. It also has electronics, plastics, and textile industries.

LEON, LUIS. Minister of Agriculture under President Elías Plutarco Calles.

LEON, NICOLAS. 1859-1929. Doctor, teacher and historian. He was born in Michoacán and was an extremely prolific writer. He practiced and taught medicine for a brief period, but later worked in many different professions, among them museum curator, ethnologist and anthropologist. Among his hundreds of works are Hombres ilustres y escritores michoacanos and Tradiciones y leyendas piadosas de México.

LEON MURILLO, MAXIMILIANO. Born in 1925 in Michoacán. A secondary and preparatory school teacher who became a leader of the Popular Socialist Party (PPS). As a PPS Deputy in Congress during 1970-73, he helped the dominant Institutional Revolutionary Party (PRI) draft key petroleum, labor, and television legislation.

LEON TORAL, JOSE DE see OBREGON, ALVARO

LEON Y GAMA, ANTONIO. 1735-1802. He was born and
   died in Mexico City. A mathematician, physicist and
   astronomer, he was a self-educated man and his scholarly papers ranged from medicine to a study of the moons
   of Jupiter.

LEPERO. Slang term applied to a person who is uncouth and
   vulgar. Other slang words conveying a similar meaning
   are "pelado" and "naco."

LERDO DE TEJADA, MIGUEL. Liberal politician and Secretary of the Treasury during the presidencies of Comonfort
   and Juárez, 1855-1859. He also served on the Mexican
   supreme court and authored the Ley Lerdo, which prohibited excessive Church ownership of land.

LERDO DE TEJADA, SEBASTIAN. 1825-1889. President of
   Mexico from 1872 to 1876, when he was overthrown by
   General Porfirio Díaz. Always regarded as a liberal
   politician, previous to this he had been a supreme court
   judge and a cabinet minister. He died in exile in New
   York City.

LEY FUGA see RURALES

LEY IGLESIAS. The reform law of 1857 which removed cemeteries from the control of the Roman Catholic Church.

LEY JUAREZ. A reform law authored by Benito Juárez and
   passed in 1855. The authority of the military and ecclesiastical tribunals was severely limited and this law was
   a major reason for the civil war which raged from 1858
   to 1860.

LEY LERDO see LERDO DE TEJADA, MIGUEL

LEYVA VELAZQUEZ, GABRIEL. Born in 1896 in Humayes,
   Sinaloa. As a young officer under General Alvaro Obregón, he fought in 1911-20 Revolutionary battles. His father was a close friend of President Francisco Madero
   and most of his relatives were precursors of the Revolution. He was acting Governor of Sinaloa 1935-37, then
   became a Deputy in Congress until 1940, then a Senator
   1940-46, and again 1970-76. When elected Governor of

Sinaloa in 1957, he was a dominant member of the national executive committee of the Institutional Revolutionary Party (PRI).   During his gubernatorial term of 1957-62, he ended longtime attempts of squatters to take over unfarmed lands, even though he had been Secretary General of the National Campesino Federation (CNC).

LIMANTOUR, JOSE YVES.   1854-1935.   French-born politician who was the Minister of Finance during the Porfirio Díaz regime.   He was the leader of the científicos and instituted many reforms, such as nationalization of the railroads, abolishment of the alcabalas and the institution of monetary reforms which enabled Mexico to attain an enviable position internationally.   In contrast to many politicians of the Díaz era, Limantour was regarded as an able, honest administrator.   He was not able to remain in government service after Díaz's resignation, was forced into exile and died in Paris.

LIVAS VILLARREAL, EDUARDO.   Born on January 21, 1911, in Monterrey, Nuevo León.   Law degree from the Monterrey Law School 1933.   A member of the organization founding the University of Nuevo León in 1933.   A longtime member of the UNL Board of Regents.   As a Senator during 1958-61, he led the congressional campaign for expropriating the electric power companies.   As Governor of Nuevo León during 1961-67, he ended the recurring strikes and unrest at the University of Nuevo León.

"LLORONA, LA."   The "Weeping Woman" or Llorona folk song from the Isthmus of Tehuantepec is nationally popular, being played at engagement parties and wedding receptions.

LOMBARDINI, MANUEL MARIA.   1802-1853.   General Lombardini was President of Mexico from February to April of 1853, when he handed over the presidency to Santa Anna.   He was always a strong supporter of the latter and died in December of the same year.

LOMBARDO TOLEDANO, VICENTE.   Born on July 16, 1894, in Teziutlán, Puebla, and died on November 19, 1968, in Mexico City.   He was Mexico's best known socialist and most successful Marxist, working within the dominant Institutional Revolutionary Party (PRI) until he founded the Popular Socialist Party (PPS) in 1948.   Law degree from the National Autonomous University (UNAM) in 1919.

UNAM law professor 1919-33.   Founder and President of
the Workers University in Mexico City 1936-38.   Member
of the Mexican Labor Party 1921-32.   Joined the PRI
when it was the Mexican Revolutionary Party in 1938.
Interim Governor of Puebla 1923.   Municipal Councilman
in the Federal District 1924-25.   Deputy in the federal
Congress from Labor Party 1926-28 and from PPS 1964-
67.   Organizer and Secretary General of the Mexican
Federation of Workers (CTM) 1936-40.   President of the
Moscow-oriented Latin American Federation of Workers
(CTAL) 1938-63.   Secretary General of the Mexican Socialist League 1944-45.   Founder in 1948 of the Popular
Party, which later added the word "Socialist" to show its
Marxist orientation.   In 1952 he was PPS candidate for
president and campaigned nationally, receiving 73,000
votes, with PRI winner Adolfo Ruiz Cortines getting 2.7
million.   Yet he helped establish the PPS strength in a
few states, such as Nayarit, in some congressional districts, and scattered municipal governments.   He wrote
profusely for the socialist magazine Avante, which closed
in 1972, for the Communist Party's Política, which ended
in 1968, and for the still prominent leftist magazine Siempre.   He founded the General Union of Workers and Campesinos (UGOCM) and in 1963 the Independent Campesino
Federation (CCI) which challenged the pro-government National Campesino Federation until co-opted in 1970.

LOPEZ MATEOS, ADOLFO.   1910-1969.   Politician and
President of Mexico, 1958-1964.   Held various political
posts previous to being elected to the presidency.   Ideo-
logically, he steered a middle course, neither veering
too far to the right nor to the left.   Under his administration the policy of free textbook distribution to millions
of public school children was initiated.   López Mateos
was well-liked by the Mexican people and succeeded in
guiding Mexico through the shock waves of the Cuban
Revolution.   He accomplished more in agrarian land reform than any president since Cárdenas and it was through
his efforts that Mexico opened important new trade with
the Far East and also became a member of L.A.F.T.A.
One of the most popular but relatively minor accomplishments of his administration was the regaining of the
Chamizal land area between Ciudad Juárez and El Paso,
Texas.

LOPEZ PORTILLO, JOSE.   Born on June 16, 1920, in Mexico City.   Law degree from the University of Santiago,

Chile, 1945. Law degree from the National Autonomous
University of Mexico (UNAM) 1946. UNAM law professor
1947-58. Founder of the UNAM Ph.D. program in public
administration. Member of the social and economic
council of the Institutional Revolutionary Party (PRI)
1958-72. Technical Director for the Ministry of National
Patrimony 1959-60. Director General of the Federal
Boards of Material Improvement in all seaports and cities
along national borders 1960-65. Director of legal affairs
for the Ministry of the Presidency 1965-68. Assistant
Minister of the Presidency 1968-70. Assistant Minister
of National Patrimony 1970-72. Director General of the
Federal Electricity Commission 1972-73. Minister of
Finance 1973-76. President of Mexico for the 1976-82
term. He is the author of two 1976 novels, both translated and published in English also in 1976. His Quetzalcoatl has the Aztec god promising Mexicans security but
they demand freedom instead. His Don Q has attorneys
questioning the efficiency of government bureaucracy. He
has a National Development Plan covering 1979 to 1990
which divided Mexico into eleven zones to decentralize
industry, giving tax credits to new investors and those
with high employment levels. Reduced rates on electricity, natural gas, and fuel oil are given to industrializing
ports. His administration is using profits from non-
renewable oil resources to invest in industries with products from renewable resources, with a goal of creating
600,000 new jobs every year to reduce the rates of unemployment and migration to the United States.

LOPEZ PORTILLO, MARGARITA. Born in 1918 in Guadala-
    jara. The sister of Mexican President José López Por-
    tillo, she has long been an established writer of televi-
    sion, radio, and film scripts and magazine articles.
    Since December 1976 she has been Director of the Bureau
    of Radio, Television, and Cinema of the Ministry of
    Gobernación (Interior). She has supervised all non-
    commercial broadcasting and the government's own daily
    news and informational programs.

LOPEZ RAYON, IGNACIO. 1773-1832. Independence figure.
    By profession he was an attorney, but dedicated himself
    to administering the family mines. Soon after the begin-
    ning of the movement for independence he became the
    secretary and confidant of Hidalgo. Later he commanded
    troops in the northern part of Mexico and was active in
    central Mexico, where he took Zacatecas. He was finally

captured by the Spaniards, but was not executed. After
independence he became Mayor of San Luis Potosí and
for a time the chief administrator of Jalisco. He died
in Guadalajara.

LORET DE MOLA, CARLOS. Born on July 30, 1921, in
Mérida, Yucatán. Nationally known as one of the few
leaders within the Institutional Party (PRI) to write spe-
cific criticism of the pressures exerted on government
officials by the establishment leadership. His 1978 book,
Confesiones de un gobernador, details inner-circle agreements. A newspaper editor and writer for Diario de
Yucatán, a Deputy in Congress 1961-63, then a Senator
1964-70. Governor of Yucatán 1970-76. He was the
most effective critic among government officials of the
Echeverría presidency.

LOYO, GILBERTO. (1901-1973). An economist from Veracruz. Dean of the School of Economics of the National
University 1944-52. Director General of the Census of
1940 and of 1950. As Minister of Industry and Commerce
1952-58, he modernized the Bureau of Statistics. He
chaired the National Commission for Minimum Wages
1963-72. He was Mexico's leading statistician from the
1940's to the 1970's. He originated courses in demogra-
phy at the National University and other Mexican universities.

LOZADA, MANUEL. 1828-1873. Guerrilla leader who resisted attempts by the federal government to regain control of his native state of Nayarit after Maximilian's fall
in 1867. Because of his cruelty he was given the name
of the "Tiger of Nayarit." He was finally caught and
executed by federal troops.

LUGO LAGUNAS, JOSE. (1871-1963). A lawyer from Guerrero who became a leader of the Anti-Reelectionist Party
in 1909 against the Porfirio Díaz dictatorship. As Governor of Guerrero during 1910-13 he opposed the growing
power of General Victoriano Huerta. In the constituent
assembly in Querétaro 1916-17, he wrote part of the Article 123 labor rights of the federal Constitution.

LUNA KAN, FRANCISCO. Born in 1926 in Mérida, Yucatán.
A physician who became an active developer of the hene-
quen, fiber, rope, and cord industries of his native state.
A Senator who became a leader in Congress during 1970-

76, he was then elected Governor of the state of Yucatán for the 1976-82 term.

LUQUE, EDUARDO. Born in 1910 in Querétaro. An attorney who became a leader in Congress as a Deputy 1943-46 and 1961-64, and as a Senator 1946-52 and 1964-70. He was dominant in congressional committees on credit, agriculture, and constitutional matters and was Senate president. He headed the Federal Conciliation and Arbitration Board and organized the customs offices for the Territory (later the state) of Quintana Roo during 1958-61.

- M -

"MACARENA, LA." At a bullfight, the band plays "La Macarena" before the action begins and between each fighting of the bulls and at the conclusion of the afternoon's six fights. This Spanish two-step was imported from Spain in the colonial era.

MACHETE. A long, wide knife, almost the size of a sword, running two or three feet in length. It is the all-purpose harvesting tool of peasant farmers (campesinos), and can cut sugar cane, brush, branches, coconuts, and serves as a repair tool for fences and houses. Machetes with engraved steel blades and decorated handles are displayed at fiestas and for other special events.

MACHISMO. The Mexican cult of male virility, manliness, personal strength and courage. Politically, it means to win over opponents, to help guide the government at various levels, to have one's policies and views predominate, and to defeat enemies domestic or foreign. Machismo is the opposite of compromise or weakness in personal or public life.

MACHO. A male who shows his vigor by dominating women sexually and in matters of love, and by siring many children with one's wife or sweetheart or with any consenting female. A macho will accept any personal, political, or social challenge and will fight to vanquish any opponent. His position is basic in Mexican culture.

MADERO, FRANCISCO INDALECIO. 1873-1913. Revolutionary and President of Mexico. Born in Coahuila and a son of landowners, he received his education in Europe

and the United States. Madero led the opposition against
General Porfirio Díaz, setting off the first major social
upheaval of the twentieth century, the Mexican Revolution.
He was elected President in October of 1911 and served
until 1913, when he was assassinated on the orders of
General Victoriano Huerta. An idealist who had no previous governmental or political experience, Madero was
unable to control the forces which he had unleashed by
forcing Díaz to resign. Although he proved to be generally inept after assuming the presidency, he is regarded
as a hero in Mexico today, although his defects are recognized. Madero is best remembered as the initiator of
the Mexican Revolution.

MADERO, GUSTAVO. Brother of Francisco. He was killed
in February, 1913, at the end of the "decena trágica."

MADRAZO, CARLOS A. (1915-1969). An attorney from
Tabasco who was a major reformer within the dominant
Institutional Revolutionary Party (PRI). He was one of
the founders of the party's National Federation of Popular
Organizations (CNOP) in 1942. As president of the PRI
1964-65, he initiated party primaries in Baja California
del Norte and Chihuahua state but could not end the inner-
circle self-replenishment system of PRI nominations for
all offices being decided on the basis of personal relationships. He was a Deputy in Congress and was Governor of Tabasco during 1959-64. His death in an airplane
crash on June 4, 1969, ended his life long efforts to make
more accessible to rank-and-file members PRI nominations for all public offices through primaries or open conventions in place of the PRI rubber-stamp conventions after party leaders have chosen candidates.

MADRINA. A godmother. Like the godfather or padrino,
she functions beyond baptisms as part of the lifelong extended family relationships of her own and the relatives
of her godchild.

MAGAÑA, GILDARDO. (1891-1939). An accountant from
Michoacán who was a general under Pancho Villa, then
became Chief of the Army of the South upon the death of
Emiliano Zapata in 1919. He was a leading intellectual
of the Zapatista reform movement. He was Governor of
Baja California del Norte, then from 1936 to 1939 Gov-
ernor of Michoacán and a major adviser of President
Lázaro Cárdenas from 1934 to 1939, a lifelong friend.

MAGAÑA NEGRETE, GUMERSINDO. He is a business executive from Irapuato, Guanajuato, who was one of the founders there in May 1971 of the right-wing Mexican Democratic Party (PDM). He helped get the PDM on the ballot for the 1979 congressional elections. Since the 1960's he has worked to get far-right Sinarquista members to join the PDM to work for a reduced bureaucracy and more private enterprise. He has been PDM president since 1978.

MAGUEY. Spanish word meaning "agave." See PULQUE.

MALDONADO SANCHEZ, BRAULIO. Born in 1903 in San José, Baja California del Norte. An attorney who became the first elected governor when BCN changed from a territory to a state in 1953, for the 1953-59 term. Founder and Secretary General of the Leftist Socialist Party 1931-32. He joined the Institutional Revolutionary Party (PRI) in 1934. From 1958 to 1963 he organized the Independent Campesino Federation (CCI) to rival the pro-government National Campesino Federation (CNC) with an unsuccessful campaign for more socialism in agrarian affairs. He led the far-left Popular Electoral Front against the PRI candidate Díaz Ordaz, who was elected Mexico's President in 1964.

MALINCHE, LA. A beautiful Indian woman who became the mistress and companion of Hernán Cortés. She was born in 1495 A.D. in Veracruz, the daughter of an Aztec governor. She is regarded by many as the key factor in Cortés's conquest of Mexico because her knowledge of the Indian languages Nahuatl and Maya enabled him to learn of the dissension and intrigues present among the various Indian nations. A woman of extraordinary beauty, she was also highly intelligent. Later, Cortés arranged for her to marry Captain Juan Jaramillo, who took her to Spain where she lived for the rest of her life, gaining the respect of the influential families of Spain. She is also known as Marina or Malintzín.

MALINCHISMO. Taken from the Aztec princess Malinche, the term means to exalt anything foreign and to undervalue anything which is native to Mexico.

"MAÑANITAS, LAS." A popular folksong, "The Dawns" is sung on a person's birthday early in the morning but also during any birthday party or celebration regardless of the time of day.

MANERO, ANTONIO. (1896-1964). A banker who directed the Regulatory Commission of the banking system in the 1920's and 1930's. Founder in 1929 of the National Labor Bank and founder in 1943 of the Industrial Bank of the state of México.

MANGA DE CLAVO. The ancestral ranch of General Antonio López de Santa Anna located in the state of Veracruz.

MANRIQUE ARIAS, DANIEL. Born in 1939. Distinguished painter who originated the "Arte Acá" movement in the Tepito region of Mexico City. It is an effort to bring muralistic art to the masses. Manrique Arias studied at the famous painting and art school, La Esmeralda in Mexico City. Among his works are "La Puerta" and "La Tapia."

MANZANILLA SCHAFFER, VICTOR. Born in 1924 in Mexico City. Law degree from the National Autonomous University (UNAM). Professor of law, sociology, then economics at UNAM. Longtime adviser on economics and politics for the Institutional Revolutionary Party (PRI), and on the PRI national executive committee. A Deputy in Congress 1967-69 and a Senator from Yucatán 1970-76. He headed the National Revolutionary Coalition in the 1960's.

MARGAIN, HUGO B. Born on February 13, 1913, in Mexico City. An attorney who became Mexico's most influential diplomat. He was director of the Retail Tax Bureau, then the Federal Income Tax Bureau 1951-59. He then served as Executive Officer, then Subsecretary of the Ministry of Industry and Commerce 1961-64. Director General of the National Commission on Profit Sharing 1962-63. Minister of Finance 1970-73. Ambassador to Britain 1973-76. He was Ambassador to the United States during 1965-70, and again since 1976. He is President López Portillo's senior diplomat, ranking right after the Foreign Relations Minister.

MARGIL DE JESUS, FRAY ANTONIO. 1657-1726. Franciscan missionary born in Spain who spent more than 50 years doing missionary work in many regions of New Spain, from Texas to Yucatán, all on foot. Among the many schools he founded was the Colegio de la Cruz, in Querétaro. Because of his profound religious works among the Indians, he has been beatified. He died in the monastery of San Francisco de México.

MARIACHIS. Mexico's prototype folklore musicians, originally from Jalisco. They wear the cowboy charro costume
of embroidered short jacket and riding trousers and large
sombrero. A mariachi orchestra consists of two violin-
ists, two trumpeters, three guitarists, and a bass guitar-
ist who plays the guitarrón string bass. Each of them
takes turns singing solos, duets, in trios, or other com-
binations. They feature songs about ranching and farm
life, and folksongs covering all the facets of Mexican
culture.

MARINA   see   MALINCHE, LA

MARQUEZ, LEONARDO. 1820-1913. General who fought on
the side of the conservatives during the Wars of the Reform (1857-1860). His wholesale shooting of prisoners
and doctors in Mexico City earned him the nickname of
the "Tiger of Tacubaya" (El Tigre de Tacubaya).

MARTINEZ, JUAN JOSE. 1782-1863. He was a hero of the
independence movement and his nickname was "El Pípila,"
a slang term for a domesticated turkey. He worked as
a miner and when Hidalgo called for independence, he
joined his movement. With the Spaniards sheltered in
the Alhóndiga de Granaditas, the revolutionaries were not
able to dislodge them until Martínez, pushing a huge stone
statue slowly forward, reached the thick wooden door of
the Alhóndiga and set it on fire, allowing the revolutionaries to gain entry. In the city of Guanajuato there is
a huge statue of Martínez overlooking the city. He died
in San Miguel Allende at an advanced age, probably of
tuberculosis.

MARTINEZ BAEZ, ANTONIO. Born in 1901 in Morelia,
Michoacán. An attorney who was legal head for the National Urban Mortgage Bank and director of indemnifica-
tions for the Agriculture Ministry in the 1930's. Head
of the National Banking Commission 1941-43, then head
of the government's sugar development bank, Financiera
Azucarera 1943-46. Minister of Industry and Commerce
1948-52. As head of the National Securities Commission,
1953-59, he reorganized Mexican stock markets. President of the Mexican Bar Association 1959-60. He represented Mexico in the Latin American Free Trade Association in 1968, getting reduced LAFTA tariffs for Mexico's
exports.

MARTINEZ CORBALA, GONZALO. Born in 1928 in San Luis

Potosí. A civil engineer who was president of the Mexican Society of Engineers and publisher of the magazine Civil Engineering in the 1960's, and head of the Mexican Planning Association. Ambassador to Chile 1972-74. As a Deputy during 1964-67, he led the move in Congress which forced Governor of the Federal District Ernesto Uruchurtu to resign in 1966 for too extensive slum clearance and street widening which left thousands of poor people homeless.

MARTINEZ DE LA VEGA, FRANCISCO. Born in 1909 in San Luis Potosí. A well-known leftist writer who was Secretary General of the Popular Socialist Party (PPS) 1951-55. He was co-founder of the leftist weekly magazine Siempre in 1951. A Deputy in Congress from the PPS 1958-59, he became Interim Governor of San Luis Potosí during 1959-61 by representing both the PPS and the dominant Institutional Revolutionary Party (PRI) as a coalition appointee to fill an unexpired term.

MARTINEZ DOMINGUEZ, ALFONSO. Born in 1922 in Monterrey, Nuevo León. A leader of the Institutional Revolutionary Party (PRI) since 1955, he was head of the PRI's Popular Organization Federation (CNOP) 1961-65, and president of the PRI 1968-70. A Deputy in Congress 1952-55 and 1964-67, where he headed the Chamber of Deputies. He was Governor of the Federal District 1970-71, and had to resign after the 1971 student riots. He was elected Governor of Nuevo León for the 1979-85 term. He built his power base as Secretary General of the Federation of Unions of Government Workers during 1949-52.

MARTINEZ DOMINGUEZ, GUILLERMO. Born in 1924 in Monterrey, Nuevo León. An economist and journalist. He was director of prices for the Ministry of Industry and Commerce, then head of the Small Business Bank. Director General of the Federal Electricity Commission 1964-70. Director General of the government's Nacional Financiera development bank 1970-76. The brother of Alfonso, Nuevo León Governor, he has been a columnist for the magazine Hoy and the daily newspapers La Prensa and Excelsior. He won the National Prize for Journalism for 1953 for exposing fraud in the Social Security Institute.

MARTINEZ TORNEL, PEDRO. (1889-1957). An engineer from Veracruz, he built the shipping port of Salina Cruz, Oaxaca in 1923 and modernized it in 1957. A top administrator of the National Railroads during 1935-43. As-

sistant Minister of Public Works 1943-45. Minister of
Public Works 1945-46. He directed Juan Almazán's unsuccessful presidential campaign in 1940, thereby cutting
himself off from the highest offices controlled by the
dominant Institutional Revolutionary Party leaders after 1946.

MARTINEZ VERDUGO, ARNOLDO. Born in 1925 in the state
of Sinaloa. A clerk in state government offices in Sinaloa in the 1940's and 1950's. National head of Communist
Youth in 1945-49. An active leader in the Communist
Party of Mexico (PCM) since 1949. A member of the
PCM Central Committee since 1955 and party head or
PCM Secretary General since 1964. After years of lobbying, he got PCM candidates certified on the ballot for
the federal congressional elections of July 1979 and then
won 10 percent of the total vote for minority or proportional representation seats.

MASSIEU, WILFRIDO. (1878-1944). An engineer who was
director of the Military Industry College, then of the College of Railroad Workers during 1920-37, which as a co-
founder he helped convert in 1937 into the National Polytechnic Institute (IPN), and then served as founding president of the IPN in Mexico City during 1937-44.

MAXIMILIAN, Ferdinand, of Habsburg. 1832-1867. Next in line
to rule the Austro-Hungarian Empire after his brother,
Franz Josef. He showed promise in maritime affairs and
was placed in charge of the Imperial Navy. He was approached by prominent Mexican conservatives to become
emperor of a soon-to-be-created Mexican Empire. He as-
sented, having been reassured that the people of Mexico
genuinely wanted his leadership. His rule lasted from May
1864 to May 1866, when he surrendered his sword to General
Mariano Escobedo at Querétaro and it was outside this city
that he was executed by firing squad on the Hill of the Bells
in June 1867. Early in his reign he alienated the conservatives by proclaiming such liberal ideas as freedom of the
press and separation of Church and State. Juárez fought him
uncompromisingly even though Maximilian had once offered
him a high position in his government. He further alienated
the liberals by finally decreeing the death penalty for anyone
supporting the Juárez government. Mexicans today generally
look on Maximilian as a well-meaning person who was completely naive about the political realities of Mexico.

MAYA. The Maya Indians concentrate in the Yucatán peninsula in the states of Yucatán, Quintana Roo, and Cam-

peche. In 1975, some 350,000 Indians in Mexico spoke
Maya, and in neighboring Guatemala three million did.
The ancient Maya empire in pre-Hispanic times included
Chiapas, the Yucatán peninsula, Guatemala, and Honduras.
During 300-900 A.D., the "Old Empire" had astronomy,
a calendar of 365 days, and temples at Palenque, Chi-
apas. After 900 A.D., the "New Empire" at Chichén
Itzá and Uxmal, Yucatán, developed pyramids and tem-
ples. Spaniard Francisco Montejo failed to conquer the
Mayas during the 1527-35 period, but his son, Francisco
the Younger, completed the conquest 1540-46.

MAZA, MARGARITA. Wife of Benito Juárez and a member
of a family who occupied a high position in society.

MAZATLAN. An important port on the Pacific Ocean in the
state of Sinaloa. Mazatlán had a 1976 population totaling
163,000. This city is a tourist resort for fishing, boat-
ing, and its beaches. It is headquarters for commercial
fishing fleets, merchant shipping, and industries related
to marine products.

MCLANE-OCAMPO TREATY OF 1859. A treaty drawn up
with the Juárez government which would have permitted
the United States perpetual right of transit across the
Isthmus of Tehuantepec, the narrowest part of Mexico.
This treaty would also have allowed United States soldiers
to be stationed in Mexico. Because of strong opposition
in both countries it was never put into effect.

MEJIA, IGNACIO. Politician, military figure and a confidant
of Benito Juárez. A very honest man, when Porfirio
Díaz could not bribe him into submission, he resorted to
levying false charges against him, forcing Mejía into exile.

MEJIA, TOMAS. 1823-1867. During the reign of Maximilian
in Mexico, Mejía was probably the best known general
after Miramón. Previously, he had fought with the conservatives against Juárez and later became genuinely devoted to Maximilian. On June 19, 1867, he was executed
on the Hill of the Bells, along with Maximilian and Miramón.

MELGAR, AGUSTIN. 1829-1847. Niño Héroe (Heroic Child).
He had lost both of his parents while very young and at
the age of sixteen he requested and was granted permis-
sion to enroll in the Escuela Militar in Chapultepec Park.
Melgar showed great valor in defending Chapultepec Castle, killing at least one invader and being wounded twice.

MELO, JUAN VICENTE. Born in 1932 in Veracruz. A physician and dermatologist, he became a fine arts critic, then a full-time writer, serving as editor of Universidad de México, and writing for other magazines, including Siempre and Revista Mexicana de Literatura. His 1956 volume of short stories, La noche alucinada, and his 1969 novel, La obediencia nocturna, made him nationally known for characterizations of lonely Mexicans.

MENDEZ DOCURRO, EUGENIO. Born in 1923 in Veracruz. Engineering degree from the National Polytechnic Institute (IPN). Master's degree from Harvard University. Director General of the IPN 1959-62. Assistant Minister of Communications 1964-70. Minister of Communications and Transportation 1970-76. In 1977, the López Portillo administration charged Méndez with stealing 80 million pesos during his service in the Echeverría cabinet. He was forced to resign his 1977 position as Subsecretary of Education, and to make restitution of one-fourth of the disputed sums. For the first time in modern history, a Mexican federal attorney general documented misappropriation of funds against a high-ranking administrator, producing false invoices and canceled checks. The case against Méndez triggered a general probe of many bureaucrats in the most extensive anti-corruption investigations and trials ever held in Mexico.

MENDIETA, FRAY JERONIMO DE. Ca. 1525-1604. He was born in Vitoria, Spain, the last of 40 children. He became famous as a Franciscan missionary and was one of the most famous religious figures of his era. He learned to speak Náhuatl so well that he became much more of an orator in that language than in his native Spanish. His Historia eclesiástica indiana is what brought him fame, being an account of the conversion of the Indians during the sixteenth century. He died in the Monastery of St. Francis in Mexico after a long illness.

MENDIETA Y NUÑEZ, LUCIO. Born in 1895 in Mexico City. A sociologist who co-founded the School of Social Sciences and the School of Economics at the National Autonomous University (UNAM). He was publisher of the Mexican Sociology Review, 1939-46.

MENDOZA, ANTONIO DE. 1493-1552. First Viceroy of New Spain. Born of wealthy parents, he became associated

with service to the Spanish royal court at a young age
and after a varied career which included diplomatic service in Hungary, he was named the first Viceroy to New
Spain in 1535, a post for which no time limit was fixed.
He was the only viceroy ever to enjoy this privilege,
since all future ones would be limited to six year terms.
Under his jurisdiction, many Indians were converted and
a more humane policy was adopted towards them. Among
his many accomplishments were the introduction of the
first printing press in New Spain, the establishment of
an imperial mint and the founding of the Colegio de Santa
Cruz de Tlatelolco for the education of Indian noblemen.
He was also responsible for the founding of the city of
Valladolid in Michoacán, today known as Morelia. He
was so successful that in 1549 the King appointed him as
Viceroy of Peru. Antonio de Mendoza is remembered
today as one of the most outstanding viceroys of New
Spain and is buried in Lima, Peru.

MENDOZA, NARCISO. Revolutionary hero born in 1800 in
Cuatla. As a boy he helped defend the city of Cuatla
against forces of the Spanish General Calleja. When the
Spaniards were about to break into the city, he fired a
cannon point blank into them and gave Morelos the opportunity to regroup his forces and defeat the Spaniards.
There is a statue of him on the outskirts of Cuernavaca.

MERIDA. The capital of the state of Yucatán and its largest
city. It lies on a low, flat plain, surrounded by henequen
plantations and has a tropical climate. The city's water
is pumped from wells by windmills. It was founded in
1542 by Francisco Montejo the Younger on the site of an
ancient Maya city called Tho. Spanish colonial buildings
were built on top of Maya temples and other native structures. The Montejo home of 1549 has been preserved at
the main plaza near the Cathedral. A center of the henequen industry, with manufacturing of rope, cordage,
coarse fabrics for sacks and bags, sack-like containers,
and fabric hats. A tourist center for the Maya archaeological sites of Chichén Itzá 72 miles east and Uxmal 55
miles south. For centuries Mérida was isolated from
most other Mexican cities except by sea at the port of
Progreso. Passenger and cargo airlines in the 1940's
and highway and railroad links in the 1950's lessened the
isolation. The city has the University of Yucatán and the
state museum.

MERINO RABAGO, FRANCISCO. Born in 1919 in Irapuato, Guanajuato. Director of credit for the National Ejidal Credit Bank 1956-58, then the Assistant General Manager of that bank 1959-60 and 1971-75, then in 1975 Director General of the Bank of Rural Credit. Minister of Agriculture and Hydraulic Resources in the López Portillo cabinet during 1976-82.

MESILLA VALLEY. The land which the United States purchased from Mexico in the Gadsden Purchase. See GADSDEN PURCHASE.

MESTIZO. A Mexican of mixed Spanish and Indian racial origins. A female is a mestiza. A majority of the citizens of Mexico are mestizos.

METATE. A carved stone for grinding corn used throughout rural and small-town Mexico and in urban homes of the poor, especially those from Indian cultures. A metate is a major household tool in Indian villages.

MEXICALI. The capital of the state of Baja California del Norte. Its 1976 population totaled 340,000. An agricultural center opposite Calexico, California, it is the only Mexican state capital on the United States border.

MEXICO CITY. One of the world's largest cities, in 1976 it had 8.7 million within its city limits and 12 million within its metropolitan area. The city lies within a Federal District only 573 square miles in area, at an elevation of 7,349 feet above sea level, on the dried bed of Lake Texcoco. It is 200 miles west of Veracruz City on the Gulf and 190 miles northeast of Acapulco on the Pacific Ocean. It was established by the Spaniards as Mexico City in 1520 on the city of Tenochtitlán, the capital built by the Aztecs in 1325 A.D. The Governor of the Federal District also serves as the Mayor of Mexico City. The city is divided into Delegations, each of which elects Councils. The chief downtown plaza or Zócalo has the National Palace housing the presidential and some cabinet offices, and the largest Cathedral in the Western Hemisphere, built 1573-1791, measuring 387 feet by 288 feet and 179 feet high. Since 1969 the city has had a subway (Metro). Its principal avenue, Reforma, runs southwest from downtown to Chapultepec Park.

MEXICO (STATE). The state of Mexico is one of the 31

states of the federal republic of Mexico. It is located in
the south central region just west and north of the Federal District, on a plateau 8,000 feet above sea level.
Its 1976 population totaled 6.3 million. A mountain range
runs northwest to southeast, separating the Valley of Mexico from the state capital of Toluca. Its economy rests
on cereals, sugar, maguey cactus, fruit, dairy products,
cattle, copper and silver mining, and manufacturing. Automobile and truck factories adjacent to the Federal District will connect with downtown Mexico City by subway
by the late 1980's. Other factories produce metal products, fibers, woolen goods, cement, and bricks.

MEZCAL. A strong alcoholic drink made from fermented
maguey cactus plants. It originated in Oaxaca but is a
standard drink throughout Mexico.

MICHELENA, JOSE MARIANO. 1772-1852. Revolutionary
and military figure. He was born in Morelia and pursued
a military career, in spite of having graduated with a law
degree. He was a key organizer in an independence
movement in 1808, the plot was discovered and he was
jailed. After being released he traveled to Spain and
took part in the liberation of Spain from Napoleon. He
remained in Spain until Mexico's independence, returning
to his native land and occupying an important post in the
government of Nicolás Bravo. Later he occupied important diplomatic posts in Europe. He died in Morelia.

MICHOACAN. A state in western Mexico with an area of
59,864 square kilometers. Its 1976 population totaled
2.8 million. Its capital is Morelia. The state has Lake
Pátzcuaro, and the republic's largest freshwater fishing
at Lake Chapala, which it shares with the neighboring
state of Jalisco. The Pátzcuaro Indians are famed for
their large nets shaped like butterflies. On its Pacific
coast the state has the government's Cárdenas Las Truchas (SICARTSA) steel complex as well as the second
largest reserves of iron ore in Mexico. This is the home
state of Lázaro Cárdenas (1895-1970), one of Mexico's
outstanding presidents (1934-40), a Revolutionary general
who became a social reformer who institutionalized the
Revolution.

MIER, FRAY JOSE SERVANDO TERESA DE. 1765-1827.
Born in Monterrey. First gained fame by giving his interpretation of how the Virgin of Guadalupe arrived in

Mexico, for which he was promptly jailed by the Inquisition. Although an opponent of Iturbide, he spoke against the liberal Constitution of 1824 and believed that it would be a disaster for Mexico.

MILPA. The word for cornfield in most of the major Indian languages of Mexico.

MINA, FRANCISCO JAVIER. 1789-1817. Spanish soldier and revolutionary who fought for Mexican independence. After fighting against Ferdinand VII in Spain, he was persuaded by Fray Servando Teresa de Mier and other Mexican liberals to take up the cause of Mexican independence. Although victorious in several battles in Mexico, he was captured and shot in October of 1817.

MIRAMON, MIGUEL. 1832-1867. The leading conservative general under Maximilian, he also served as provisional president 1859-1860. He enjoyed the reputation of being a very capable general, but was captured and shot on the Hill of the Bells, along with Maximilian and General Tomás Mejía, in June of 1867.

MITLA see OAXACA CITY

MIXTEC. The Mixtecs are the second largest Indian group in the state of Oaxaca and related ethnically and linguistically to the largest group, the Zapotecs. The two tribes had a pre-Hispanic kingdom replete with temples and other large structures at Monte Albán and Mitla in Oaxaca state from 600 to 1521 A.D.

MOCIÑO, JOSE. He was born in the latter part of the eighteenth century and died around 1820. He was an outstanding scientist who was most famous for his work in botany. He was a student and colleague of the famous French botanist Sessé and accompanied him on scientific expeditions throughout New Spain, where both men contributed greatly in discovering and categorizing many flora of New Spain. Mociño accompanied Sessé to Spain, and after the latter's death he settled in France for a time. He died in Spain after having written numerous scientific works, the most famous one being Flora mexicana.

MOCTEZUMA CID, JULIO RODOLFO. Born in 1927 in Mexico City. An attorney who was assistant director of planning for the Ministry of the Presidency in 1964, then

director of investments for the Presidency Ministry 1965-
70. He became legal consultant for the Ministers of Finance and of the Presidency and for the head of the Basic
Commodities Corporation (CONASUPO) during 1971-73,
thereby influencing major policies of the Echeverría administration. From December 1976 to November 1977
he was Minister of Finance and Public Credit, then became coordinator for that ministry and the Ministry of
Planning and the Budget, as President López Portillo's
chief adviser on finance and economics.

MODERADOS. From the beginning of Mexican republicanism
in 1823, until the Reform Wars, beginning in 1857, they
played a very important role in Mexican politics. They
were middle-of-the-roaders, and at times found themselves attacked by both liberals and conservatives. The
Moderados were principally upper class Creoles opposed
to both a monarchical form of government and the privi-
leged status of the clergy.

MOLINA ENRIGUEZ, ANDRES. 1866-1940. Mexican lawyer
who later became an insurgent general in the Mexican
Revolution. Los grandes problems nacionales, published
in 1910, a book dealing with the chief social ills of the
time, had a great effect on the developing ideology of the
Revolution. He is regarded as the chief architect of
agrarian reform and had great influence in the drafting
of Article 27 of the Constitution of 1917.

MONCAYO, JOSE PABLO. Born 1912. Composer who wrote
"Huapango."

MONTE ALBAN see OAXACA CITY

MONTEJO, FRANCISCO DE. 1448-1550. Spanish conquistador and one of Hernán Cortés's principal allies, de Montejo was sent to Spain by Cortés to defend the interests
of the latter. In 1527 the Spanish king authorized his
exploration and colonization of Yucatán. At one time he
had command over Yucatán, Cozumel and Honduras, but
was forced to give up Honduras by Pedro de Alvarado.
When he was very old, his lands were taken away from
him and he returned to Spain, dying there.

MONTENEGRO Y NERVO, ROBERTO. 1885-1968. Mexican
painter who was born in Guadalajara, his specialty was
surrealistic mural painting. He was the first director
of the Museum of Mexican Popular Art, 1934.

MONTERREY. The third largest city in Mexico and the second largest industrial center in the republic. The capital of the state of Nuevo León. Founded in 1596 by Luis de Carvajal, a Spanish governor who later was condemned by the Inquisition as a Jewish convert to Catholicism who continued to practice his old faith and was killed. The city was the viceroyalty's control point for trade routes through the Sierra Madre Oriental. Modernization began in 1888 when the railroads from Texas and Mexico City reached Monterrey. In 1903, the city got Latin America's first integrated iron and steel plant, Fundidora. A large supply of natural gas from the adjacent state of Tamaulipas and a large supply of iron ore from Nuevo León and the adjacent state of Coahuila have aided industrialization. Monterrey has the largest cement and glass factories in Mexico and the Cuauhtémoc company, which produces Carta Blanca and other beer brands in Latin America's largest brewery. Other factories produce paper, plastics, automobile equipment, and electronic and electrical appliances ranging from television receivers to refrigerators. The historic Obispado or Bishop's Place downtown was headquarters in 1846 for the unsuccessful defense against United States troops in the U.S.-Mexican War. The National Productivity Center, second only to the one in Mexico City, trains skilled workers. The city has the University of Nuevo León and a private university, Monterrey Institute of Technology, Mexico's leading higher institution for engineering education. Monterrey's 1976 population totaled 1.1 million within the municipality and its greater metropolitan area had 1.5 million. The city is 150 miles south of the Texas border.

MONTES DE OCA, FERNANDO. 1829-1847. Born in Atzcapozalco, he died in defense of Chapultepec Park and along with the other Niños Héroes is a national hero. In spite of the orders of his commander to retreat, he remained to fight when there no longer was any hope of victory.

MONTES DE OCA, LUIS. (1894-1958). An accountant who became the finance envoy of President Carranza in the United States in 1915. As Comptroller General 1924-27, he was the republic's monetary reformer. Founder in 1937 of the government's National Bank of Foreign Commerce. Director General of the Bank of Mexico 1935-40. Longtime spokesman for Mexican presidents to the National Banking Council. He initiated the widespread appointment of public accountants in federal high-level offices.

MONTEZUMA II. 1475-1520. He is officially known as Moctezuma Xocoyotzin to distinguish him from his predecessor, Moctezuma Ilhuicamina, the "Old One." It was during the reign of Moctezuma II that the first hotels were
established in Tenochtitlán and a botanical garden built
in Oaxtepec, Morelos. He lived in extraordinary luxury,
being attended by 300 servants, his daily meals consisting
of hundreds of different courses from which he chose a
sampling. His plates were silver and gold and he enjoyed
ocean fish the same day they were caught and brought to
Tenochtitlán by special relays of runners. He was killed
by a stone thrown from one of his own followers, while
trying to persuade them to surrender to the Spaniards.

MORA, JOSE MARIA LUIS. 1794-1850. Politician. A liberal who worked closely with Valentín Gómez Farías and
recognized as the principal theoretician of Mexican liber-
alism. He was banished into exile by Santa Anna but returned when the latter was forced into exile. Mora died
in Paris and it wasn't until 1963 that his remains were
brought back to Mexico.

MORALES BLUMENKRON, GUILLERMO. Born in 1908 in
Puebla. A broadcaster who directed government programs
and stations during 1934-36, then originated the government's "National Hour" over all radio stations on Sunday
night, still running in 1979. President of the Association
of Advertising Agencies 1957-59 and head of the National
Chamber of Broadcasters 1968. Interim Governor of
Puebla 1973-74. Owner of twenty leading radio stations
and a leading network official.

MORDIDA. Spanish word literally meaning "bite." In Mexico it refers to a bribe paid to government employees.

MORELIA. The capital of the state of Michoacán. In 1976
its population totaled 221,000. The city has preserved
colonial buildings, including a Spanish governor's palace.
Its University of San Nicolás, which is the state university, claims to be older than the National Autonomous
University of Mexico (UNAM), which was founded in 1551
as a Spanish pontifical university. San Nicolás traces
its origin to a college founded in 1538. The city is 125
miles west of Mexico City in a fertile valley at an elevation of 6,200 feet above sea level. It was founded in
1541 as Valladolid and renamed for José Morelos, a hero
of the war of independence against Spain. Its 1976 population totaled 220,000.

MORELOS (STATE). The second smallest state in Mexico
with an area of 4,941 square kilometers. Its 1976 population was 866,000. It lies just south of the Federal District, bounded on the southwest by Guerrero and on the
southeast by Puebla state. Its mountainous cities have
springlike mild climate. A major producer of sugar cane
and rice. Its capital, Cuernavaca, is a tourist resort.
It is the native state of Revolutionary leader Emiliano
Zapata (1877-1919), born in the town of San Miguel.

MORELOS Y PAVON, JOSE MARIA. 1765-1815. Born in the
city of Valladolid, Michoacán, which is today known as
Morelia. Although regarded as a Creole, he was probably a mestizo with some black ancestors. He was a mule
driver in his younger years, and his knowledge of the
terrain in southern Mexico enabled him to become an outstanding military and guerrilla leader during the initial
struggle for independence. Morelos studied under Miguel
Hidalgo at the Colegio de San Nicolás and afterwards became a priest. After Hidalgo's insurrection began, Morelos volunteered as a chaplain, but was ordered to head
the revolutionary movement in the south. He became the
leader of the independence movement after Hidalgo's death
in 1811 and proved to be a very capable military and political leader.
      Probably Morelos y Pavon's outstanding military feat
was the victory at Cuatla over the Spanish General Calleja. After capturing the port of Acapulco he convened
the Congress of Chilpancingo, which declared the nation
independent under a republican form of government. In
contrast to the prideful nature of his predecessor, Morelos used the title of "Servant of the Nation." After a
series of defeats a constitutional congress was convened
in the city of Apatzingán, and the constitution drawn up,
although never put into effect, contained many of the political ideas of Morelos. Outstanding among them were
the abolishment of the caste system and of tribute.
      Mexico regards Morelos second only to Hidalgo as a
hero of the independence movement. In fact, particularly
in the military sector, Morelos had far greater ability
than his predecessor. On his way to Tehuacán he was
captured, tried and was shot by a firing squad on December 22, 1815.

MORENO, PEDRO. 1775-1817. Revolutionary leader. He
became active in the independence movement in 1814 and
worked closely with Javier Mina. He took part in many
military campaigns and it was after his attack on Guana-

juato in October of 1817 that he was captured and executed by the Spaniards. Lagos de Moreno in the state of Jalisco is named after him.

MORONES, LUIS N. 1890-1964. Mexican labor leader who founded the CROM (Confederación Regional Obrera Mexicana), the labor union which was the most powerful in Mexico in the 1920's. A short, extremely overweight individual, Morones was known for his corruption, but continued to wield decisive labor influence because he managed to maintain good relations between labor and President Plutarco Calles. Under the regime of the latter he was made Minister of Industry, Commerce and Labor, further enhancing his power. Even though the CROM lost power and influence under the Portes Gil administration, Morones continued to be wealthy. When Cárdenas rose to power he was exiled to the United States in 1936, but returned later to head the now powerless CROM. He died in Mexico City.

MORROW, DWIGHT. 1873-1931. Appointed American ambassador to Mexico in 1927. His appointment marks the beginning of the best era of cooperation between the United States and Mexico and is an excellent example of how much one man can influence relations between two countries in a favorable manner. Morrow had a genuine love and respect for the Mexican people and was greatly instrumental in settling the dispute between the Cristeros and the Calles government.

MOTION PICTURES. As early as 1900 feature-length silent films were produced in Mexico occasionally. Despite the fighting of the Revolution, documentaries were produced during the 1910-20 period. In 1915 the México-Lux production company started, with an active silent-film industry from 1918 to 1923. The first Mexican talking picture was Miguel Contreras' "El Aguila y la Serpiente" in 1929. In the 1930's, Hollywood and foreign films with dubbed Spanish soundtracks limited the number of Mexican film features. However, in 1936 "Allá en el Rancho Grande" starring Tito Guízar launched the genre of ranch or rural-life comedies which flourished into the 1960's, reaching its heights in the 1940's and 1950's with such singing stars as Jorge Negrete and Pedro Infante.
From the 1940's through the 1970's, the industry was developed by directors such as Emilio ("El Indio") Fernández, comedian Mario ("Cantinflas") Moreno, and ac-

tress Dolores Del Río. In 1946 the major modern studios of Churubusco, Azteca, Clasa, Tepeyac, Cuauhtémoc, and México opened, giving the republic the largest movie industry in Latin America. Production of feature-length films increased every year until the largest number produced in a single year totaled 122 in 1950. In that same year, daily television broadcasting began, and soon in every nation producing feature films, the annual total began to shrink in the face of video competition and rising production costs. By 1972, Mexico's annual total was down to 64 films, and by 1979 not half that number. Outstanding films have ranged from "Mecánica Nacional" directed in 1971 by Luis Alcoriza to "María Candelaria" directed in 1943 by Emilio Fernández. In 1975 the government expropriated production studios under its agency National Cinema Company or CONACINE.

MOTOLINIA see BENAVENTE, FRAY TORIBIO DE

MOYA, LUIS. Hero of the Mexican Revolution who was born in the state of Zacatecas, he won numerous battles at the beginning of the Revolution, major ones being the freeing of the city of Zacatecas and Ciudad Lerdo. He was killed in 1911 by a stray bullet in the town of Sombrerete as he was dismounting to visit relatives, just after having liberated the town.

MOYA PALENCIA, MARIO. Born in 1933 in Mexico City. An attorney who was public relations administrator for the National Railroads 1955-58. Then assistant director of real estate for the Ministry of National Patrimony 1959-61. He was director general of the Cinema Bureau for the Ministry of the Interior (Gobernación) 1964-68. Assistant Minister of Gobernación 1969-70. Minister of Gobernación 1970-76. He was the preference of President Echeverría to receive the presidential nomination of Institutional Revolutionary Party (PRI) until the PRI inner circle chose José López Portillo.

MUGICA, FRANCISCO. Mexican general who fought on the insurgent side during the Mexican Revolution. He fought strongly for land and labor reform and was a delegate to the Constitutional Convention held at Querétaro in 1916-17.

MUGICA, FRANCISCO JOSE. 1884-1954. An officer in Revolutionary battles 1910-20. He was Governor of his native state of Michoacán 1920-22, then director of federal

prisons. An army general and close friend of President
Lázaro Cárdenas, he was Minister of Industry and Commerce 1934-35, then Minister of Public Works 1935-39.
Governor of Baja California del Sur 1940-46. The Institutional Revolutionary Party considered him a possible
presidential candidate for 1940 but rejected him as being
too radical after he helped bring Leon Trotsky from the
Soviet Union to settle in Mexico.

MUGICA MONTOYA, EMILIO. Born in May 1926 in Mexico
City. Economics degree from the National Autonomous
University (UNAM). Economics professor at UNAM 1951-
73. Economist for the Ministries of Communications,
then National Patrimony 1948-52, then for the development bank Nacional Financiera. Administrator for the
Basic Commodities Corporation (CONASUPO), then for
the National Railroads, then the Finance Ministry 1959-
75. He was coordinator for all publicly-owned industries
in 1975-76, and since 1976 has been Minister of Communications and Transportation.

MUNICIPIO. In Mexico a municipio is translated as municipality. It is a county-wide area with one or more cities
and towns within it and constitutes the smallest unit of
government. The municipal council or ayuntamiento functions in the largest city within the municipio and administers for all other towns and cities within the municipality.
This unit combines the concepts of city and county government as understood in the United States. The republic
has 2,359 municipios.

MUÑOZ LEDO, PORFIRIO. Born on July 23, 1933, in Mexico City. Law degree from the National Autonomous University. Graduate studies in economics and political science at the University of Paris 1956-59. Political adviser and analyst for the Institutional Revolutionary Party
(PRI) 1960-72. Envoy to UNESCO. Assistant Director
of graduate education, Ministry of Education 1961-65.
Secretary General of Social Security 1966-70. Assistant
Minister of the Presidency 1970-72. Minister of Labor
1972-75. President of the PRI 1975-76. Adviser on
federal housing throughout the 1970's. In 1976 he became
Minister of Public Education and pushed expansion of vocational training and institutions of higher learning. He
resigned in December 1977 over policy disagreements.

MURILLO VIDAL, RAFAEL. Born in 1904 in Veracruz. An

attorney who was a judge in the state courts of Veracruz
and Nayarit, a Deputy in Congress, Postmaster General
of Mexico, then a Senator 1964-68, and Governor of
Veracruz 1968-74. Since 1946 he has been a leader of
the popular organizations (CNOP) sector of the Institutional Revolutionary Party (PRI) and helped federal bureaucrats control the dominant political party.

MUSEUM OF ANTHROPOLOGY. The National Museum of
Anthropology opened at its present site in Chapultepec
Park in 1962 in one of the world's best designed museum
complexes, after decades of being housed in several colonial era buildings in downtown Mexico City. Its exhibits, maps, artifacts, and dioramas depict both ancient and
modern Indian cultures from throughout Mexico. Simula-
tions of the pyramids of Teotihuacán and of Maya, Zapotec, and Aztec temples combine scaled-down structures
and murals. The museum has the original Aztec sacrificial stone and the codices of Aztec, Maya, and Zapotec
hieroglyphics. Taped music, mannequins in typical clothing, and household and work scenes from present-day
cultures include Yaquis, Totonacas, Tarahumaras, Tarascans, Huicholes, Seris, Mayas, Mixtecs, Zapotecs, and
every other Indian group found in Mexico.

MUSEUM OF HISTORY. The National Museum of History occupies Chapultepec Castle atop the hill in Chapultepec
Park and adjacent modern buildings. With paintings,
maps, dioramas, flags, weapons, uniforms, documents,
furniture, and a multitude of other artifacts, this museum
traces Mexico's history through the Spanish colonial era
of viceroys, the struggle for independence from Spain,
the eras of Juárez, Emperor Maximilian, Porfirio Díaz,
and the Revolutionary era of 1910-20, including governments, battles, and civilian and military leaders.

- N -

NACIONAL FINANCIERA (NAFIN). This is the official agency
of the Mexican government whose purpose is to foment
economic development, both in the public and private sectors. It was created in 1934 initially only as a government agency to buy real estate, but has expanded into
such diverse fields as transportation, electrical energy
and irrigation. It also founded the Mexican stock market.
Since 1947 it has been the only government agency author-

ized to negotiate foreign loans, and it has been highly successful in this.   One of its greatest strengths is the low interest rate it charges for loans.

NACIONAL NEWSPAPER.   A Mexico City daily newspaper owned by the government and established in 1929.

NAFIN   see   NACIONAL FINANCIERA

NARCOTICS.   Since the 1950's, Mexico has been a major exporter of marijuana into the United States.   Since 1972, Mexico replaced Turkey as the major transporter and source of heroin in illegal traffic into the United States. A vigorous Mexican-United States control program, however, reduced the percentage of heroin coming into the U.S. from Mexico from 90 to 50 percent of the total imports by 1979.

NARVAEZ, PANFILO DE.   1470-1528.   Spanish conquistador who helped Diego Velázquez conquer Cuba.   The latter sent Narváez to pursue Cortés in Mexico and to arrest him, but Cortés succeeded in having Narváez imprisoned. He was noticed years later in Spain, after many had believed he was dead.   He was granted royal authority to explore lands from northern Mexico to Florida and a year after beginning his explorations he was drowned off the coast of Florida.

NATERA, PANFILO.   1882-1951.   A general in Revolutionary battles from 1913 to 1920, second in command to Pancho Villa.   He was Governor of his native state of Zacatecas 1940-44.

NATIONAL ACTION PARTY (Partido de Acción Nacional).   A basically conservative political party and the second largest in Mexico, it was founded on September 15, 1939, by Manuel Gómez Morín.   It supports the ideas of private enterprise and is against the use of government as a tool to effect social change.   It is very small in comparison to the official government party, but it has shown strength in the states of Yucatán and Baja California del Norte. Although identified with conservative elements of Mexican society, it has moved more towards the political center during the last ten years, principally under the guidance of Christlieb Ibarrola.

NATIONAL BANKS   see   BANCO NACIONAL ...

NATIONAL BASIC COMMODITIES CORPORATION see COMPAÑIA NACIONAL DE SUBSISTENCIAS POPULARES

NATIONAL CAMPESINO FEDERATION see CAMPESINO NATIONAL FEDERATION

NATIONAL CHAMBER OF COMMERCE FEDERATION see CAMARA DE COMERCIO

NATIONAL COMMISSION FOR PROFIT SHARING see INCOME DISTRIBUTION

NATIONAL FEDERATION OF GOVERNMENT WORKERS. The Federación de Sindicatos de los Trabajadores en el Servicio del Estado (FSTSE) is the Federation of Unions of Government Workers, the voice of organized civil servants.

NATIONAL FEDERATION OF INDUSTRIAL CHAMBERS see CAMARA INDUSTRIAL

NATIONAL FEDERATION OF MEXICAN WORKERS see CONFEDERACION DE TRABAJADORES MEXICANOS

NATIONAL FEDERATION OF POPULAR ORGANIZATIONS see CNOP

NATIONAL FUND FOR HOUSING see INFONAVIT

NATIONAL FUND FOR WORKERS CONSUMPTION see FONDO NACIONAL DEL CONSUMO DE LOS TRABAJADORES

NATIONAL PALACE. The federal government building in Mexico City on the principal plaza or Zócalo which houses the offices of the President of the Republic and certain key cabinet ministers.

NATIONAL POLYTECHNIC INSTITUTE see INSTITUTO POLYTECNICO NACIONAL

NATIONAL PROLETARIAN DEFENSE COMMITTEE OF MEXICO. A committee set up in 1935 at the suggestion of President Lázaro Cárdenas. Its purpose was to organize Mexican labor into a general confederation and it should be regarded as a kind of forerunner of the CTM, or Mexican Federation of Labor.

NAVA CASTILLO, ANTONIO.   Born in 1906 in Puebla.   One
of the co-founders of the National Federation of Popular
Organizations (CNOP) of the Institutional Revolutionary
Party (PRI) in 1943, and CNOP Secretary General 1944-
46.   Director of the Federal Penitentiary in Mexico City
1955-58.   A Deputy in Congress.   Elected Governor of
the state of Puebla in 1963 for a six-year term but he
was forced to resign in 1964 after failing to end university student strikes which brought chaos and federal
troops.

NAVARRETE ROMERO, ALFREDO.   Born July 24, 1923, in
Mexico City.   An economics degree from the National
University of Mexico and a Ph. D. in economics from
Harvard University.   Director of the government's devel-
opment bank, Nacional Financiera, 1953-70, under three
presidents of Mexico, Rúiz Cortines, López Mateos, and
Díaz Ordaz.   Director of the government's National Sugar
Bank or Financiera Azucarera 1970-72.   Subdirector of
finances for Petróleos Mexicanos 1972-76.   Economic ad-
visor for the United Nations, the Organization of Ameri-
can States, the World Bank, and the Mexican Ministry of
Finance.

NAVARRETE ROMERO, IFIGENIA MARTINEZ DE.   Born in
1930 in Mexico City as Ifigenia Martínez.   The wife of
Alfredo Navarrete.   One of Mexico's leading economists,
she is a professor of economics at the National Autonomous University (UNAM), and the only woman to be Dean
of the UNAM School of Economics 1970-72.   She was a
member of the Council of Economic Advisers for President Díaz Ordaz during 1964-70.   She is an economic
adviser for the Institutional Revolutionary Party (PRI).

NAVARRO, HECTOR.   Painter and educator.   He teaches at
the University of Guadalajara.   Navarro has had many
exhibitions in both the United States and Mexico and his
works can be seen at many museums in the two countries.
Of note are his paintings entitled, "Personaje Mitomano"
and "Situación de Ubicuidad. "

NAYARIT.   A state on the south-central Pacific coast which
until 1917 was the Territory of Tepic.   Its capital is the
city of Tepic.   The state's population in 1976 totaled
699,000.   The Sierra Madre Occidental traverses the
state northwest to southeast, making the eastern portion
a mountainous region of forests and valleys producing

lumber. The western portion has tropical agriculture, producing cotton, sugar, coffee, and palm oil. San Blas is the major port. Some sixty miles off the coast, the state's Tres Marías Islands are a federal penitentiary.

NERVO, AMADO. 1870-1919. His complete name is Amado Ruiz de Nervo. Poet and diplomat, he started out as a journalist, but became famous initially as a novelist with the publication of El bachiller (1896). After the turn of the century he became a diplomat and around the same time gained fame as a poet, becoming a good friend of Rubén Darío. His style is modernistic and he followed in the path of Gutiérrez Nájera. One of his most famous poetic works is La amada inmóvil (1912), inspired by the death of his loved one, Ana Cecilia Luisa Daíllez, his companion of ten years. This latter work is his most popular one in Mexico today.

NEZAHUALCOYOTL. Poet and king of Texcoco. When he was young he was a brave warrior, and later in his youth he showed outstanding ability as a poet and scientist. His father was deposed from his throne by Tezozómoc of Azcapotzalco and Nezahualcóyotl and his father had to flee for their lives, eventually finding refuge in Tenochtitlán. For more than ten years Netzahualcóyotl lived in exile, but eventually regained the throne which his father had occupied, ruling from 1431 until his death in 1472. He was responsible for many public works, among them the most famous hanging gardens in America, plus numerous palaces, aqueducts and public baths.

NEZAHUALPILLI. King of Texcoco and son of Nezahualcóyotl, he ruled Texcoco in the latter part of the fifteenth century.

NIAGARA CONFERENCE (1914). A meeting which took place at Niagara Falls, Ontario, Canada for the purpose of ending the Mexican Revolution, the hope being that peace could be established between the Huerta and Carranza factions. Argentina, Brazil, Chile and the United States called the meeting, but it failed, primarily because Carranza demanded the unconditional surrender of Huerta.

NIERMAN, LEONARDO. One of Mexico's most outstanding contemporary painters, he prepared for his career by studying physics and the psychology of color at the National University in México, D.F. He has had exhibitions all over the world and his paintings are characterized by brilliant colors which at times seem to emit fire. Representative of his works are "Pájaro de Fuego" and "Influencia Solar."

NIGROMANTE, EL see RAMIREZ, IGNACIO

NISHIZAWA, LOUIS. Born in the state of México in 1920, he studied at the Escuela Nacional de Artes Plásticas de México and the Center of Japanese Artists in Tokyo. He has had art exhibitions in many parts of the world and one of his most famous works is "Naturaleza Muerta."

NOGALES. A city in Sonora on the United States border, opposite Nogales, Arizona. In 1976 its population totaled 120,000, whereas its U.S. twin had only 12,000. The two communities cooperate in fighting fires, traffic control, and other daily tasks of the municipal area despite the international boundary. They form a natural pass in the mountains for north-south road connections. In the 1960's and 1970's, the Sonora city was cited often by U.S. investigators as a corridor for illegal drug shipments.

NOREÑA, MIGUEL. 1843-1894. One of the most famous Mexican sculptors of the nineteenth century, his most famous work is the statue of Cuauhtémoc on the Paseo de la Reforma in Mexico City. Some of his other works are the statues of Benito Juárez in Oaxaca and in the Palacio Nacional in Mexico City.

NOVO, SALVADOR. 1904-1974. A prolific author of essays, plays, poems, novels, and popular histories. Master's degree in literature, National Autonomous University. Professor of drama at the National Conservatory 1930-33. Director of public relations for the Foreign Relations Ministry 1930-34. Head of theatrical productions and director of the School of Drama of the National Institute of Fine Arts 1946-56. Official historian of Mexico City 1965-74. An editor and writer for Contemporáneos literary magazine 1928-33. His 1928 novel, El joven, portrays Mexico City as seen by a young man. His 1948 Nueva grandeza mexicana is a popular history of Mexico.

NUEVA ESPAÑA. The name for Mexico under Spanish colonial rule from 1521 to 1821 was the Viceroyalty of New Spain or Nueva España.

NUEVO LAREDO. A city in the state of Tamaulipas on the

United States border opposite Laredo, Texas.   Its 1976
population totaled 220,000.   This municipality in recent
decades has shown independence from the dominant Institutional Revolutionary Party (PRI), electing a Mayor and
Council members from the minority Party of the Authentic Mexican Revolution (PARM) in 1973 and showing some
strength in the 1960's for the opposition, conservative National Action Party (PAN).   A processing center for agricultural exports into the United States, the city has
several assembly plants which are twins of plants on the
U.S. side of the border, assemblying appliances, which
are imported into the U.S.   Parts are manufactured in
the U.S. and supplied to the Mexican assembly lines.

NUEVO LEON.   A northern state touching Texas and bordered
by the states of Tamaulipas on the east, San Luis Potosí
on the south, and Coahuila on the west and north.   Its
area totals 64,555 square kilometers, and its 1976 population totaled 2.4 million.   Its western and southern regions are crossed by the Sierra Madre Oriental.   The
northern portion is desert, with hot, dry climate.   The
Salinas, Salado, and San Juan rivers are tributaries of
the Río Grande on the United States border.   Irrigated
farming crops include cotton, citrus, fruits, wheat, and
corn.   Silver and lead are mined.   The state's capital,
Monterrey, in 1976 had a greater metropolitan population
totaling 1.5 million, making it the third largest city in
the republic and second only to Mexico City as an industrial center.   The state's industrial economy benefits
from large oil and natural gas reserves in the adjacent
state of Tamaulipas, with gas and oil pipelines running
from Tampico on the Gulf Coast to Monterrey.   The state
produces steel, glass, beer, tiles, batteries, automobile
and truck parts, radios, television receivers, and various
other electronic and electrical appliances.   It has cement
and construction materials industries.   The capital has
the famous, privately-owned Monterrey Institute of Technology, Mexico's leading institution of higher learning for
engineering.

NUÑEZ CABEZA DE VACA, ALVAR.   Born in Jerez de la
Frontera, Spain around 1490.   Explorer and colonial administrator.   Treasurer of the Narváez expedition of
1527-28.   Was captured by Indians after being shipwrecked
off the Florida coast in 1528, escaped and arrived in
Mexico in 1536, completing a journey which took him
eight years.   He occupied numerous administrative posts
in the New World.

NUÑEZ KEITH, GUILLERMO. Born in 1921 in Guaymas,
    Sonora. The leading network radio announcer in Mexico
    City in the 1940's and 1950's and for the television net-
    works in the 1950's. Head of the Inter-American Con-
    gress of Announcers in 1952. A Deputy in Congress
    1967-70. Owner of several leading radio stations through-
    out the republic and the Publimex public relations agency.
    Periodically the official radio-TV announcer when a Pres-
    ident of Mexico broadcasts.

NUNO, JAIME. 1824-1908. Composer of the music of the
    Mexican National Anthem. He was Spanish by birth, hav-
    ing been born in a small town in the province of Cata-
    lonia. Nunó was very well thought of because of his mu-
    sical ability and held important musical posts in Spain,
    Mexico and the United States, where he died in New York
    City.

                        - O -

OAXACA CITY. The capital of the state of Oaxaca in south-
    ern Mexico, at an elevation of 5,000 feet above sea level.
    Most houses are built with extra thick walls as protection
    against earthquakes, such as those in 1931 and 1957.
    Most public buildings are constructed with gray-green
    stone from the area. Spaniards founded the city in 1521
    on the sites of Zapotec and Mixtec Indian centers founded
    in 1486 A. D. A huge bronze statue by sculptor A. A.
    Cencetti constructed in 1891 is atop a hill on the edge of
    the city, honoring Benito Juárez (1806-72), Mexico's
    greater reformer, and a native of the state. Six miles
    to the west lies Monte Albán and 20 miles southeast Mit-
    la, archaeological sites built by Zapotecs, then occupied
    by Mixtecs, in the 14th century. Their highly developed
    civilization left huge buildings and temples, including Mit-
    la's Hall of Columns with mosaic designs and hieroglyphic
    drawings. The 1931 excavations by Alfonso Caso at Monte
    Albán of delicate gold, silver, and jade jewelry, masks,
    and implements are now in the state museum in Oaxaca
    City.

OAXACA (STATE). A state on the southern Pacific coast with
    an area of 95,363 square kilometers. Its 1976 population
    totaled 2.4 million. Mountain ranges running through the
    state northwest to southeast create two watersheds. The
    Papaloapan and Coatzacoalcos rivers flow through the

state of Veracruz into the Gulf of Mexico. The Tehuantepec River flows into the Pacific. The economy stresses
cereal, fruit, sugar, coffee, and tobacco production.
Mexican reformer President Benito Juárez (1806-72) was
born at San Pablo Guelatao near Oaxaca City. The state
has hundreds of thousands of Zapotec and Mixtec Indians.

OBREGON, ALVARO. 1880-1928. President and revolutionary hero. A native of Sonora, he began his political career as the municipal president of Hutabampo, and in
1912 became an active participant in the Mexican Revolution. He allied himself with the forces of Venustiano
Carranza and defeated Pancho Villa in the Battle of Celaya, where he lost an arm. He became president in
1920 and succeeded in putting together a working coalition which would later evolve into the official revolutionary party of Mexico. However, he showed a heavy hand
against the rebellious Cristeros and also signed the un-
popular Treaties of Bucareli, which guaranteed the interests of United States citizens living in Mexico, even
though these interests might interfere with the aims of
the Revolution. He was planning to run again for the
presidency in 1928, when he was assassinated by the religious fanatic, José de León Toral.

OCAMPO, MELCHOR. 1814-1861. A native of the state of
Michoacán, he studied law and natural science before ded-
icating himself to politics beginning in 1840. He opposed
the peace treaty with the United States which ended the
Mexican-American War of 1847. Later, he was exiled
by Santa Anna to New Orleans, where he met Benito
Juárez and became a dedicated liberal. When Juárez
assumed the presidency, Ocampo became Secretary of
the Interior and acting Secretary of Commerce and Foreign Relations. He was one of the prominent liberals of
his day and worked closely with Juárez in writing the Reform Laws. However, he does come in for criticism for
previously having taken part in the McLane-Ocampo Treaty. He retired from government work in 1861 and the
same year he was captured by the forces of Leonardo
Márquez and shot. See also MCLANE-OCAMPO TREATY.

OCAÑA, SAMUEL. Born in Arivechi, Sonora on September
7, 1931. Medical degree from the National Polytechnic
Institute. Graduate studies in respiratory diseases. In
1964 he became director of the Regional Hospital in
Navojoa, Sonora. Director for Sonora of economic and

social studies of the Institutional Revolutionary Party (PRI). Sonora head of the PRI 1978-79. Mayor of Navajoa 1973-76. Assistant Secretary of State Government 1977-78, Sonora's Secretary General 1978-79. Elected Governor of Sonora for the term 1979-85.

OCARANZA, FERNANDO. (1876-1965). A physician who was Dean of the Medical School of the National Autonomous University (UNAM) 1925-34, then President of UNAM 1934-38. A longtime leader of the Mexican Red Cross and the National Health Council. He pioneered in comparative physiology in Mexico.

OFFICIAL MAYOR. The executive officer or chief administrator of any governmental ministry, agency, or public office in Mexico.

OIL see PEMEX

OJEDA PAULLADA, PEDRO. Born on January 19, 1934, in Mexico City. An attorney who was assistant director of the Federal Betterment Boards in ports and border cities, 1958-61. Legal adviser for the Communications and Transportation Ministry 1964-70. Attorney General of Mexico 1971-76. Since 1976 the Minister of Labor. Mexico's top legal expert on communication and transportation laws during the 1960's and 1970's.

OLACHEA AVILES, AGUSTIN. (1893-1974). Governor of Baja California del Sur 1929-31, 1946-52, 1952-56. Governor of Baja California del Norte 1931-35. President of the Institutional Revolutionary Party (PRI) 1956-58. A former army general, he became an inner-circle adviser for presidents and cabinet ministers during 1944-1958, influencing tourism, mining, and public works policies.

OLIVARES SANTANA, ENRIQUE. Born in 1920 in San Luis, Aguascalientes. Teacher's diploma. Deputy in the Aguascalientes State Legislature, then Deputy in Congress 1958-61. Governor of the state of Aguascalientes 1962-68. Senator in Congress 1970-76. Head of the government's National Public Works Bank 1976-79. Since May 16, 1979, the Minister of the Interior (Gobernación), and head of the cabinet of President López Portillo. Secretary General of the Institutional Revolutionary Party (PRI) 1968-70 and a key official of the PRI's national executive committee since 1970, he has formulated PRI policies and the PRI structural reforms of 1972 and 1979 which broadened the base of popular participation.

OLLOQUI, JOSE JUAN DE. Born November 5, 1931, in Mexico City. Law degree from the National University (UNAM). Master's degree in economics from George Washington University. Professor of economics at UNAM and at Iberoamerican University. Director of Currency for the Minister of Finance, then head of the National Securities Commission. He was executive director of the Inter-American Development Bank 1966-70. He was Ambassador to the United States 1970-76 and helped reduce tension prompted by President Echeverría's policies. Since 1976 he has been Undersecretary of Foreign Relations.

OLMEC. The Olmec Indians built the first pre-Hispanic high civilization in Mexico between 1200 B. C. and 100 B. C. on the La Venta coastal plain of Veracruz, with pyramids, spacious temples, jaguar mosaics, and colossal carved heads ten or more feet high. Their mathematics had the concept of zero. Olmec culture penetrated as far south as Chiapas. By 300 A. D. their culture had been absorbed by the Mayas.

OÑATE, JUAN DE. 1549-1624. Explorer born in Guadalajara, he colonized large sections of New Mexico and traveled as far north as Kansas, founding many settlements along the way.

OPERADORA DE TEATROS. A nationwide chain of motion picture theaters in which a major stockholder is the government. It competes with the Películas Nacionales and Oro theater chains, in which the government also holds large blocks of stock.

ORDAZ, DIEGO DE. Born in 1480 and died around 1532. Spanish military leader who accompanied Cortés in the conquest of Mexico, he eventually became one of Cortés's most trusted officers, although originally he had been arrested by the latter because of his loyalty to Diego Velázquez. After giving valuable service to Cortés, he eventually took on the conquest of what today is Colombia and Venezuela, but was not successful. He died while on his way back to Spain.

ORIVE ALBA, ADOLFO. Born in 1907 in Mexico City. An

engineer who constructed the hydroelectric dams in Sonora
1935-38. He was director of the National Irrigation Commission 1940-46, then Minister of Hydraulic Resources
1947-52. Since 1970 he has been director of the government's Cárdenas Las Truchas steel and iron complex
(SICARTSA) in Michoacán.

ORIZABA. A city in the state of Veracruz 81 miles west of
the Gulf of Mexico and 182 miles southeast of Mexico
City, at an elevation of 4,030 feet above sea level. Its
1976 population was 110,000. Founded in 1774, it is a
center of the coffee industry, and has sugar and jute
mills, cigar factories, and marble quarries.

ORIZABA VOLCANO. An inactive peak 60 miles west of
Veracruz City on the boundary between the states of
Puebla and Veracruz, with an altitude of 18,700 feet above
sea level. Its largest eruptions were between 1545 and
1566 A.D. Being Mexico's highest peak, it was called
Citlaltépetl or "Mountain of Stars" by the Aztecs and had
a pre-Hispanic temple dedicated to the "sacred fire."

ORLANDO, FELIPE. Born in 1911. Although he was born
in Mexico, he grew up in Cuba, where he studied art
under Cuban masters in his formative years. Besides
being an accomplished painter, he has also studied music, archaeology and is considered an authority on African transculturation in America. A measure of the recognition he has received is that many museums, among
them the Museum of Modern Art in New York City, have
permanent exhibitions of his works.

OROZCO, JOSE. (1883-1949). A painter of murals of the
Mexican Revolution who became world famous in the
1930's depicting Mexico's struggle for social justice.

OROZCO, PASCUAL. 1882-1915. A general closely identified with the opening years of the Mexican Revolution.
He supported Madero, winning several key battles in the
north and capturing Ciudad Juárez in 1911. Eventually
he broke with Madero and recognized Huerta. He was
finally forced to seek exile in Texas, where he died.

OROZCO Y BERRA, MANUEL. 1816-1881. Lawyer, engineer, historian and archaeologist. Among his many important posts was that of Chief Justice of the Supreme
Court just before Maximilian's rise to power. He also

gained fame for his historical work Historia antigua y de
la conquista de México, published in four volumes in
1880-1881. When Maximilian was driven out, Orozco
served a brief prison term, but was soon back in official
favor.

ORTIZ DE DOMINGUEZ, JOSEFA. 1768-1829. Independence
heroine and wife of Miguel Domínguez, the mayor of
Querétaro. She always defended the downtrodden and very
early began to work for independence from Spain. She
convinced her husband of the righteousness of her beliefs
and the mayor's house was used frequently to plan for
independence. When the conspiracy was discovered by
the Spaniards it was she who warned the other insurgents,
thus causing the rebellion to begin much earlier, on September 16, 1810. She was eventually captured and held
in a convent, but freed when she promised to cease her
revolutionary activities. She died in Mexico City, disappointed by the emergence of the Mexican Empire under
Iturbide, a man she had never supported.

ORTIZ MENA, ANTONIO. Born in 1908 in Parral, Chihuahua. An attorney who directed nationalization of properties 1940-45. He ran the National Mortgage Bank 1946-
52. Director General of Social Security 1952-58. Minister of Finance for President López Mateos 1958-64 and
for President Díaz Ordaz 1964-70. Since 1971 he has
been the president of the Inter-American Development
Bank, in Washington, D. C.

ORTIZ RUBIO, PASCUAL. 1877-1963. Politician and president. A native of Michoacán and originally an engineer
by profession, he became a politician and supporter of
Madero during the early years of the Revolution. His
political star continued to rise until he finally became
president of Mexico, serving from February, 1930 to September of 1932, when Calles forced him to resign. Actually, this resignation was not as serious as it may appear to be, since Calles was the one who had really governed the country unofficially by telephone from his residence in Cuernavaca. A mild, ineffectual man, the Mexicans referred to him derisively as "don Nopalitos."
Nevertheless, notable accomplishments of his regime were
promulgation of the Estrada Doctrine and the Federal
Work Law. He did spend a period of exile in the United
States immediately after his ouster. Ortiz Rubio died in
Mexico City.

OSORIO PALACIOS, JUAN. Born in 1920 in Mexico City.
A leading concert violinist in the 1960's and 1970's.
Concertmaster with the National Symphony Orchestra
1939-48. Member of the National University Symphony.
Secretary General of the Music Workers Union 1946. A
Deputy in Congress 1952-55 and 1958-61, promoting the
national development of fine arts.

OTEYZA, JOSE ANDRES. Born on November 21, 1942, in
Mexico City. Economics degree, National Autonomous
University (UNAM) 1965. Master's in economics, University of Cambridge, England. UNAM economics professor 1968-70. Economist for the Ministry of National
Patrimony 1965-68. Economist for the Bank of Mexico
1968-70. Chief analyst for government-owned enterprises
1970-71. Director General of research for the National
Patrimony Ministry 1974-75. Since December 1976 he
has been Minister of National Patrimony and the chief
policy formulator for government-owned enterprises.
Since 1969 he has been an editor and writer for the republic's leading economics journals: Investigación Económica, El Trimestre Económico, and El Economista Mexicano. Since 1972 he has been an advising editor for the
Carta de México which the Mexican President's office
publishes.

OTOMI. The Otomí Indians from the states of México and
Hidalgo are famous for their weaving of red woolen gar-
ments. Men and women wear red wool sashes with white
work clothes or fancy party costumes. They weave fiber
made from cactus into bags. They are Mexico's leading
weavers of fancy baskets.

- P -

PACHECO, JOSE EMILIO. Born in 1939 in Mexico City. A
nationally known writer, editor, and literary critic since
the 1960's. He won the 1969 National Prize for Poetry.
His 1967 novel, Morirás lejos, condemned persecution of
religious minorities. His 1972 volume of short stories,
El principio del placer, evoked national nostalgia for sim-
pler times.

PADILLA, EZEQUIEL. Born in 1890. Diplomat and politician who served under Zapata and Villa in the Revolution.
Among his many diplomatic posts were those of ambas-

sador to the United States, delegate to the United Nations
and foreign minister. He was the main opposition candidate to Miguel Alemán, running as the nominee of the
Mexican Democratic Party in the campaign of 1946. Although the Partido de Acción Nacional (PAN) supported
him and he ran a vigorous campaign, the outcome was
never in doubt, the official party taking close to 75 percent of the total vote. His being identified too strongly
as pro-American probably hurt his presidential chances.

PADILLA NERVO, LUIS. Born in 1898 in Michoacán. Degree from the National Autonomous University (UNAM),
and graduate studies at the University of London and
George Washington University. A veteran diplomat to
Latin American and European nations since 1918. Ambassador to Uruguay, El Salvador, Panama, Costa Rica,
Denmark, Spain, Argentina. Headed the Mexican delegation to the United Nations 1945-52, 1958-64. Minister
of Foreign Relations 1952-58. Justice of the International
Court of Justice at The Hague 1964-72. President of the
UN General Assembly 1951-52.

PADILLA SEGURA, JOSE ANTONIO. Born in 1922 in San
Luis Potosí. An electrical engineer who was Vice-
President of the National Polytechnic Institute (IPN) during the 1950's, then IPN President until 1964. Minister
of Communications and Transportation 1964-70. Director
of the government's steel industries since 1971. He expanded doctoral-level education in engineering.

PADRINO. A godfather at the christening of the children of
a close friend becomes as the padrino the lifelong unofficial relative in the offspring's family and relates to that
family socially and politically.

PALACE. A palace or palacio in Mexico is any governmental
building from municipal on up to presidential.

PALACE OF FINE ARTS. The leading opera house and fine
arts theater in Mexico, the Palacio de Bellas Artes was
built in 1934 from marble, designed by Italy's leading
architects to resemble the La Scala Opera House in Milan. The federal government administers it through the
National Institute of Fine Arts. It is home for the Ballet
Folklórico de México and the National Symphony. Its
muraled glass curtain came from Tiffany's of New York.

PALACIO see PALACE

PALENQUE. A Maya archaeological site in the southernmost state of Chiapas in a tropical rain forest. Temples and other large buildings were constructed during 514-784 A. D. The Mayas achieved artistic innovation and indicated elaborate knowledge of astronomy in an observatory. By 800 A. D. the Mayas had abandoned the site and moved to the Yucatán peninsula.

PAN. Partido de Acción Nacional. See NATIONAL ACTION PARTY.

"PAN O PALO." Phrase used during the long rule of Porfirio Díaz, literally meaning "bread or club." If one cooperated with the Díaz regime he received rewards; those who didn't were punished.

PAN-AMERICAN UNION. The Pan-American Union centered in Washington, D. C. , was the outgrowth of the Third Pan-American Conference held in Rio de Janeiro in 1906. The association of Latin American nations meeting with the United States took the name of the Union of American Republics and created the Pan-American Union to act as the central coordinating agency. A Pan-American conference was held on Mexican soil in early 1945, when the Chapultepec Conference, known officially as the Inter-American Conference on Problems of War and Peace, was held. Its most important accomplishment was the Act of Chapultepec, a defensive military alliance which bound together all signatories. See also CHAPULTEPEC, ACT OF; CHAPULTEPEC CONFERENCE.

PANI, ALBERTO J. 1878-1955. Politician and diplomat. Served in various government posts after the beginning of the Mexican Revolution and distinguished himself as finance minister in the government of General Alvaro Obregón, replacing Adolfo de la Huerta, who led an unsuccessful coup against Obregón. He strengthened the power of the Treasury Department and through his efforts a strong national bank was funded.

PARACAIDISTA. Paracaidista literally means a parachutist but in Mexican public life the word means a squatter, one who invades unguarded or disputed land and begins to farm it as his own.

PAREDES ARRILLAGA, MARIANO. 1797-1849. General and politician who supported Santa Anna in 1841 and deposed

him in 1844. He also seized power from Herrera in
1845. He was president of Mexico from January of 1846
until the end of July 1846. Sympathetic to the idea of a
monarchy in Mexico, he was accused of diverting military
forces away from the war against American forces and
using them to overthrow Herrera, thus weakening Mexico
against the common enemy. Paredes Arrillaga lived in
exile for a time in the United States and died in Mexico
City.

PARM. The Party of the Authentic Mexican Revolution or
    Partido de la Auténtica Revolución Mexicana (PARM) was
    founded in 1954 by Generals Jacinto B. Treviño and Juan
    Barragán to take a moderate approach to the institution-
    alized social revolution. PARM has won a handful of
    congressional district seats from 1958 to 1976 and since
    1964 a few minority-party Deputy seats and four mayoral
    races.

PARTIDOS. Partidos (Mexican political parties) are mostly
    listed under their initials in Spanish, such as the Institu-
    tional Revolutionary Party under "PRI." For decades,
    a party in the last century only needed a few members
    to qualify for the ballot if the president in power permit-
    ted it. In this century, the electoral laws until 1977 re-
    quired only 75,000 members with some members in two-
    thirds of the states to qualify a party for the ballot. The
    1978 Law of Organic Politics and Processes gives a party
    temporary registration for federal congressional elections
    if it has been functioning prior to 1974. Failure to ob-
    tain 1.5 percent of the total national vote cancels a par-
    ty's registration. For decades, four parties qualified
    for the ballot but in the 1979 elections, seven parties
    were on the ballot. The conservative and moderate par-
    ties are headed by presidents and the leftist parties by a
    secretary general. Each party in Mexico gets its own
    two distinctive colors and symbol for the ballot, so that
    the illiterate may mark a straight-party vote.

PASTRY WAR. The popular name given to a minor war be-
    tween France and Mexico fought in 1838. French nation-
    als had been subjected to losses in Mexico during pre-
    ceeding years and were suing for 600,000 pesos. The
    war draws its name from the accusation of a French
    pastry maker in Tacubaya who claimed that his business
    had been shot up by a group of Mexican officers. The
    French took possession of the island of San Juan de Ulúa,

and with the help of British mediation received a guarantee of the 600,000 pesos claimed. After this agreement, the French left San Juan de Ulúa and sailed back to Europe.

PATERNALISM. An integral part of personalism, it refers to the personal interest a leader takes in his followers, to the point where the former can effect changes simply by deciding to implement them, irrespective of any political institutions which are available for this purpose, such as legislative and judicial branches of a government. See also PERSONALISM; PULQUE.

PATIÑO, ANTENOR. Born in La Paz, Bolivia, Patiño was the wealthiest owner of tin mines in Bolivia until that republic's 1952 expropriation of the tin industry. He then moved to Mexico, where he developed the port of Manzanillo in the state of Colima into a resort for wealthy tourists with the Las Hadas hotel complex. During 1960-62, he developed the luxury María Isabel Hotel in Mexico City, then sold his majority stock to the Sheraton Hotel chain and to the Mexican government.

"PATRIA CHICA." The phrase literally means "small fatherland" and is the tendency, very prevalent in Mexico, to place one's loyalty primarily in the immediate environs where one lives, instead of in the national government. A phenomenon generally associated with agricultural societies, the "patria chica" idea can be expected to have less importance as Mexico becomes a more strongly urbanized, industrialized country.

PATZCUARO. A town in the state of Michoacán located on the lake of the same name. It has a population of over 35,000 and is a favorite tourist attraction.

PATZCUARO, LAKE. One of the most beautiful lakes in Mexico, it occupies an area of 422 square kilometers and at its greatest extension is 20 kilometers long and 14 kilometers wide. It is a rather shallow lake, averaging 7.6 meters in depth and is famous for its white fish caught by men who use the very distinctive and traditional "butterfly" nets.

PAZ, OCTAVIO. Born in 1914 in Mexico City. Studied literature, social sciences, and humanities at the National Autonomous University. In 1943 he obtained a Guggen-

heim Fellowship to study literature in the United States,
then in Europe.   He wrote essays, poetry, popular history, political commentary, novels, and non-fiction books
about Mexican and international public life and by the
1960's became Mexico's most distinguished writer and one
of the republic's most influential writers of this century.
His 1950 book The Labyrinth of Solitude, on daily life and
widespread attitudes in Mexico, influenced mass demands
for reforms and government responses.   His 1970 book
Boscdata stirred national consciousness about technological development.   After having been Ambassador in major
European nations, he resigned as Ambassador to India in
1968 to protest the handling of the student riots.   He has
written for Excelsior and via syndication most other Mexican papers and every major Mexican magazine, including
Proceso since 1978 and Hoy and Siempre in earlier years.

PCM.   The Partido Comunista Mexicano (PCM) or Mexican
    Communist Party was founded in 1919.   In 1920 it at-
    tempted to build a labor base with the General Labor Fed-
    eration (CGT) and during 1921 CGT leaders were trained
    in Moscow, but fewer than 80,000 workers joined CGT
    unions before it began to dissolve in 1928.   In 1958, a
    PCM member, Demetrio Vallejo, as leader of the Rail-
    road Workers Union, caused millions of dollars of damage
    to the economy through slowdown and unauthorized stop-
    pages of trains until he was jailed under the federal penal
    code for social dissolution.   During the 1950's and 1960's,
    the muralist painter David Alfaro Siqueiros was PCM
    Secretary General.   For the participation of the PCM in
    the 1959 railroad strikes, Siqueiros was also convicted
    of social dissolution and jailed 1960-62.
        The PCM had remained legal but off the ballot until
    1979 because for decades it listed only 5,000 members.
    In 1978 it claimed 80,000 members and fielded minority-
    party proportional representation candidates for the 1979
    federal Deputy elections.   Valentín Campa ran as a PCM
    write-in candidate in the 1970 presidential election.   Ar-
    noldo Martínez Verdugo has been PCM Secretary General
    since 1964, a member of the PCM Central Committee
    since 1955, and a PCM official since 1949.   The PCM
    publishes a weekly Oposición.   The PCM consistently re-
    mains pro-Moscow.   Its Communist Youth of Mexico
    (JCM) is active within student federations and helped en-
    large the bloody 1968 riots against the government.   Since
    the first in 1921, the PCM has held eighteen congresses.
    The PCM rejects Trotskyite and pro-Peking rival groups

and denies any connection with the Communist September 23rd League of guerrillas.

PDM. The Partido Democrático Mexicano (Mexican Democratic Party) was shaped in 1946 by presidential hopeful Ezequiel Padilla. This party soon faded. A different far-right party with the same initials, the Partido Demócrata Mexicano (Mexican Democrat Party) was begun in 1971 and by 1975 the new PDM had 100,000 registered members and ran candidates for federal Deputy in congressional races in all 31 states and the Federal District. In Irapuato, Guanajuato, on May 23, 1971, Juan Aguilera Azpeitia convened a national meeting of former members of the fascist Sinarquista Movement and convinced them that discredited rightists could gain status and political influence through the proposed PDM. The conference adopted a party charter and elected Baltasar Ignacio Valádez as PDM president. In 1978 the PDM chose an Irapuato business executive, Gumersindo Magaña Negrete as president and he directed the 1979 PDM congressional campaigns. The PDM became one of the seven registered parties. It advocates expanding private enterprise and using traditional Catholic values in government policies and programs.

PEMEX. Pemex or Petróleos Mexicanos was created in 1938 after President Lázaro Cárdenas expropriated the entire petroleum industry on March 18, 1938. This government entity operates all oil reserves, drilling, transporting, refining, and marketing of petroleum. It leases concessions for retail service stations. No private domestic or foreign oil company can operate in Mexico. The director of Pemex is a member of the presidential cabinet. The agency also has a monopoly authority on natural gas in all aspects of conservation, development, production, and marketing.

PENINSULAR. During colonial times, the name given to a Spaniard born in Spain but who lived in the New World.

PERALTA, ANGELA. 1845-1883. She was one of the most famous Mexican opera singers of the nineteenth century and began her professional career at the age of fifteen. She sang at La Scala Opera House in Milan and became a favorite in Europe. She died at the height of her career from a plague of cholera which was sweeping Mexico at that time.

PEREZ MARTINEZ, HECTOR. 1906-1948. A dentist from
Campeche who became a very influential journalist. A
reporter for the government's daily newspaper El Nacional, 1929-31, he became its editor 1932-37. A Deputy in
Congress, then Governor of Campeche 1939-44, and Minister of the Interior (Gobernación) 1946-48. He was an
inner-circle adviser for Presidents Avila Camacho and
Alemán from 1940 to 1948.

PERSONALISM. The practice, common in Mexico and all of
Latin America, of following an individual because of his
personal traits and not necessarily because of any ideo-
logical or political beliefs which he may possess. In
Mexico, outstanding examples of those who commanded
wide following in this manner are Emiliano Zapata, Pancho Villa, Plutarco Elías Calles and Lázaro Cárdenas.

PESO. The Mexican unit of currency. From 1876 to 1906,
one peso was worth one U.S. dollar. During the 1910-
20 Revolutionary fighting, the value varied. From 1920
to 1933, the rate was two pesos to the dollar. From
1933 to 1940, 3.60 pesos to the dollar. During 1940-49,
4.85 to the dollar. From 1949 to 1954, 8.65 to the dollar. For 22 years, from 1954 to 1976, the rate was
12.50 pesos to the dollar. Since September 1976, the
peso has floated, but remained at 22 or 23 to the dollar.

PETROLEUM RESERVES. From 1938 to 1974 Mexico's governmental agency Pemex struggled to produce enough
petroleum to meet domestic needs but since 1974 Mexico
has become a major exporter of oil. Incomplete geological research had indicated from 6 to 11 billion barrels
of proven petroleum reserves in the ground. Modern
geological exploration flourished in Mexico, and by 1976
the reserves totaled at least 30 billion barrels. By 1979,
the total of proven reserves had been raised to 60 billion
barrels. For the 1980's, Mexico planned to produce 2.25
million barrels of oil a day and to export 1.1 million bar
rels a day.

PINO SUAREZ, JOSE MARIA. 1869-1913. Lawyer, politician
and Vice-president of Mexico, 1911-1913. Along with
President Madero, he was assassinated by agents of General Victoriano Huerta.

PIPILA, EL see MARTINEZ, JUAN JOSE

PISTOLERO. It literally means "man with a pistol." See
RURALES.

PNR. Partido Nacional Revolucionario (PNR) or National
Revolutionary Party was founded by former Mexican President Plutarco Calles, whose term had ended in 1928.
When former President Obregón was assassinated in 1928,
Calles returned for a second term in violation of the
Revolutionary Constitution. He dominated interim presidents until 1934 but needed to cohere the military, agrarian, and labor leaders into one dominant party to keep
the social Revolution permanent. A convention convened
in March 1929 in Querétaro to charter the PNR. In 1938
the PNR changed its name to the Mexican Revolutionary
Party (PRM), and in 1946, to the Institutional Revolutionary Party (PRI).

POINSETT, JOEL ROBERTS. 1779-1851. American diplomat
from South Carolina who occupied a number of posts in
Latin America, he was the first American minister to
Mexico, from 1825 to 1829. He supported President
Guadalupe Victoria and opposed the liberals. Poinsett
supported the York Lodge of masonry as a way to coun-
teract English influence in Mexico. Probably because of
this move he was accused of meddling in Mexico's internal affairs. The poinsettia (la flor mexicana de noche-
buena) was named after him.

PORFIRIATO. Refers to the administration of Porfirio Díaz,
who with the exception of the years 1880 to 1884, ruled
from 1876 to 1910, the longest anyone was president of
Mexico.

PORTES GIL, EMILIO. President of Mexico, 1928-1930.
Born in Ciudad Victoria, Tamaulipas in 1891, he was
active in the Mexican Revolution and in national life both
before and after his presidency. Although Calles largely
controlled his administration, Portes Gil played a significant role in settling the Cristero rebellion, made a serious effort at instituting land reform, and broke with the
Soviet Union because of propaganda attacks against the
Mexican government. He served for a time as ambassador to India after leaving the presidency and died in Mexico City in 1978.

POSADAS ESPINOSA, ALEJANDRO. Born on May 29, 1939,
in Mexico City. A certified public accountant who has

helped modernize administrative procedures throughout
the federal government.   He was president of the National
Public Accountants Association 1969-71 and director of
financial and social research for the Institutional Revolutionary Party (PRI) popular sector 1971.   He was an administrator for the Ministry of Agriculture 1954-58, for
the Finance Ministry 1960-62, for National Warehouses
then for the Basic Commodities Corporation (CONASUPO)
1962-73, and since 1973 director of the National Commission of the Corn Industry, coordinating consumer prices
with those on all other foods with price ceilings.   He has
been one of Mexico's top experts on the cost of basic
foods and their relationship to subsidies and government
policies.

POSITIVISM.   The philosophy originated by the French philosopher Auguste Comte.   His idea was that society could
be improved by the social sciences, provided it was not
corrupted by religion, theology or any other metaphysical
influence.   Positivism became strong in Mexico during
the nineteenth century and one of its strongest advocates
was Gabino Barreda.   Under his direction it became the
official doctrine of Mexico's educational system in the
1870's.   Because it embodied belief in principles of hierarchy and authority, it found favor with the administration
of Porfirio Díaz and in particular with the científico fac-
tion, mainly José Yves Limantour and Justo Sierra.   It
declined in influence with the advent of the Mexican Revolution, but still attracts interest in Mexico today.   Its
most prominent spokesman is Leopoldo Zea, whose work
Positivism in Mexico is still widely read.

PPS.   The Partido Popular Socialista (PPS) or Popular Socialist Party was founded as the Popular Party by Marxist labor leader Vicente Lombardo Toledano on June 20,
1948, when an assembly of socialists and leftists voted
for the party's charter.   Later the word "Socialist" was
added to the party name.   In 1952 Lombardo was the PPS
candidate for President of Mexico but got only 73,000
votes to the winner's 2.7 million for the candidate for
the Institutional Revolutionary Party (PRI).   In subsequent
presidential elections, the PPS fielded candidates for Deputies and Senators in Congress, state Legislatures, and
municipal governments but supported the PRI presidential
candidate.   Since 1964 the PPS has won a few Deputy
seats every three years.   With the death of Lombardo in
1968, Jorge Cruickshank became PPS Secretary General,

and in 1976 became the first PPS member to be a Senator.
From 1962 to 1972, the PPS published the magazine Avante,
and since 1972 the magazine Nueva Democracia. One Mexico
City daily newspaper, El Día, editorially supports the
PPS. One of Mexico's leading news magazines, Siempre,
also editorially supports the PPS jointly with the PRI.
The party's greatest strength in membership and political
activists has been found in the states of Nayarit, Oaxaca,
and selected areas of Morelos, Mexico, and the Federal
District.

PRESIDENCY. The Ministry of the Presidency was created
in 1958 and abolished in December 1976 by President
López Portillo, who assigned its functions and duties to
the new Ministry of Planning and the Budget.

THE PRESIDENTIAL SUCCESSION of 1910. A rather mod-
erate book published by Francisco Madero in 1908. Although criticized in some quarters as very critical of
Porfirio Díaz, all it called for was that the people should
have a hand in choosing the vice-president if Porfirio Díaz
should choose to run again in 1910.

PRI. The Partido Revolucionario Institucional (PRI) or Institutional Revolutionary Party was established in 1929 as
the National Revolutionary Party (PNR) to unite labor,
agrarian, and military groups into one dominant party to
insure that the social Revolution would continue. In 1938
the PNR changed its name to the Mexican Revolutionary
Party (PRM) and in 1946 to the PRI to emphasize the
institutionalized Revolution. The PRI has a National Executive Committee (CEN), 31 State Committees, a Federal District Committee, and 2,359 Municipal Committees.
During the presidency of Manuel Avila Camacho (1940-
46), the military sector was phased out and replaced by
the popular sector. In 1943 the National Federation of
Popular Organizations (CNOP) became that sector, and
dominates the labor and agrarian sectors, inasmuch as
CNOP contains the government bureaucrats and the professional class. The CEN controls the geographical hierarchy of the party as well as the three vocational sectors.
The CEN consists of the party President, a Secretary
General, and Secretaries for Agrarian, Labor, Popular,
Political, Press and Public Relations, Recruitment, Financial, and Social Action. A National Council consists
of the party President and Secretary General, 32 State
Committee Chairmen, and 15 representatives from each

of the agrarian, labor, and popular sectors. Every three years a PRI General Assembly of 3,000 delegates and alternates representing the general membership endorses the programs and principles which the CEN and the Council have proclaimed. Since 1929 the PRI has dominated government, winning every presidential election, every governor's race, every senate race but one, most state legislative and municipal elections, and a vast majority of the federal Deputy seats. In 1979, under a constitutional amendment, 100 minority-party Deputies were elected along with 300 congressional-district Deputies, 294 of whom were from the PRI.

PRIETO, GUILLERMO. 1818-1897. Liberal politician, literary figure and a close supporter of Benito Juárez. He backed the Plan of Ayutla and was a delegate to the assembly which drafted the Constitution of 1857. Besides being a senator, he held cabinet posts in various liberal governments. Prieto was also an accomplished poet, one of his most famous works being La musa callejera (The Street Muse), a valuable contribution to the establishment of Mexican folklore as a significant literary genre of that country.

PRM. Mexican Revolutionary Party. See PRI.

PRONUNCIAMIENTO. A Spanish word meaning "pronouncement." It refers to a revolt accompanied by a declaration of what the new leader will do once he comes to power. Except for the porfiriato era, the pronunciamiento was common in Mexico until the 1920's.

PRUN. The Partido Revolucionario de Unificación Nacional (PRUN) or Revolutionary Party of National Unification was founded in 1940 by General Juan Almazán for his presidential candidacy against the winner, Manuel Avila Camacho. The party dissolved after the election.

PST. The Partido Socialista de los Trabajadores (PST) or Socialist Workers Party was founded in 1973 by Rafael Aguilar Talamantes, a former head of the National Democratic Student Federation, a Marxist group. As PST Secretary General, he got the party registered on the ballot for the 1979 congressional elections and fielded candidates for Deputy in all 31 states and the Federal District. The PST seven co-founders and Central Committee members came from the 1972 Mexican Workers

Group, led by Herberto Castillo, which was composed of
dissidents from the Communist Party (PCM) who could
not recruit enough members for legal registration for a
Workers Party.   A National Committee for Opinion Surveys and Coordination led to the forming of the PST.

PTM.   The Partido de Trabajadores Mexicanos (PTM) or
Mexican Workers Party was founded in 1974 by Herberto
Castillo, a Marxist civil engineer from Veracruz.   The
PTM membership grew from the National Committee for
Opinion Surveys and Coordination, which Castillo and
Rafael Aguilar Talamantes founded in 1972.   The PTM
has not yet qualified for legal registration as a party and
was not on the ballot in the 1979 elections.

PUEBLA, BATTLE OF.   1862.   This victory of the Mexican
forces over the French at Puebla on May 5, 1862, represents one of the most glorious episodes in Mexican military history.   The invading army, composed of a large
number of soldiers from the French Foreign Legion, was
in the process of securing Mexican territory from Veracruz to Mexico City, in order to establish Maximilian as
the head of an empire which would comprise all of Mexico.   Expecting no serious resistance, the French closed
in on Puebla, but were repulsed by poorly equipped soldiers under the direction of General Ignacio Zaragoza and
forced to retreat back to the coast.   General Laurencez,
the head of the defeated French army, was replaced by
the more capable General Forey, and a year later he
laid siege to the city.   Under attack by a force of over
50,000, the Mexicans held out for three months and only
surrendered after all ammunition and food had been ex-
hausted.   To commemorate the initial victory over the
French, May 5th (El Cinco de Mayo) is celebrated as a
national holiday in Mexico.   See also ZARAGOZA, IGNA-
CIO.

PUEBLA CITY.   The capital of the state of Puebla, 70 miles
southeast of Mexico City.   A major industrial and commercial city, famous for its ceramics and Talavera tiles,
with auto, steel, and chemical industries.   Founded in
1531 by Spanish Franciscan friars, it soon displaced the
nearby Indian city of Cholula as the religious center of
the Puebla basin.   The Cathedral and the University of
Puebla typify its baroque architecture.   Its 1976 population of 500,000 made it Mexico's fifth largest city.   On
May 5, 1862, General Ignacio Zaragoza's Mexican troops

used the city as a base from which to defeat the French army of Emperor Maximilian. Although the final ouster of the French did not come until 1867, this battle has become the Fifth of May (Cinco de Mayo) annual national holiday, commemorating Mexico's resistance to foreign intervention.

PUEBLA (STATE). An inland state of south central Mexico, and the fourth most populous state, with a 1976 population of 3.1 million in an area of only 33,929 square kilometers. That is, in territory Puebla is one of the smallest states. A mountainous terrain, with the center crossed by an east-west range of volcanoes, including the republic's three highest peaks--Orizaba, Popocatêpecl, and Ixtlaccíhuatl--each rising more than 17,000 feet. The pre-Hispanic center of Cholula, near Puebla City, the capital, has the private University of the Americas. Manufacturing accounts for 60 percent of the state's gross product. Onyx, silver, lead, coffee, corn, and livestock are produced.

PUERTO VALLARTA. A fishing resort and port on the Pacific Coast of the state of Jalisco. Its Banderas Bay has been a port since early Spanish colonial times. In 1800 Jesuits built the ornate Guadalupe Church. Since the 1950's, it has become a fashionable resort for foreign and Mexican tourists, with luxury hotels.

PULQUE. An alcoholic beverage dating back to pre-Columbian times and made from the fermented juice of the maguey plant. It is popular particularly among the lower classes. An interesting example of paternalism involves the use of pulque and happened some years ago in the state of Mexico. Because the governor felt that workers were spending too much on this beverage and not providing enough for their families, he unilaterally prohibited the sale of pulque in public places, and to ensure that his decision was being carried out he made frequent inspection flights in a government helicopter to many out-of-the-way places. Thereafter, it was legal to purchase the drink only in private homes.

- Q -

QUEMADA, LA. The pre-Hispanic archaeological site near the city of Zacatecas, with monuments and destroyed edifices.

QUERETARO CITY.   The capital of the state of Querétaro,
135 miles northwest of Mexico City, at an elevation of
5,904 feet above sea level.   Its 1976 population totaled
160,000.   It has cotton and woolen mills and in the vicinity opal mines.   Its water supply comes from mountains through a stone aqueduct 5 miles long, built in
1735.   Its colonial Santa Rosa Church and federal building
are made of basalt.   The city was founded by the Aztecs
on the site of an Otomí Indian town conquered by Emper-
or Moctezuma in 1440 A.D.   It was conquered by Spanish
general Fernando Tapia in 1531.   In the U.S.-Mexican
War of 1846-48, the city became the temporary federal
capital.   Its Iturbide Theater was the site of the trial in
1867 of Emperor Maximilian, condemned for usurping
power.

QUERETARO LITERARY SOCIETY.   An organization formed
in 1808 in the city of Querétaro, 135 miles north of Mexico City.   Ostensibly, its purpose was to encourage the
fine arts, but it was really a cover for revolutionary activity against the Spanish colonial government.   Members
of this organization finally convinced Hidalgo that he
should accept the leadership of the insurgent movement.
This organization was the prime mover behind the 1810
uprising.

QUERETARO (STATE).   A state in central Mexico with an
area of 11,769 square kilometers.   Its 1976 population
totaled 618,000.   This was the land of the Otomí Indians
in pre-Hispanic times.   The state produces hides, cotton,
corn, and cattle.   Near its capital is a growing industrial
area producing automobile parts, and since 1975 the largest producer in Mexico of truck and automobile gearshift
units.

QUETZAL.   A tropical bird with long green plumes, native
to southern Mexico.

QUETZAL DANCE.   Indian folk dances performed in Veracruz, Puebla, and Hidalgo.   Dancers wear a headdress
of paper and ribbons depicting the quetzal bird.

QUETZALCOATL.   A feathered serpent god of the Aztecs,
Mayas, and earlier, the Toltecs.   The god of the air and
the water.   Also the morning and evening stars god.
There are two entities associated with this name and they
are as follows:

1. Quetzalcóatl the legendary god. According to tradition, Quetzalcóatl was a fair haired, light skinned, bearded folk hero who ruled the Aztecs and preached virtue and a high code of ethics. He departed suddenly, with a promise to return at some time in the indefinite future. Legend has it that he departed in disgrace for having succumbed to temptation by Tezcatlipoca, the God of Darkness. Whatever the reason for his departure, his promise to return was a significant factor in the Spanish conquest of Mexico, since Hernán Cortés resembled the description of Quetzalcóatl, and Montezuma (the Aztec emperor at the time of the Spanish invasion in 1519) believed that Cortés was actually Quetzalcóatl, who had returned to reclaim his throne, thus completing his promise made centuries earlier.

2. Quetzalcóatl, the person. There are many versions of who he was, the most accepted one being that he was a Toltec king who ruled around the beginning of the thirteenth century A.D. He was a ruler of extraordinary ability, being a scientist, metallurgist and jewelry artisan. Perhaps his most lasting contribution was his introduction of the use of chocolate and rubber. There are so many versions of the legend of Quetzalcóatl that at this point in time it is virtually impossible to really present an accurate account of him.

QUEVEDO MORENO, RODRIGO. Born in 1889 in Chihuahua. He joined the Revolution in 1912 under General Pascual Orozco and fought against the Madero forces. He fought alongside Juan Almazán against the Constitutionalists. In 1920 he became a key supporter and advisor for President Alvaro Obregón. He became Governor of Chihuahua in 1935. As a Senator in the federal Congress 1958-64, he was a leader of the formulators of new laws on agriculture, immigration, mining, and national defense.

QUINTANA ROO, ANDRES. 1787-1851. Born in Yucatán. Politician, literary figure and independence leader. He was president of the 1813 Congress of Chilpancingo, which declared Mexico independent and after independence he served in various political posts, among them being senator and supreme court justice. Quintana Roo was noted for his honesty and keen judgement and showed great courage by criticizing the government, particularly for the assassination of Vicente Guerrero. He was also an accomplished poet, particularly of the independence movement. His ode, "The Sixteenth of September," is one of his best-known poems.

QUINTANA ROO (STATE).   The newest state of the Mexican
republic, the Territory of Quintana Roo had remained
relatively empty of population during the last century and
the first two-thirds of this century.   On October 10,
1974, the territory became the 31st state.   Its 1976 population totaled 131,000.   Its area covers 50,350 square
kilometers, taking up the eastern third of the Yucatán
peninsula.   Its capital is Chetumal, with a 1976 population of 48,000.   In 1955, Mexican President Rúiz Cortines
ended the campaign of the state of Yucatán to absorb
Quintana Roo.   Not until 1958 did modern roads adequate-
ly connect the two states.   Off its coastline lie the Mu-
jeres and Cozumel resort islands.   The Hondo River
forms its boundary with British Honduras (Belize).   The
state produces half of Mexico's tobacco, plus chicle, lumber, coffee, cotton, and sisal.

QUINTANILLA, LUIS.   Born on November 22, 1900, in Paris,
France.   Degree in philosophy and Ph.D. in political
science at the Sorbonne, Paris.   Professor of international relations at the National Autonomous University of
Mexico (UNAM), then at Johns Hopkins, Virginia, Kansas,
and George Washington universities, 1937-42.   Became
a diplomat in 1922, serving in Guatemala, Brazil, then
in the United States.   Head of the Mexican delegation to
the League of Nations 1932.   Chairman, Inter-American
Peace Commission 1948-49.   Ambassador to Colombia,
then to the United Nations.   Ambassador to the Organization of American States 1945-58.   Director of the National
Housing Institute 1958-64.   Author of the widely read book
A Latin American Speaks, published in 1950.

QUIROGA, VASCO DE.   1470-1565.   Born in Spain, he graduated from the University of Valladolid with a degree in
law and went to New Spain in 1531 as an oidor.   He was
interested in administering to the sick and founded the
Hospital of Santa Fe, complete with a church and an or-
phanage.   He then became a priest and was named Bishop
of Michoacán in 1538, a position which he held until his
death.   Apart from numerous hospitals, he founded the
Colegio de San Nicolás Obispo, which ultimately became
the Universidad de San Nicolás de Michoacán.   He encouraged the development of Michoacán along lines of a
kind of "primitive Christianity," with each community developing a certain specialty, like the tannery industry in
Uruapan.   He believed in non-violence and was loved so
much by the Tarascan Indians that he was affectionately

called "Tata Vasco," a term used to indicate a beloved
father of a family. His death was the occasion of a long
and profound period of mourning.

- R -

RABASA, EMILIO O. Born on January 23, 1925, in Mexico
City. Law degree from the National Autonomous University (UNAM). Law professor part-time at UNAM for 15
years. Legal adviser for the Ministry of Finance, then
the Ministry of Health, then for the Department of Agrarian Affairs, then for the National Bank for Ejido Credit.
Director General of the government's National Cinematography Bank 1964-70. Ambassador to the United States
1970. Minister of Foreign Relations 1970-76. During
the Echeverría administration, he was the leader of those
trying to keep the President from applying increasingly
negative policies towards the United States.

RADICAL PARTY. The political party of 1824 opposed to any
Mexican amnesty for Spaniards accused of crimes during
the War of Independence (1810-21). The Radicals supported President Santa Anna in 1828. In 1846 the Radical
Party championed the plan for nationalization of church
property. In 1857 the party supported the Plan of Tacubaya, which tried to annul the 1857 Constitution and supported President Ignacio Comonfort. When Comonfort
left Mexico in 1858, and Benito Juárez came to power,
the Radicals were discredited and their party began to
fall apart.

RAFFUL, FERNANDO. Born in 1935 in Campeche. An
economist for the Ministry of National Patrimony 1965-
67. Director of Federal Government Decentralized Agencies and Businesses 1970-73. Assistant Minister of National Patrimony 1973-76. In December 1976 he was
named by President López Portillo as the first Director
of the newly-created Department of Fishing, an autonomous agency allied with the Ministry of Agriculture.

RAILROADS. Under the direction of dictator President Porfirio Díaz, Mexico's first railroad line connected Mexico
City with the port of Veracruz, which in a pre-air, pre-
automobile age was the republic's front door to the world,
via ships. In the 1890's, this pioneer line increased the
volume of trade and visitors to the federal capital and

encouraged Díaz to construct railroad lines to major provincial cities throughout the republic, in partnership with Southern Pacific and Missouri Pacific Railroads. In 1937, President Lázaro Cárdenas expropriated the privately-owned railroads into the government's National Railroads of Mexico, leaving the Railroad of the Pacific, from Nogales to Guadalajara, operating semi-autonomously during a long period of transition. In 1961, the Chihuahua-al-Pacífico, another government railroad line, opened. It connected Chihuahua City with the Pacific Coast of Sinaloa, and crossed Mexico's "Grand Canyon," the Copper Canyon in Chihuahua state.

RAMIREZ, IGNACIO. 1818-1879. Born in San Miguel Allende and known as "El Nigromante" (The Necromancer). He was a liberal writer who was strongly anti-clerical and originally pro-Juárez, serving in his cabinet. But eventually he turned against him and ended up supporting Porfirio Díaz. He played a major role in writing the Constitution of 1857 and among the publications he founded were El Clamor Progresista and La Insurrección. One of his disciples was Ignacio de Altamirano. Ramírez died in Mexico City.

RAMIREZ VAZQUEZ, MARIANO. Born in 1903 in Mexico City. An attorney who during the 1930's, as Secretary General of the Federal Board of Arbitration and Conciliation, set the pattern of government dominating all labor-management negotiations. A justice of the federal Supreme Court 1947-49 and 1954-76 under five presidents.

RAMIREZ VAZQUEZ, PEDRO. Born on April 16, 1919, in Mexico City. An architect and city planner, he directed school construction in Tabasco state 1944-47, then directed building construction for the Ministry of Education 1947-64. He was manager for all school pre-fabricated buildings in the republic 1964-66, then director of UNESCO's school construction for Latin America 1966-69. He was chairman of Mexico's 1968 Olympics Committee. In 1973 he founded Metropolitan Autonomous University. Since 1976 he has been Minister of Human Settlements and Public Works.

RAMOS ARIZPE, MIGUEL. 1775-1843. Priest, economist-politician and a prominent liberal figure in Mexico's initial period of independence. He was elected representative to the Spanish Cortes in 1812, but was imprisoned

by Ferdinand VII because of his desire for Mexican independence. His release came about in 1820, when the
Spanish liberals again became a dominant force. Ramos
Arizpe was one of the drafters of the federalist Constitution of 1824, which was patterned after the United States
Constitution. He, along with Valentín Gómez Farías, was
the dominant force behind this document, which called for
a strongly decentralized government and divided Mexico
into nineteen states and four territories. Ramos Arizpe
was also named as the deputy from Puebla to the Constitutional Congress of 1832. Among the many political
posts he occupied was that of Minister of Justice. He
was one of the most honest and dedicated politicians of
his time, during an era when political corruption was the
overwhelming norm.

"RANA." For centuries this folk song of Mexican children
about a frog and a spider was a favorite.

RANGEL FRIAS, RAUL. Born in 1913 in Monterrey, Nuevo
León. An attorney who was law professor, then president of the University of Nuevo León 1939-43. Governor
of the state of Nuevo León 1955-61. He pioneered the
offering of civics courses for those in skilled trades at
Workers Centers in Mexico City and throughout northern
Mexico to increase working-class leadership in public
life.

RAYON, IGNACIO LOPEZ. 1773-1832. Revolutionary and
politician. He joined Miguel Hidalgo in the initial struggle for independence, becoming Secretary of State in the
first revolutionary government. After Hidalgo's death he
attempted to set up a separate Mexican government in
Zitácuaro, but was forced to resort to guerrilla warfare
because of overwhelming Spanish power. He attended the
Congress of Chilpancingo and fought the Spaniards until
1817, when he was captured. He was released in 1820.

REBOLLEDO, EFREN. 1877-1929. Poet and diplomat. The
various diplomatic posts he held around the world inspired
much of his literary work, such as Rimas japonesas and
the novel, Saga de Sigfrida la blonda, the latter inspired
by his diplomatic appointment in Norway. His literary
works are characterized by the great care and choice of
words that he used to compose them. He died in Madrid.

REBOZO. A woman's shawl, often dark blue or purple, used

among rural and working class Mexicans. Among urban middle and upper class women fancy rebozos come in bright colors with embroidery. Among Indian and village mestiza
women, the rebozo is the standard overcoat-raincoat, as
well as head covering and wrap for infants. The rebozo
is an integral part of folk dance costumes.

REDUCCION. Name given by the Spaniards during the colonial period to Indian towns. The Spaniards segregated
the Indians by forcing them to live in these settlements
for the following reasons: 1) to protect them from being
taken unfair advantage of; 2) to assure a readily-available
supply of labor; 3) to facilitate their conversion to Christianity. In Mexico the greatest resettlement of Indians,
not always accomplished peacefully, took place at the end
of the sixteenth and the beginning of the seventeenth centuries under the direction of Viceroy Gaspar de Zúñiga
y Acevedo.

REFORM, LAWS OF. Laws issued by Juárez in 1859, which
called for the confiscation of Church property not used
for worship, the nationalization of cemeteries and the
conversion of marriage into a civil contract administered
by the state. These laws were bitterly fought and led to
a very destructive, three-year war.

REGENERACION. In 1900 the clandestine Liberal Party
founded this newspaper, which served as its vehicle to
rally support against Porfirio Díaz. It was promptly
suppressed and its editor, Ricardo Flores Magón, escaped and took asylum in the United States, where he
died in 1922, a very embittered man.

RENDON, SERAPIO. 1867-1913. Lawyer, politician and
revolutionary figure. From Yucatán, he originally gained
literary fame under the pen name of León Roch. He was
a strong supporter of Madero and Pino Suárez, and when
they were killed by Huerta he turned against the latter.
He was surprised by Huerta's followers and assassinated
on August 22, 1913.

REPARTO DE UTILIDADES. Profit sharing. See INCOME
DISTRIBUTION.

REVILLAGIGEDO ISLANDS. A group of uninhabited islands
located in the Pacific Ocean almost 500 miles to the west
of the city of Manzanillo and belonging to the state of

Colima. They are composed of three main islands,
Clarión, San Benedicto and Socorro. There are also
several smaller ones. Socorro Island is the largest of
the group, measuring 24 by 9 miles and rising to a
height of almost 4,000 feet.

REVOLUTION, THE. When spelled with a patriotic capital
"R," in Mexico the Revolution means not only the fighting
from 1910 to 1920, but also the ongoing or institutionalized social reforms mandated by the Constitution of 1917.
It is the permanent quest for social justice, the dynamic
process receiving the public allegiance of every political
and governmental leader of the past 60 years. It is entwined in the name of the dominant Institutional Revolutionary Party and the modified goal by different emphasis
of the minority opposition parties.

REVOLUTIONARY COALITION. The power elite of Mexico.
The interlocking leadership of the federal government,
the dominant Institutional Revolutionary Party, the state
and local governments, organized labor, and industry.
This coalition or elite is self-replenishing. Outsiders
gain admittance through apprenticeships in coalition
cliques.

REVUELTAS, JOSE. Born in 1914 in Durango. As a Communist Youth, his violence put him in prison. His 1941
novel, Los muros del agua, based on his experiences at
the Tres Marías Islands prison, won him national fame
as a writer. In 1968 he helped organize the student
strikes and violence during July-October, and publicly
announced his goal of trying to force the cancelation of
the Olympics to discredit the government. His unsuccessful campaign aimed at discrediting the Revolutionary Coalition and bringing a Marxist dictatorship to power. He
was convicted of sedition and was in prison during 1968-
74. The far leftists continued to distribute his essays
throughout the 1970's.

REVUELTAS, SILVESTRE. 1899-1940. One of Mexico's
leading composers, he developed an original, uncompli-
cated style based upon Mexico's deep folkloric tradition.
Among his most famous works are "Janitzio," "Ventanas"
and "Colorines." His "Homenaje a García Lorca" (1935)
was written for chamber orchestra.

REYES, ALFONSO. 1889-1959. Born in Monterrey. One

of Mexico's outstanding intellectuals, he was known for
his work as a diplomat, historian and philosophical writer. Along with other Mexican writers, in 1909 he
founded the Ateneo de la Juventud (Athenaeum of Youth),
a society interested in revitalizing the intellectual cur-
rents of Mexico. In 1914 he worked in the Center for
Historical Studies in Madrid under the direction of Menéndez Pidal. In 1920, Reyes began his diplomatic career as second secretary of the Mexican embassy in
Madrid. Later, he was to occupy many diplomatic posts,
including those of ambassador to Argentina and Brazil.
He was also a member of numerous intellectual societies
and for a time was president of the prestigious Colegio
de México. In 1945 he was awarded Mexico's national
prize for literature and in the same year was a candidate
for the Nobel Prize for Literature. Alfonso Reyes was
a most prolific writer, his works occupying more than
ten volumes. One of his most famous works is Visión
de Anáhuac, published in 1917 when he was 28 years old.

REYES, BERNARDO. 1850-1913. Born in Monterrey. General and politician during the regime of Porfirio Díaz.
While he was governor of the state of Nuevo León he
passed the first workmen's compensation law in Mexico.
He had aspirations to be Díaz's successor and the latter
made him Secretary of War in 1903. However, his inability to get along with the men composing Díaz's inner
circle, particularly José Yves Limantour, caused him to
fall from favor. Reyes continued to be a strong supporter of Díaz, the latter sending him to Europe in 1910.
Upon his return he led an unsuccessful rebellion against
Madero, attempted another one in 1913 and was killed.
He was the father of Alfonso Reyes.

REYES HEROLES, JESUS. Born on April 3, 1921, in Tux-
pan, Veracruz. Law degree from the National Autonomous University. Graduate studies at the University of
Buenos Aires. Administrator for the Institutional Revolutionary Party (PRI) national executive committee 1940-
61. President of the PRI 1972-76. Head of the Mexican
Institute of Books. Key adviser to President Rúiz Cortines 1952-58. Director of Petróleos Mexicanos 1964-70.
Minister of the Interior (Gobernación) 1976 to May 1979.
At the 1972 PRI National Assembly, he tried to broaden
the base of popular participation but his reforms were
more cosmetic than substantive.

REYNOSA. A city on the U.S. border opposite McAllen,

Texas. Its 1976 population totaled 207,000. It is a commercial center in northeastern Tamaulipas state.

RINCON, VALETIN. (1901-1968). An attorney from Chiapas, a Deputy in Congress, a judge in Veracruz state and in Federal District courts. Known throughout the republic as the Grand Master of the Mexican Masonic Lodges 1949-68.

RIO GRANDE. The river serving as the border between the United States and Mexico from Matamoros, Tamaulipas to Ciudad Juárez, Chihuahua, it winds 1,600 miles northwestward, then turns northward into the state of New Mexico. Also known to Mexicans as the Río Bravo.

RIVA PALACIO, VICENTE. 1832-1896. Politician and writer. His liberal tendencies caused General Miramón to incarcerate him, although after obtaining his freedom he continued to fight on the side of Juárez. He occupied important political positions when Porfirio Díaz came to power, but because of his attacks on President Manuel González he was again incarcerated, during which time he wrote significant portions of México a través de los siglos. Other representative works are Los cuentos del general and the poem, "Al viento."

RIVAS, GENOVEVO. 1886-1947. From San Luis Potosí. As a colonel in the Revolution, he fought the U.S. troops under General John Pershing in Chihuahua in 1916. As a general, he subdued the far-right fanatical Cristeros 1926-28, helping to suppress this clerically-led anti-Revolutionary movement. He was interim Governor of San Luis Potosí 1938-39.

RIVERA, DIEGO. 1886-1959. Born in Guanajuato. Rivera was a painter who became famous in the 1920's, primarily as a muralist. It was José Vasconcelos's idea of using mural paintings to depict the ideals of the Mexican Revolution which provided Rivera with a potential audience of millions, since every blank wall of a building, every university, were potential sights for his muralistic genius. He was so successful that this technique became the most important development in Latin American painting.

Among the themes he treats are Mexico's social turmoil, its Indian heritage and the quest for social justice. Some of his paintings criticize the United States and capitalism. His works can be seen in such diverse places

as the Alhóndiga de Granaditas in Guanajuato, the Palace
of Cortés in Cuernavaca and the Palace of Fine Arts in
Mexico City. Many consider his greatest painting to be
the mural done at the National Agricultural School in
Chapingo. However, he considered his greatest to be
the unfinished work, "Market in Tenochtitlán," which
hangs in the National Palace.

He supported international communism, but was expelled twice from the Mexican Communist Party for sym-
pathizing with the Trotskyists. Less than three years
before his death he announced that he was a Catholic,
this announcement coming shortly after he had painted
out the words "Dios no existe" ("God doesn't exist") from
his mural hanging in the Del Prado Hotel in Mexico City
entitled, "Sunday in the Alameda." He is considered to
be the greatest painter that Mexico has produced.

ROA BARCENA, JOSE MARIA. 1827-1908. Poet and writer.
He had supported Maximilian, and when Juárez triumphed
Roa Bárcena spent some months in prison. In 1875,
when the Mexican Academy of the Spanish Language was
founded, he served as treasurer. He is famous for such
works as Leyendas mexicanas and Recuerdos de la inva-
sión norteamericana (1846-1848).

ROBLES PEZUELA, MANUEL. 1817-1862. Born in Guanajuato. General and President of Mexico in 1858-1859.
He was considered one of the most refined individuals to
ever occupy the presidency and was highly respected.
He fought against the Americans in the War of 1846-1848,
was later president for only one month, and after joining
the cause of Maximilian was captured and shot as a traitor by General Ignacio Zaragoza on March 23, 1862.

ROCABRUNA, JOSE. 1879-1957. Violinist and composer
who was born in Barcelona, but once he arrived in Mexico he never left his adopted country. Rocabruna won
numerous honors because of his musical abilities and held
a chair at the National Conservatory for more than 50
years. He died in Mexico City.

ROCAFUERTE, VICENTE. 1788-1847. Diplomat and book
publisher. An Ecuadorian, Rocafuerte at times acted in
official capacities for the Mexican government, even
though he also occupied important positions in the Ecuadorian government during his lifetime. He headed the
Mexican legation in London in 1826. Perhaps his most

important contribution was the books he published, a fore-most example being a reprint of Las Casas's work, the Destruction of the Indies.

ROCH, LEON.   Pen name for Serapio Rendón.

ROCHA, JUAN NEPOMUCENO.   1810-1859.   General who fought against Santa Anna, he supported the Plan of Ayut-la and in later years commanded a division in Jalisco. He was assassinated while retreating after the Battle of La Albarrada.

ROCHA, SOSTENES.   1831-1897.   A military figure who eventually attained the rank of General de Brigada, he originally fought against the liberals, but early in his career became a strong supporter of President Benito Juárez.   When Porfirio Díaz assumed power he sent Rocha to Europe, ostensibly to study military affairs, but probably because he had inflicted military defeats on Díaz years earlier.   He was also an author of military books and his remains rest in the Rotonda de los Hombres Ilus-tres.

RODRIGO, ISABEL see RODRIGUEZ, ISABEL

RODRIGUEZ, ABELARDO K.   1889-1967.   Born in Guaymas, Sonora.   General and president.   Served as provisional president of Mexico from 1932 to 1934, after Calles forced Pascual Ortiz Rubio to resign.   He fought in the Mexican Revolution and was a close associate of Alvaro Obregón.   During his political career leading up to the presidency he was governor of the Northern Territory of Lower California and occupied several other political posts.   During his presidency a notable member of his cabinet was General Lázaro Cárdenas.   Although his re-gime was considered to be generally uneventful, it was responsible for the first minimum salary for the Federal District, $1.50 pesos a day, passed on January 5, 1934. He was also responsible for creating the Mexican Civil Service, in the same year.

RODRIGUEZ, AGUSTIN.   A Franciscan priest, he opened up the territory through what is now El Paso, Texas in 1598.   In that year he gave that location the official name of El Paso del Río del Norte.

RODRIGUEZ, AGUSTIN.   1842-1919.   One of Mexico's most

outstanding jurists, he was the first rector of the Escuela Libre de Derecho and occupied various juridical positions throughout his career.

RODRIGUEZ, DIONISIO. 1810-1877. A lawyer by profession, he was an outstanding philanthropist and educator. He began the Escuela de Artes y Oficios in his native Guadalajara and was instrumental in founding various hospitals.

RODRIGUEZ, ISABEL. It is possible that her last name was Rodrigo. She accompanied the army of Hernán Cortés during his conquest of Mexico, serving as a nurse and at times even bearing arms.

RODRIGUEZ, JOSE GUADALUPE. Rural teacher and a strong believer in agrarian reform. He fought on the side of the Mexican Revolution and organized farmers as a bulwark of government support. However, in 1929 he was executed for insubordination.

RODRIGUEZ, MARIANO. A famous bull fighter of the nineteenth century, his nickname was "La Monja" (The Nun).

RODRIGUEZ, PEDRO L. 1841-1918. From the state of Mexico, he became a strong political leader in the state of Hidalgo, becoming governor. He was removed from office as a result of the Mexican Revolution.

RODRIGUEZ AGUILAR, MANUEL. 1909-1956. An engineer for Petróleos Mexicanos, he founded the Department of Exploration within Petróleos Mexicanos and managed it until his retirement. He died in Mexico City.

RODRIGUEZ ALCONEDO, JOSE LUIS. 1762-1815. He was a silversmith and painter who fought on the side of Morelos in Mexico's War of Independence and was shot by the Spaniards. One of his most famous works, a silver medallion with a picture of Carlos IV, can be seen at Chapultepec castle in Mexico City.

RODRIGUEZ ARANGOITY, EMILIO. 1833-1891. A military man who occupied important posts in the Mexican Corps of Engineers. Some of his most famous fortifications were those constructed in Puebla and which led to the victory over the French on May 5, 1862. He was officially recognized by President Benito Juárez for his valuable support of the Republic.

RODRIGUEZ DE VELASCO Y OSORIO BARBA, MARIA IGNA-
CIA. A woman of extraordinary beauty, she was known
as the "Güera Rodríguez" ("the Blond Rodríguez"). She
was a supporter of Hidalgo and a close friend of Iturbide.
Baron Alexander Von Humboldt, during his travels through
Mexico, commented on her beauty.

ROEL GARCIA, SANTIAGO. Born in 1919 in Monterrey,
Nuevo León. A law professor at the University of Nuevo
León, he became head of the Chamber of Deputies in
Congress, then a Senator. He was Assistant Secretary
General of the Institutional Revolutionary Party. Ambas-
sador to India. Minister of Foreign Relations from De-
cember 1976 to May 1979. He was the key presidential
adviser working for Mexico's resumption of diplomatic
relations with Spain after the 1975 death of Francisco
Franco.

ROJAS, LUIS MANUEL. 1871-1949. Supporter of President
Francisco Madero and an elected deputy of his government. He publicly accused American Ambassador Henry
Lane Wilson of being personally responsible for the deaths
of President Madero and Vicepresident Pino Suárez. Because of his opposition to General Victoriano Huerta he
was encarcerated, but was freed in time to head the Constitutional Congress of 1917. Rojas occupied various political posts afterwards and for a brief time headed the
Mexico City newspaper El Universal.

ROJO GOMEZ, JAVIER. (1896-1970). An attorney who was
Governor of his home state of Hidalgo 1937-40. Ambassador to Indonesia 1952-55. Ambassador to Japan 1956-
58. Governor of Quintana Roo 1967-70. A founder of
the National Campesino Federation (CNC) in 1936. CNC
Secretary General. As Governor of the Federal District,
in 1947 he was charged with illegal land sales. Scandal
cost him serious consideration by the Institutional Revolutionary Party as a presidential candidate.

ROMERO, JOSE RUBEN. 1890-1952. Poet, novelist and diplomat, he was born in Michoacán. Although he is known
principally as a novelist, his career was very diverse.
He supported Madero and later became the governor of
Michoacán. He continued to be active politically and was
appointed to various federal posts after he was no longer
governor. One of his earliest works is his collection of
poems in the book Tacámbaro. He was also rector of

the University of Michoacán and ambassador to Brazil and
Cuba. However, his fame came as the result of his
prose ability, his most famous and widely-read work being the picaresque novel, The Useless Life of Pito Pérez
(La vida inútil de Pito Pérez), published in 1938. It is
still quite popular in Mexico.

ROMERO RUBIO, MANUEL. 1828-1895. Liberal politician
and father-in-law of Porfirio Díaz. He aspired to the
presidency during the long period of the porfiriato, but
never received the approval of Díaz, thus negating his
chances. He was Secretary of the Interior from 1884 until his death.

ROSAS, JUVENTINO. 1868-1894. Violinist and composer.
He came from a family of musicians and earned a great
deal of his livelihood playing in the family orchestra.
His most famous work is the waltz, "Over the Waves, "
a work which at one time or another has been attributed
to many other composers. He never attained the fame
and wealth in life which he justly deserved, his life being
cut short by tuberculosis.

ROSAS MORENO, JOSE. 1838-1883. Poet, journalist and
politician. He was regarded as an outstanding fable writer and lyrical poet of his time. His poem "La vuelta a
la aldea" is representative of his work. He is also an
accomplished dramatist. Rosas Moreno supported Juárez
and after the latter's return to power served in various
political posts and in the legislature.

RUBIO, CARMEN. The second wife of Porfirio Díaz, whom
she married in 1883. She served as a moderating influence on Díaz vis-à-vis his feelings toward the Roman
Catholic Church.

RUIZ CORTINES, ADOLFO. 1890-1973. Born in Veracruz.
President of Mexico from 1952 to 1958. He supported
Madero and fought against Huerta after the latter had
seized power. A close friend of Miguel Alemán, who
helped him become governor of Veracruz and later president of the Republic. Ruiz Cortines also served as Minister of the Interior during the administration of President
Alemán. After his inauguration President Ruiz Cortines
set about to reestablish credibility in government and was
largely successful. He was not a flamboyant leader by
any means, but the Mexican people did not resent this in

the least, since the time was appropriate for a paternal
image in the presidency.   Ruiz Cortines' administration
stressed industrialization, the development of the country's hydraulic resources and the consequent increase in
electric power.   The danger of floods was also decreased
and he provided irrigation for millions of acres of farm
land, thus increasing food production.   Women were
granted the right to vote for the first time and his administration combatted the perennial balance of payments def-
icit by devaluating the peso to 12. 50 to the dollar, a new
exchange rate which was to last for 22 years.

RUIZ DE ALARCON Y MENDOZA, JUAN   see   ALARCON Y
MENDOZA, JUAN RUIZ

RULFO, JUAN.   Born in 1918 in Sayula, Jalisco.   From the
Centro de Escritores Mexicanos he became in the 1950's
Mexico's leading short story writer.   He is known for
his 1953 volume of 15 stories, El llano en llamas, depicting the violence of life in rural Mexico and the atti-
tude of resignation of peasants.

RURALES.   The term used for the rural police of Mexico
during the presidency of General Porfirio Díaz.   Previous
to the porfiriato, Mexico's rural areas were considered
unsafe and highwaymen were numerous.   It was for this
reason that President Díaz instituted the rurales, many
of them actually having been highwaymen, or pistoleros.
This new force actually did make the country's rural
areas safe, and it is still said in Mexico that it wasn't
even necessary to lock one's door at night.   But the poor
and underprivileged frequently suffered at their hands and
eventually they became greatly feared and despised.   The
pistoleros frequently resorted to the ley fuga, a free
translation being the "law of flight."   The pistoleros at
times would purposely leave the cell door of a prisoner
unlocked, so that when he attempted to flee they would
shoot to kill.

- S -

SAENZ, AARON.   Born in 1890.   One of the key advisers of
President Plutarco Calles 1920-24.   The dominant Revolutionary Party in 1929 strongly considered Sáenz as a
presidential candidate to succeed interim President Portes
Gil, but former President Calles, still unofficially gov-

erning Mexico after Alvaro Obregón's assassination in
1928 for attempting a second term as president, decided
that Pascual Ortiz Rubio of Michoacán would be a better
choice. He followed the orders of Calles better than did
Sáenz and the latter therefore lost his chance to be interim President of Mexico.

SAENZ, MOISES. 1888-1941. Educator and diplomat. He
    was known principally for the many posts he held in Mex-
    ican education, among them being Director of the National
    Preparatory School (La Escuela Nacional Preparatoria),
    organizer of the First Interamerican Indigenous Congress
    and President of the Committee on Indigenous Research.
    He was a principal figure in the development of Mexico's
    secondary school system. Sáenz died while serving as
    ambassador to Peru.

SAHAGUN, BERNARDINO DE. 1500-1590. His real name
    was Bernardino Ribeira and he was born in the Kingdom
    of León. He became a Franciscan priest at an early age
    and arrived in New Spain in 1529, where he preached to
    the Indians in their own language and taught Latin at the
    Colegio de Santa Cruz de Tlatelolco. In spite of his
    great reputation as a missionary and teacher, he is best
    known for his historical writings, the most famous one
    being Historia general de las cosas de la Nueva España,
    a history of New Spain dealing with all phases of life in
    the New World. It went through three major revisions,
    in which he constantly amplified what he had written pre-
    viously. He died in the Monastery of St. Francis at a
    very advanced age.

ST. PATRICK BATTALION. A group composed of Irish-
    American prisoners of war who fought on the Mexican side
    in the War of 1846-48. After the end of hostilities they
    were executed by the Americans as traitors. However,
    they are regarded as heroes by the Mexican people.

SAINZ DE BARANDA, PEDRO. 1787-1845. Politician and
    maritime figure. A Creole, he was born in Campeche of
    wealthy parents and studied to be a naval officer in Spain,
    participating in the Battle of Trafalgar, where he was
    wounded. With the advent of Mexican independence he
    took charge of the navy and succeeded in dislodging the
    Spaniards from the island of San Juan de Ulúa. After-
    wards, he became the Vicegovernor of Yucatán and occu-
    pied other political posts in that region. He died in
    Mérida.

SALAS, JOSE MARIANO. 1797-1867. He had a long military
career before being named president during the latter
part of 1846, only to give it up to Santa Anna in December of the same year. A strong conservative, he later
became part of the Regency which governed with the help
of the French until Maximilian was officially installed as
the Emperor of Mexico. He died in Mexico City.

SALAZAR, RUBEN. Born in 1905 in Veracruz. A popular
author who became nationally known with his 1947 book,
La democracia y el comunismo. His fame rests on his
1968 novel, Viva México, which exposes police brutality
and incompetence among journalists.

SALTILLO. The capital of the northern state of Coahuila.
Its 1976 population totaled 223,000. The city has preserved some colonial era buildings.

SAN BLAS BATTALION see CHAPULTEPEC, BATTLE OF

SAN FELIPE DE JESUS. 1575-1597. Franciscan priest who
was Mexico's first saint. He studied to be a Franciscan
priest, but when he abandoned his studies his wealthy
parents sent him to the Philippines, where he led a life
of ease and followed the whims of the flesh. He eventually mended his ways and was ordained, but on his way
back to Mexico City to celebrate his first mass the boat
was intercepted near the coast of Japan and he and four
other priests were tortured and killed.

SAN JACINTO, BATTLE OF. The deciding battle of the Texas war for independence, it was fought on April 21, 1836.
A Mexican force of about 1500 under the command of
General Antonio López de Santa Anna was crushed by a
force of Texans numbering about that many. With memo-
ries of the massacre at the Alamo, the Texans surprised
the Mexicans, killed many hundreds and took the rest
prisoner, including Santa Anna. Actually, Mexican care-
lessness was just as responsible for their defeat as was
the bravery shown by the Texans under the command of
General Sam Houston. Santa Anna succeeded in talking
his captors out of executing him and negotiated an end
to the war. See also SANTA ANNA, ANTONIO LOPEZ
DE.

SAN JUAN DE ULUA. A small island one mile offshore from
the port of Veracruz on which the Spaniards constructed
a fortress in the sixteenth century. Originally it was

used as a loading and unloading point for ships and also
to protect the city from sea attack. Through the years
it has been used as a prison, a customs house and a
presidential mansion. It no longer serves any active
function and is now preserved as a national historic monument. See PASTRY WAR.

SAN LUIS POTOSI, PLAN OF. This was the manifesto of
Francisco Madero containing the principal changes demanded of Porfirio Díaz and was issued in San Antonio,
Texas in October of 1910. It declared the recent elections to be invalid and called on the Mexican people to
rise up against Díaz, fixing November 20th as the day
for the rebellion to begin. Since in effect it was the rallying cry for the beginning of the Mexican Revolution, it
called for effective suffrage and no re-election, land reform and the reinstatement of the Constitution of 1857.

SAN LUIS POTOSI (CITY). The capital of San Luis Potosí
state in north central Mexico. An important mining center 225 miles northwest of Mexico City at an elevation of
6,100 feet above sea level. The Governor's Palace and
state and municipal buildings have baroque architecture,
built of rose-colored stone. The city's many towers are
covered in colored tile. Founded in 1550 A.D., the word
"Potosí" was added alluding to Bolivian mining wealth.
Gold was discovered in 1590. After 1620, a major silver
mining center. During the struggle against Emperor Maximilian in the 1860's, the city was briefly the provisional
capital of the government of Benito Juárez. Its 1976 population was 294,000.

SAN LUIS POTOSI (STATE). A state in north central Mexico
on a plateau averaging 6,000 feet above sea level, crossed
by the Sierra Madre Oriental in its southeastern portion.
Its area is 63,670 square kilometers, and its 1976 population totaled 1.5 million. The state's Pánuco River
flows eastward into the Gulf of Mexico at Tampico. The
economy includes mining of silver, lead, mercury, and
copper, and production of coffee, sugar, fruit, and fiber
plants. In its capital was drawn up the "Plan of San
Luis" calling for the 1910 Revolution.

SANCHEZ DE TAGLE, FRANCISCO MANUEL. 1782-1847.
Poet, educator, politician. His ability as a poet was
recognized when his poem "La lealtad americana" won
first place in a contest. Contrición poética is represen-

tative of his later works. He taught at the Colegio de San Juan de Letrán and held various political positions in the government after independence.

SANCHEZ TABOADA, RODOLFO. 1885-1955. A longtime official of the Institutional Revolutionary Party (PRI) national executive committee. From Puebla. Director of the Budget for President Cárdenas 1934-36. President of the PRI 1946-52. Key adviser for Presidents Alemán and Ruiz Cortines. Governor of Baja California del Norte 1937-40, 1940-44. One of the few men never an admiral nor naval officer to be Minister of the Navy 1952-55.

SANCHEZ VITE, MANUEL. Born in 1915 in Hidalgo. School teacher, attorney, and Deputy in the federal Congress. Legal adviser to the National Teachers Union. As Governor of Hidalgo 1969-70, he got a leave of absence in order to be President of the Institutional Revolutionary Party (PRI) from 1970 to 1972, then returned as Governor 1972-74.

SANDOVAL, GONZALO DE. 1497-1528. Spanish conqueror who was a close confidant of Cortés. He accompanied the latter during the conquest of Mexico and was the key figure in the defeat of Pánfilo de Narváez, who had been sent to Mexico to arrest Cortés. After the fall of Tenochtitlán, Sandoval continued the conquest towards the southeast, arriving as far as Coatzacoalcos. On Cortés's orders, he established peace in Colima and later accompanied him on his conquest of Honduras. Upon returning to Spain, he died in the port of Palos after a brief illness.

SANSORES PEREZ, CARLOS. Born in 1918 in Campeche. An attorney who was a Deputy in the federal Congress 1946-49, 1955-58, 1961-64, and 1973-76. A Senator during the period 1964-67. He was Governor of Campeche 1967-73, and resigned in 1973 to become majority leader of the Chamber of Deputies. President of the Institutional Revolutionary Party (PRI) from December 1976 to February 1979. He resigned, disputing the economic policies of President López Portillo.

SANTA ANNA, ANTONIO LOPEZ DE. 1794-1876. Born in Veracruz. Soldier, politician, revolutionary and president. He dominated Mexican politics for 25 years and was president eleven times. The epitome of political opportunism, he supported liberals and conservatives alike, although he tended to espouse the cause of the conservatives and the Church. Santa Anna originally was opposed to Mexican independence and fought against Hidalgo. Later, he played a key role in deposing Agustín Iturbide in what was the beginning of a career of alternating support for conservative and liberal factions. He supported Vicente Guerrero in 1829, but later turned against him and supported Bustamante. In one of the many political revolts in which he took part, he ended up by being President from 1833 to 1835.

It was under his leadership that Texas was lost to Mexico, due to serious political and military errors. For example, when Stephen Austin went to Mexico City to plead for more aid from the government, he was summarily imprisoned, thus worsening relations between Texas and the Mexican central government. The Battle of San Jacinto, which completed the Texas secessionist movement, was lost because Santa Anna did not bother to post a guard and allowed his soldiers to take a siesta without observing any precautions.

He enjoyed surrounding himself with sycophants, but once he tired of them and government work in general, he would retire to his ancestral ranch of Manga de Clavo, there to await the "wishes" of the Mexican people to return once more to govern them. He succeeded in using his military experience to gain publicity, at times adding to his detriment. One of the best examples of this practice was the loss of one of his legs due to a French cannon explosion during the Pastry War. He alienated many of his followers by having the leg interred in a special vault in Mexico City. Shortly afterwards, he was exiled and did not return to his native land until 1846, when he led his country against the North American invaders. Although he proved himself to be a capable military leader on occasion, he lost the key battles of Buena Vista and Cerro Gordo. He was exiled again in 1848, but was recalled and served as President between 1853 and 1855. Santa Anna again was forced into exile by the Revolution of Ayutla and remained outside of Mexico until 1862, the year when attempts began to establish a monarchy in Mexico. As a measure of his duplicity, he first offered his services to Juárez, but was rebuffed. Then he approached Maximilian, with the same result. Destitute, ignored and nearly blind, he lived out his last years in Mexico City, behind the old Basilica of the Virgin of Guadalupe. As an indication of the scorn in which he continues to be held

by the Mexican people, there is no statue dedicated to
him in any part of the country.

SANTOS, GONZALO N.   Born in 1898 in San Luis Potosí.
A Deputy in the federal Congress, then a Senator 1934-
40.   Governor of San Luis Potosí 1943-49.   He became
the unofficial political boss or cacique of his home state,
controlling major policies and state government contracts
from 1949 to 1959.   President Adolfo López Mateos
pledged in his 1958 campaign to break the power of such
regional bosses.   The Chief Executive encouraged the
protests of the Potosí Civic Union (UCP).   In 1959, after
periodic closings of businesses by UCP members, the
Governor of the state, Manuel Alvarez, had to resign,
and the power of Santos ended.

SARTORIO, JOSE MANUEL.   1746-1828.   Priest, poet and
writer.   Before Mexico's independence, he was appointed
to serve on various censorship boards.   He was also
president of the Academy of Moral Sciences of San Joaquín.   In spite of these appointments he favored Mexican
independence.   Although Sartorio wrote a great deal of
poetry, he was never considered an outstanding writer in
this genre.   A representative work is Rasgo en honra de
Nuestra Señora de los Dolores.

SENTIES, OCTAVIO.   Born in 1915 in Veracruz.   An attorney
who was a Deputy in the federal Congress.   Mexico's
chief spokesman on automobile and truck transportation
at international conferences in the 1950's and 1960's.
Governor of the Federal District 1970-76.

SERDAN, AQUILES.   1876-1910.   Military figure and politician.   He was born in the city of Puebla and because of
his pro-Madero sentiments was imprisoned.   He was a
co-founder of the Antireelection Party of Puebla and was
killed on November 18, 1910, when his house was surrounded and stormed by Díaz's soldiers.

SERRANO, FRANCISCO.   General and Minister of War under
General Alvaro Obregón.   He fought against General Victoriano Huerta and held various political posts.   He was
a presidential candidate of the opposition party and in 1927
was arrested and shot in Cuernavaca, along with several
of his followers.

"SICK FAMILY."   Name given to Juárez and his inner circle

of government officials, Melchor Ocampo and Guillermo Prieto, as they retreated across Mexico in a black carriage with the curtains drawn, seemingly always only one step ahead of the French invaders.

SIERRA MENDEZ, JUSTO. 1848-1912. Born in Campeche. Positivist and one of the outstanding members of the cabinet of Porfirio Díaz, where he served as Minister of Education. His literary achievements were truly prodigious and he became known as a poet, essayist and historian, just to name the principal genres in which he excelled. His most famous and widely read book is the Evolución política del pueblo mexicano (Political Evolution of the Mexican People). He will also be remembered for having reopened the Autonomous National University of Mexico in 1910.

SIETE LEYES. In English the phrase means "Seven Laws" and it refers to the Constitution of 1837, a centralist, highly conservative document which created the Poder Conservador, a fourth branch of government which was all-powerful.

SIGÜENZA Y GONGORA, CARLOS DE. 1645-1700. A Jesuit priest, he was born in Mexico City and was truly a learned man, being a recognized authority in many fields of the arts and sciences. Although a close friend of the great poetess Sor Juana Inés de la Cruz and a poet in his own right, he is remembered more for his prose, his most famous work being Mercurio volante. His 28 volumes of history are still used by many historians. He died in Mexico City.

SILVA HERZOG, JESUS. Born in 1892 in San Luis Potosí. Economics degree from the National Autonomous University (UNAM). Graduate studies in New York 1912-14. He became one of Mexico's leading economists. One of the founders of the UNAM School of Economics, and its Dean 1940-42. UNAM professor 1924-60. Assistant Minister of Education 1932-34. Ambassador to the Soviet Union 1928-30. General Manager of Petróleos Mexicanos 1939-40. Assistant Minister of Finance 1944-46. Publisher of one of Mexico's leading academic magazines, Cuadernos Americanos, 1948-71. Economics adviser for the Ministries of Finance, National Patrimony, the Customs Department, and for six Presidents of Mexico.

SINALOA. A state in northwestern Mexico extending 350 miles

along the Gulf of California and the Pacific Ocean.   Bordered on the north by the state of Sonora and on the south
by the state of Nayarit.   Its area is 58,480 square kilometers in a long, narrow shape.   On its eastern boundary, the Sierra Madre Occidental separates it from Chihuahua and Durango states.   The state's 1976 population
totaled 1.7 million.   Its largest city and capital, Culiacán, had 264,000 population in 1976.   The city of Mazatlán is a major Pacific port and tourist resort.   Sinaloa
became a state in 1830, being separated from Sonora.
It produces sugar cane, tobacco, coffee, cotton, rice,
and fruit.   It is the major supplier of winter vegetables
for Canada and the major supplier of tomatoes during the
winter for the United States.   The state is drained by the
Sinaloa, Culiacán, and Fuerte rivers.   It has iron ore,
lead, silver, hardwoods, textile plants, sugar refineries,
and cereals.   It is Mexico's chief transporter of narcotics
to the United States, in illegal operations by organized
crime.

SINARQUISMO.   The word literally means "without anarchy."
A fascistic movement which originated in Mexico in 1937
under the German Helmut Oscar Schreiter and the Mexican José Angel Urquiza.   The official party was known
as the National Sinarquist Union and the height of its power corresponded with the zenith of Nazi success, 1939-
1943.   It favored a strong law and order program and
supported the conservative elements of society.   The decline of this movement is directly related to the decline
of Nazi power and after World War II it ceased to be a
threat to Mexico's established governmental institutions.

SIQUEIROS, DAVID ALFARO.   1889-1975.   Born in Chihuahua.   Painter, revolutionary and political activist.   Up
to his death in early 1975, he was generally regarded as
Mexico's greatest living painter and will go down in history as one of its greatest artists.   It is impossible to
separate his professional life from his political activities
He fought in the Mexican Revolution, became an officer
on the Republican side during the Spanish Civil War and
even led a group of 20 gunmen in an unsuccessful attempt
to assassinate Leon Trotsky at his home in Mexico City.
His specialty was mural painting and the recurrent
theme in his works is man's progress through the ages
and his struggle for social justice.   Major works can be
seen in the National Preparatory School and the National
Institute of Fine Arts.   By his own admission, his major
work is "The March of Humanity," a mural which covers

the eighteen-sided poly-forum building in the Hotel de México complex.

The following incident illustrates the ability of Mexico to recognize genius in its citizens while at the same time punishing them for acts which it considers dangerous to the country. In 1960 Siqueiros was commissioned by the government to do a mural painting in Chapultepec Park and during this same period had been involved in anti-American demonstrations. While working on this mural painting he was arrested for his part in these demonstrations and imprisoned. Eventually, the matter ran its legal course and he was freed. Years later, just before his death, he was paid a courtesy visit by President and Mrs. Luis Echeverría, this visit indicative of the dual feelings that Mexico held for one of its greatest artists.

SOCIALIST EDUCATION. A term used in the 1930's to refer to Mexican education. The phrase was used nebulously and referred to a Marxist-type orientation which Mexican education was supposed to follow.

SOLDADERAS. The Indian women who accompanied their men in the barracks and during battle, cooking and caring for them wherever they might be. Clemente Orozco vividly portrays them in his painting entitled, "Las Soldaderas."

SONORA. A state in northwestern Mexico with an area of 184,000 square kilometers. The second largest state in the republic. Bordered on the north by Arizona and New Mexico and on the west by the Gulf of California. Its 1976 population was 1.4 million. Eastern Sonora is mountainous. The western region is flat with a rocky coastline. The capital is Hermosillo. The city of Guaymas is a major Mexican port. The island of Tiburón and the adjacent mainland are the homes of the Seri Indians. Sonora has the third highest state income among the 31 states. Since colonial days its mining includes copper, coal, and iron ore. Since the 1940's, nine hydroelectric dams have brought extensive irrigated farming. Sonora supplies 70 percent of Mexico's wheat. It has cotton, cattle, cereals, commercial fishing, and frozen shrimp processing. At Nogales on the border, assembly plants turn out electrical appliances and musical instruments. Spanish explorer Vásquez de Coronado traveled around Sonora in 1540. Juan de Anza, born in Sonora in 1735, in 1775 marched northward, across Southern California and up to San Francisco, helping establish missions and

forts. Sonora is the home state of four Mexican Presidents: Alvaro Obregón 1920-24, Plutarco Calles 1924-28,
Abelardo L. Rodríguez 1932-34, and Adolfo de la Huerta
in 1920. Sonora's historic colonial mining town is Alamos. Several important battles in the Revolution occurred
in Sonora during the period 1910-15.

SOTO Y GAMA, ANTONIO DIAZ. 1880-1967. Politician, educator and agrarian leader. He was a close adviser of
Emiliano Zapata and took over the leadership of Zapata's
movement after he was assassinated. He organized the
Confederación Nacional Campesina.

STEPHENS GARCIA, MANUEL. Born in 1925 in Bellavista,
Nayarit. Secondary school teacher who became one of
the national leaders of the Popular Socialist Party (PPS).
A Deputy in the federal Congress 1961-64 and 1970-73.
A regional secretary of the National Union of Workers in
Education (SNTE). In 1975 a PPS candidate for Governor
of Nayarit, the state which is the party stronghold. He
continued to claim victory and charged fraudulent vote
counting. In 1976, the controversy ended when the PPS
elected its first federal Senator from Oaxaca, Jorge
Cruickshank, which Stevens claimed was recompense from
the dominant Institutional Revolutionary Party for his loss
in Nayarit.

THE STREET OF ALI BABA AND THE FORTY THIEVES. A
term used derisively by Mexicans when referring to the
street in Cuernavaca where President Calles and his followers lived in a very ostentatious manner, displaying
their wealth by constructing huge mansions and generally
practicing conspicuous consumption.

STUDENT FEDERATIONS. Since the 1930's, a majority of the
university and preparatory school student federations in
Mexico have been leftist-led, either Communist or otherwise anti-establishment. Exceptions are in private universities. Most student federations utilize strikes over
national political issues.

SUAREZ, VICENTE. 1833-1847. Niño Héroe (Heroic Child).
A cadet of the Escuela Militar in Chapultepec Park, he
died in hand-to-hand combat against the American invaders
while defending the Escuela Militar in Chapultepec Park.
There is a street named in his honor in the Colonia Con-
desa neighborhood in Mexico City.

"SUFRAGIO EFECTIVO; NO REELECCION!" A Spanish
   phrase meaning, "Effective suffrage; No Reelection!"
   Porfirio Díaz used it as a rallying cry when he came to
   power in 1876. Ironically, it was used as a rallying cry
   to force him from office in 1910. It has remained a cor-
   nerstone of governmental policy and since 1910 no Mexican president has ever succeeded himself.

SUN STONE. The "Sun Stone" is the Aztec calendar, a huge
   disc now found in the National Museum of Anthropology.
   It contains the concepts of chronometric and cosmological
   systems handed down by the Toltecs and expanded and refined by the Aztecs. It was the sacred almanac of their
   polytheism. Weighing 20 tons, it is 12 feet in diameter.
   At the center is the sun. The twenty day names encircle
   the central symbols.

- T -

TABASCO. A state in southeastern Mexico, bordering the
   Gulf of Mexico on its north, Campeche to its east, and
   the states of Chiapas to the south and Veracruz to the
   west. Its area is 24,661 square kilometers. Its 1976
   population totaled 1,055,000. Its capital, Villahermosa,
   had a 1976 population of 153,000. In pre-Hispanic times,
   the Maya Empire included Tabasco. It has humid, tropical climate and produces sugar cane.

TABLADA, JOSE JUAN. 1871-1945. Poet, political writer
   and satirist. An extremely prolific writer, his political
   satires were published in numerous magazines and newspapers, such as El Mundo Ilustrado and Excelsior. His
   poem "Onix" is one of his most famous. He was also
   active in New York in publicizing and disseminating information about Mexican life and culture.

TACUBAYA, BATTLE OF. On April 11, 1858, during the
   War of the Reform, in the Mexico City suburb of Tacubaya, General Leonardo Márquez's conservative forces defeated liberal troops, keeping the capital under the authority of clericals, and delaying the return to power of
   liberal reformer Benito Juárez.

TACUBAYA, CONFERENCE OF. After meeting for the first
   in 1826, members of the Panama Congress agreed to
   meet at a later date in Tacubaya, a part of greater Mexico City. However, the meeting never took place.

TALAMANTES, GUSTAVO L. 1880-1958. A Senator from
Chihuahua, then Governor of Chihuahua 1935-40. A key
policy maker for the government's National Ejido Bank
during 1935-50.

TAMAULIPAS. A state in northeastern Mexico on the Gulf
of Mexico, just south of Texas. Its area totals 79,600
square kilometers. Its 1976 population totaled 1.9 million. It has an extensive coastal plain but a mountainous
center crossed by the Sierra Madre Oriental. With irrigation from the Rio Grande on the U.S. border, the state
produces cotton, sugar cane, and citrus fruit. Tamaulipas was the first petroleum-producing state in Mexico
in the 1900's, but now furnishes more natural gas than
oil and has major pipelines running south to Veracruz and
southwestward to Monterrey. It has the second-highest
income among the 31 states, trailing only Baja California
del Norte during 1970-78 and just ahead of Sonora. Its
port of Tampico is the second largest port in the republic
and a major oil-refinery center. The capital is Ciudad
Victoria, a commercial and agricultural center. Major
cities for trade and tourist traffic from the United States
into Tamaulipas are the border cities of Nuevo Laredo,
Reynosa, and Matamoros. The state was named for the
pre-Hispanic Tamaulipas Indians and colonized by the
Spaniards in 1746.

TAMAYO, RUFINO. Born in 1899. One of Mexico's most
famous painters and together with Orozco, Rivera and
Siqueiros represents a level of achievement in painting
rarely achieved by one nation in so short a period of
time. In contrast to the others, Tamayo is known for
his reflective spirit and not for expressing great contrasts
in his art form. Some of his most famous paintings are
"Homage to the Race" and "The Birth of Our Nationality,"
both of them being at the Palace of Fine Arts in Mexico
City. Tamayo is well-known abroad and the Museum of
Modern Art in New York City possesses representative
examples of his work. His best artistic qualities are the
use of color and his ability to bring out suggestion.

TAMPICO. One of Mexico's major ports, a city in Tamaulipas almost at the border of that state and the state of
Veracruz. Its 1976 population totaled 232,000. It has
the second largest port facilities in the republic and is
a major oil refinery center. Tampico has pipelines for
petroleum and for natural gas connecting to Monterrey,
Mexico City, and Veracruz.

TAMPICO INCIDENT.   In 1914, the crew of the U.S.S. Dolphin was arrested in Tampico and when Huerta refused to honor the American flag with a 21-gun salute President Wilson sent American ships into the Gulf of Mexico, even though the sailors had been released.   These ships eventually were used to occupy Veracruz.

TAPIA, ENGUERRANDO.   Born in Hermosillo, Sonora.   A reporter for the Hermosillo daily newspapers El Imparcial and El Regional in the 1950's, in the 1960's and 1970's he built up the rival Hermosillo daily El Sonorense as publisher and editor.   From the 1950's through the 1970's he has been an adviser on public relations for the Institutional Revolutionary Party (PRI) leaders in Sonora and for many top state government leaders.

TAPIA CAMACHO, MANLIO.   Born in 1928 in Veracruz.   An attorney, judge, briefly a Senator, Mayor of Veracruz 1964-67.   Also a journalist and public relations adviser for the Institutional Revolutionary Party (PRI) in Mexico City since the 1960's.

TARAHUMARAS.   The Tarahumara Indians, concentrated in the state of Chihuahua but found elsewhere in the Sierra Madre Occidental, are noted for their physical stamina as foot racers.   They can run for miles without rest.

TARASCANS.   The Tarascan Indians concentrate in the state of Michoacán.   They have lived around Lake Chapala and Lake Pátzcuaro for centuries and are noted fishermen.

TARRAGO, LETICIA.   Born in 1940 in Orizaba, Veracruz.   A painter and engraver, she first won international recognition in 1957 for winning a twelve-nation competition by KLM Airlines entitled, "This Is My Country."   She has studied engraving in Warsaw, Poland and also studied with Dr. Atl.   Her fame is such that she now has several permanent exhibitions in Europe and the United States.   Representative of her color etchings are "8:45 A.M." and "Burbujas."

TAXCO.   A city in the state of Guerrero which has preserved most of its downtown and commercial areas with the colonial era buildings and cobblestone streets which have made it a tourist resort.   Taxco is famous for its many silversmith artisans, who turn out the most elaborate jewelry in the republic.

TELEVISA. The private-public broadcasting corporation Televisa is an umbrella management entity overseeing
privately-owned television stations Channels 2, 4, and 5
plus the government's Channel 8 in Mexico City. Televisa retains corporate ownership but encourages each
channel to compete for advertising revenue and audiences.
In addition, each anchor outlet feeds a network of provincial affiliates. Televisa also produces feature films for
showing in theaters or on television.

TELLEZ BENOIT, MARIA EMILIA. Born on December 27,
1921, in Washington, D. C. A lawyer, she became a
pioneer woman foreign service officer in 1946. She became director of the United States Section of the Foreign
Relations Ministry, then the Europe-Asia-Africa Section.
She was Third Secretary of the embassy in Washington,
then Second Secretary in Havanna. In 1970 she became
Director General of International Organizations for the
Foreign Relations Ministry.

TELLEZ CRUCES, AGUSTIN. Born on November 15, 1918,
in Guanajuato. Law degree from the National Autonomous
University. District Court judge in the states of Hidalgo,
Puebla, Chiapas, Sonora, México, and then the Federal
District. A justice of the federal Supreme Court, he was
re-elected annually Chief Justice of Mexico in 1977, 1978,
and 1979. He toured all federal prisons and got improved
medical care and vocational rehabilitation for inmates.
He originated the treaty with the United States under which
Americans convicted of narcotics crimes in Mexico can
serve their terms in U.S. prisons and vice-versa for
Mexicans convicted of narcotics crimes in the U.S.

TELLO, MANUEL J. 1898-1971. A lawyer from Zacatecas
who became a distinguished career diplomat in the United
Nations, Belgium, West Germany, and Japan. He was
Ambassador to the United States 1952-58. Minister of
Foreign Relations 1951-52 and 1958-64. He set the policy
for President López Mateos of keeping diplomatic relations
with Castro's Cuba when all other Latin American republics broke relations in 1962.

TELLO MACIAS, CARLOS. Born on November 4, 1938, in
Mexico City. The son of Manuel J. Tello, he has a
master's degree in science from Columbia University and
an economics degree from the University of Cambridge,
England. An economist for the Nacional Financiera de-

velopment bank, then for the Ministry of National Patrimony, then for President Díaz Ordaz 1964-70. Undersecretary of Finance 1970-76. From December 1976 to November 1977 he was the first Minister of Planning and the Budget, the entity converted from the defunct Ministry of the Presidency.

TENOCHTITLAN. The capital of the Aztec Empire. The literal meaning of this word is "prickly pear over rocks." The city lasted from its traditional date of founding in 1325 until its conquest by the Spaniards in 1521. Mexico City was built over its ruins. Tenochtitlán was an unbelievably beautiful city which at the height of its growth had about 250,000 inhabitants. It was situated in the center of Lake Texcoco and could be entered only by four broad causeways. Anyone visiting the floating gardens of Xochimilco today will have an idea of what Tenochtitlán was like. It was a very clean city and enjoyed a high division of labor among its artisans. One of the more exotic handicrafts was the art of feather weaving, long since lost. An abundant water supply was available to the city and was brought in by ducts, but the vulnerability of these ducts proved to be the undoing of the city, since a major factor in the Spanish conquest of Tenochtitlán was their ability to cut off this water supply.

TEOTIHUACAN. A pre-Hispanic city, 25 miles northeast of Mexico City, which arose in 100 B.C. and flourished to 750 A.D. A religious and political center for Teotihuacán people descended from Olmecs, who influenced succeeding Toltec and Aztec cultures. Its area covered 85 square miles and had a population of 50,000. Its north-south axis, called Street of the Dead, is crossed by an east-west axis at the center. At its Citadel lies the Temple of Quetzalcóatl. The largest structure is the Pyramid of the Sun, 200 feet high, with five concentric terraces to a top platform. Nearby is the smaller Pyramid of the Moon. The site has 4,000 apartment-like lime-plastered rooms.

TEQUILA. An alcoholic beverage distilled from century plants or maguey cactus. It is the symbolic national drink of Mexico. Clear in color, it originated in the town of Tequila, Jalisco. It is closely related to the Mexican drinks pulque and mezcal. Traditional drinking of tequila requires one to squeeze lemon juice onto the tongue, add salt, and then swallow the liquor.

TERRAZAS, EDUARDO. Born in 1936 in Guadalajara. He is a painter who was a professor of architectonic design at Columbia University from 1963 to 1966 and has had many one-man exhibitions in Europe, North and South America. Representative of his paintings are "Danzantes" and "Arco Iris."

TERRAZAS, FRANCISCO DE. Sixteenth-century poet and the first poet born in New Spain. Most of his works have been lost, but "Nuevo mundo y conquista" ("New World and Conquest"), an epic poem, survives. The poem "Dejad las hebras de oro ensortijado" ("Leave Behind the Strands of Woven Gold") is representative of his work.

TERREROS, PEDRO. Mine owner who in 1762 reopened the Vizcaína Vein in San Luis Potosí. He eventually made a multi-million dollar profit and was given the title of Conde de Regla.

TEXAS. The territory which eventually became known as Texas was a sparsely populated area the Spaniards began to colonize around the middle of the seventeenth century. After the independence of Mexico, American settlers were encouraged to settle there, the principal conditions being that they become Mexican citizens and Roman Catholics. The latter condition was almost impossible to enforce, resulting in many Protestants colonizing the area, a factor which later contributed to the alienation of Texans and Mexicans. However, Texans were allowed to engage in slavery, at least for the time being, a practice which had been eliminated in Mexico many years previously.

As the 1830's approached, the central government in Mexico City became apprehensive and in 1829 a decree by President Vicente Guerrero abolished slavery in the area, but it was impossible to enforce. By 1830 there were some 25,000 to 30,000 settlers living in Texas, plus their slaves. Conditions worsened, the Mexicans prohibiting further immigration and attaching Texas to the Mexican state of Coahuila, moves which further incensed the Texans. Relations continued to worsen, so that on March 2, 1836, a Texas convention proclaimed independence, a move which Mexico refused to accept. Within a month's time two historic battles were fought which forced Mexico to accept the independence of Texas. In March of 1836 over 300 Texans were surrounded and annihilated by Santa Anna's forces at the Alamo fortress in San Antonio. However, the following month saw Sam Houston defeat Santa

Anna at the Battle of San Jacinto. In return for his life, the Mexican general agreed to recognize the independence of Texas. It continued as a separate country for nine years, when it was annexed to the United States, leading to the war with Mexico in 1846.

"TIERRA Y LIBERTAD." Spanish phrase meaning "Land and Liberty." It was the rallying cry of the forces of Emiliano Zapata.

TLALOC. The Toltec god of rain and water, absorbed into the Aztec religion. Even today Mexican Indians sometimes consider Tláloc a Catholic saint and patron for rain.

TLAXCALA (CITY). The capital of the state of Tlaxcala in central Mexico. A picturesque small city famous for its textiles. Its Church of San Francisco, built in 1521, claims to be the oldest church in Mexico.

TLAXCALA (STATE). An inland state in central Mexico, east of the Federal District. The smallest state in the republic with only 3,914 square kilometers. Its 1976 population totaled 498,000, making it densely populated. In the Aztec language, Tlaxcala means "rocky place." It is on a plateau with a mean elevation of 7,000 feet above sea level. In its southern rim is the dormant Malinche volcano.

TOLSA, MANUEL. 1755-1816. Spanish architect, sculptor and the dominant figure of his period. In 1790 he was named director of the recently formed Academia de las Tres Nobles Artes de San Carlos and contributed a great deal of his genius to near completion of the facade of the Mexico City Cathedral. However, his most famous work is the equestrian statue of Carlos IV ("El Caballito"), located on the Paseo de la Reforma in Mexico City. Even though it is considered to be one of the finest works of its kind in the world, it had to be hidden during the wars of independence in Mexico for fear that it would be destroyed by anti-Spanish mobs.

TOLTEC. The Toltec Indians built a pre-Hispanic civilization from the 9th century A.D. radiating out from Tula, north of the Valley of Mexico. They worshiped Quetzalcóatl, the feathered serpent. Their culture was absorbed by the Aztecs.

TOLUCA. The capital of the state of México, to the west of

the Federal District.   Its 1976 population totaled 149,000.
From its suburbs to Mexico City runs an industrial corridor with automobile and truck factories and related auto
parts plants.

TORREON.   A city in Coahuila state, which serves as an industrial and trade center for the Laguna region of northern Mexico, including the state of Durango.   The hydroelectric dams on the Nazas River allow irrigated cultivation of cotton and grapes.   Torreón has flour mills, cotton gins, chemical plants, copper smelters, and the University of Coahuila medical school.   In the 1950's and
1960's, 900 peasant families from its communal farms
(ejidos) were relocated in Campeche state after a lengthy
drought.

TORRES BODET, JAIME.   1902-1974.   Born in Mexico City.
Diplomat, scholar and statesman.   He was Professor of
French Literature at the National University of Mexico
during the 1920's and went on to have a distinguished career in politics and diplomacy.   He was Minister of Education during the presidencies of Manuel Avila Camacho
and Adolfo López Mateos and will be remembered for his
successful efforts to focus attention on Mexico's educational shortcomings, particularly the problems of illiteracy
and low teachers' wages.   He served as Minister of Foreign Affairs under Miguel Alemán and was Director-
General of UNESCO from 1948 to 1952.   Torres Bodet is
regarded in Mexico as one of that country's outstanding
educators of the twentieth century.

TORRES MANZO, CARLOS.   Born in 1923 in Michoacán.
Economics degree from the National Autonomous Univer-
sity (UNAM).   Graduate studies University of London.
UNAM economics professor 1955-70.   Director of the
Basic Commodities Corporation (CONASUPO) 1964-70.
Minister of Industry and Commerce 1970-74.   Governor
of Michoacán 1974-80.   He formulated the policies of
selling work clothes and non-food consumer goods in
CONASUPO retail stores for poor families.

TORTILLA.   A thin pancake made of corn meal used as bread
or a basic food by Indians and mestizo peasants, as well
as other Mexicans.   It is eaten plain or folded and filled
with vegetables or chopped meat.

TRESGUERRAS, FRANCISCO EDUARDO.   1758-1833.   He was
a kind of renaissance man who excelled in many fields,

but was regarded as an outstanding sculptor and architect.
He preferred the neoclassical style and his famous archi-
tectural works are the Church of Our Lady of Carmen in
Celaya (1807) and the Alarcón Theater in San Luis Potosí
(1827).

TREVIÑO, JACINTO B. 1883-1971. A Revolutionary general
in 1914 who supported Alvaro Obregón and fought Francisco Villa. Minister of Industry, Commerce and Labor in
1918. For supporting General Escobar's unsuccessful revolt in 1929, he went into temporary exile in Texas. He
supported Juan Almazán for President in 1940. He and
General Juan Barragán in 1954 founded the minority opposition Party of the Authentic Mexican Revolution (PARM).

TRUEBA URBINA, ALBERTO. Born in 1906 in Campeche.
Professor of law at the National Autonomous University
(UNAM) 1937-45. A Deputy in the federal Congress.
Governor of Campeche 1955-61. Attorney General of
Yucatán. He is nationally known as the author of the
leading textbooks on constitutional law. For many years
he has been legal adviser to Mexican presidents, labor
leaders, and cabinet ministers.

TUXTEPEC, PLAN OF. Porfirio Díaz's proclamation of
January 1, 1876, signalling the beginning of an armed rebellion against President Sebastián Lerdo de Tejada.
Among the principal points were the call for his resignation, effective suffrage and no re-election of presidents.
Díaz was finally successful towards the end of 1876 and
the following year was installed as constitutional president. Ironically, the effective suffrage and no re-election
issues were to be the rallying cries in forcing Díaz's
resignation in 1910.

TUXTLA GUTIERREZ. The capital of the southernmost state
of Chiapas. An agricultural and commercial center.

- U -

UNAM. The Universidad Nacional Autónoma de México
(UNAM) or National Autonomous University of Mexico.
It was founded in 1551 as the Royal Pontifical University
of New Spain by a decree of Emperor Charles V of Spain,
who also authorized in the same decree the University of
San Marcos in Lima, Peru. Ever since, Peru and Mex-

ico have disputed which had the first university in the New
World. During the Porfirio Díaz dictatorship of 1876-
1911, the National University suspended most operations.
On May 1, 1917, Mexican President Venustiano Carranza
revived it and appointed Natividad Macías as President
with orders to the attorney and educator to expand all
professional courses. During the 1920's, philosopher José
Vasconcelos helped upgrade the programs. On July 10,
1929, Mexican President Emilio Portes Gil had Congress
pass a law making the university autonomous in its administration instead of under the Ministry of Education.
From the 1950's on, radical leftist-led student federations
and unions of both non-teaching and teaching staffs have
plagued UNAM with many serious strikes. By the 1960's,
enrollment exceeded 100,000 students, making UNAM administration unwieldy. Since 1975, Dr. Guillermo Sobe-
rón, a physician and medical professor, as UNAM President (Rector) has been able to reduce tensions and work
stoppages. The vast UNAM campus, with colorful murals
across high-rise buildings and Olympic-sized swimming
and track facilities, opened on a site eleven miles south
of downtown Mexico City in 1952, moving from crowded
colonial-era buildings scattered downtown. The UNAM
campus is adjacent to the Pedregal suburb and is noted
for its modern architecture.

UNION FEDERATIONS see CONFEDERACION DE TRABAJA-
DORES MEXICANOS; LABOR UNION PLURALISM

UNION LIBERAL. A political party formed in 1892 for the
purpose of legitimizing the rule of Porfirio Díaz and dis-
pelling the belief that his was purely a one-man rule.
No other political parties were tolerated.

UNITED STATES-MEXICAN WAR. 1846-1848. This was the
most disastrous war ever fought by Mexico and resulted
in the loss of more than half its territory. Nationalist
fervor was a key factor in both countries. The idea of
Manifest Destiny was popular in the United States and
there were those in Mexico who believed strongly that
Mexican forces would be in Washington, D.C. in a short
period of time.
President Polk's dispatching of American troops into
the area between the Nueces and Rio Grande rivers led
to a formal declaration of war in April of 1846. After
conquering northern Mexico as far as Saltillo, the United
States invaded the interior of Mexico through the port of

Veracruz and forced harsh peace terms on Mexico after
the conquest of Mexico City. See SANTA ANNA, ANTON-
IO LOPEZ DE and GUADALUPE-HIDALGO, TREATY OF.

UNIVERSIDAD AUTONOMA METROPOLITANA. In the 1970's,
the Metropolitan Autonomous University (UAM) was developed in Mexico City to relieve the pressures of more than
100,000 students enrolled in the National Autonomous University of Mexico (UNAM). This UAM in Mexico City,
also was created by and is financed by the federal government.

UNIVERSIDAD NACIONAL AUTONOMA DE MEXICO see
UNAM

UNIVERSITIES. Each of the 31 states of the republic maintains a state university, but the federal government provides more funds for these institutions than do the state
governments. In addition to the UNAM and the Metropolitan University, the federal government also operates the
National Polytechnic Institute (IPN), a National Agricultural College, and several technological institutes and
centers. The republic has 41 privately-owned universities, e.g. Ibero-American University, a Catholic institution in Mexico City, and the distinguished Monterrey Institute of Technology.

UNIVERSITY OF THE AMERICAS. Established in Mexico City
by Professor Paul Murray in 1940 as Mexico City College, the University of the Americas later moved to its
extensive campus at Cholula, Puebla, near Puebla City.
It is a privately-owned institution offering courses in both
English and Spanish, organized with the degree programs
and semester-hour or quarter-hour concepts of universities in the United States. In the 1970's, it has increased
the proportion of Mexican students, but still draws hundreds of students from the U.S., Canada, and other foreign countries.

UNO MAS UNO. After the associates of Mexican President
Luis Echeverría purged the editorial staff of publisher
Julio Scherer García from the leading daily newspaper
Excelsior in July 1976, these staffers established the
Mexico City daily Uno Más Uno to preserve an editorial
voice independent of the Echeverristas. As of late 1979,
the new daily had built a circulation of readers seeking
editorials moderately independent of the Revolutionary
coalition and of liberal reform viewpoints.

URAGA, JOSE L. An army general who was chosen in 1853 by Mexican President Mariano Arista to defend the government, but instead switched to the opposition forces of General Santa Anna. In 1860 the pro-clerical conservative forces of President Miguel Miramón defeated the rebel forces of Uraga. In 1864 Uraga assumed command of an army committed to the liberal reform cause of Benito Juárez but when faced with a larger number of French troops of Emperor Maximilian in western Mexico, Uraga defected, ending his career in disgrace after the French withdrew from Mexico and the republic was restored in 1866.

URBINA, LUIS GONZAGA. 1864-1934. Poet and journalist. A close friend of Gutiérrez Nájera, he also admired Justo Sierra greatly. He spent the first decade of the Mexican Revolution (1910-1920) outside of the country, but wrote and published a great deal. His more famous poems are "Lámparas en agonía" and "El poema de Mariel." The two-volume Antología del centenario (1910) was planned in cooperation with Justo Sierra and to this day is regarded as a masterpiece of literary research.

URBINA, TOMAS. A Revolutionary general who in 1914 became the executive officer for General Francisco Villa's Army of the North. In late 1915 Urbina deserted his post, going into hiding and taking the army's payroll funds, which were never recovered. Before becoming an officer under Villa, Urbina had been a cattle rustler in Chihuahua.

URBINA Y FRIAS, SALVADOR. (1885-1963). An attorney who became Attorney General for President Carranza in 1914. A justice of the federal Supreme Court for 21 years, from 1923 to 1935 and from 1940 to 1951, and Chief Justice during 1941-51.

URDIÑOLA, FRANCISCO DE. Spanish colonizer who was one of the first to develop a wine industry in New Spain. He had extensive holdings in Parras, Coahuila.

URUCHURTU, ERNESTO P. Born in 1906 in Hermosillo, Sonora. An attorney who was a justice of the Sonora Supreme Court. Then legal adviser for the Ministry of Agriculture and for the National Bank of Ejido Credit. Assistant Minister of the Interior (Gobernación) 1946-51. Minister of Gobernación 1951-52. Governor of the Federal District under Presidents Ruiz Cortines, López

Mateos, and Díaz Ordaz, from 1952 to 1966. He was forced to resign because his vigorous urban renewal destroyed Mexico City slums which had yielded high profits to those in the power elite, though official charges were for misadministration of squatters and failure to relocate all affected slum dwellers.

USIGLI, RODOLFO. Born on November 17, 1905, in Mexico City, and died there on June 18, 1979. Mexico's leading playwright of the 20th century. He wrote more than 40 plays, including Medio tono in 1937, La mujer no hace milagros in 1939, and La familia Cena en casa in 1942. His El gesticulador, written in 1937, was Mexico's first theatrical satire of 1910 Revolutionary leaders. His Corona de sombras in 1947 dealt with the tragedy of Empress Carlota. His 1961 Corona de fuego dealt with Aztec rulers, and his 1965 Corona de luz with the Virgin of Guadalupe. His plays El niño y la niebla, A dónde van nuestras hijas, and Otras primaveras were also made into films. Between 1944 and 1973 he held diplomatic posts periodically, including ambassadorships to Norway, Lebanon, and Belgium, and posts in Britain and France.

UXMAL. An ancient Maya city in the state of Yucatán 55 miles south of Mérida. Founded between 980 and 1007 A.D. by Maya prince Hun Uitzil Chac. Its architecture reflects the high civilization of the Maya Empire. The largest building is the Governor's House, one of the most important pre-Hispanic monuments in Mexico. It rests on a terrace 500 feet north and south and 590 feet east and west. The building is 300 feet long, and decorated with complex designs telling about Maya history. Masks, dates, and historical incidents are carved into the cornices and doorways. Adjacent is the House of Turtles. There is a ball court 115 feet long on which an ancient form of basketball was played. Four buildings comprise the Houses of the Nuns, in which Maya girls lived cloistered lives dedicated to their religion. A pyramid called the House of the Magician or Sorcerer is 102 feet high and is decorated with ornamented carved stones and detailed symbols. Depicted are serpents and a rain god. There are interior chambers and an interior stairway as well as a steep exterior stairway. Artifacts from Uxmal have revealed much pre-Hispanic history of Maya kings, princes, and the priesthood, as well as their beliefs and philosophy.

- V -

VALDES MUÑOZ, JORGE. Born in Hermosillo, Sonora, in
1926. Vocational school. Owner of a printing shop in
Hermosillo. Municipal and state committee member for
the National Action Party (PAN) and since 1958 on the
PAN national council. He became the first opposition-
party Mayor of a state capital in modern Mexican history
in 1967 when he defeated the PRI candidate. Mayor of
Hermosillo 1967-70. PAN candidate for Governor of
Sonora in 1979.

VALENCIA, FRAY MARTIN DE. 1453-1534. Spanish missionary who was very active in New Spain, he was the
head of the first group of Franciscan missionaries to ar-
rive in Mexico City. He also established the first monastery and the first school dedicated to Indian education.
He never stopped fighting to obtain better living conditions
for the Indians and won their respect and cooperation.

VALENZUELA ESQUERRO, GILBERTO. Born in 1922 in
Mexico City. A civil engineer. He was Assistant Director of construction for the Public Works Ministry 1952-
59. He directed public works for the Federal District
1959-64. Minister of Public Works in the presidential
cabinet 1964-70. He was a key consulting engineer for
Mexico City's expanding system of expressways in the
1950's and 1960's.

VALLEJO, DEMETRIO. A labor leader active in the Communist Party while head of the Railroad Workers Union
from 1950 into 1958. He ordered the slow-down work
stoppages on all the railroads in 1958 and the various
railroad strikes in 1959 which threatened to keep major
Mexican crops from reaching domestic and foreign markets before spoiling. President Adolfo López Mateos in
1959 had the federal Attorney General indict and jail Vallejo for sedition under the federal penal code. He was
convicted and served a prison term, with efforts of various leftist groups in the early 1960's petitioning for his
release. As a result of these protests, Article 145 of
the Penal Code was changed, making similar convictions
more difficult.

VAQUERO. A Mexican cowboy or cattle rancher.

VASCONCELOS, JOSE. 1882-1959. Philosopher, educator

and politician. Born in Oaxaca. A member of the Ateneo de la Juventud (The Athenaeum of Youth), after the
Mexican Revolution broke out he supported Madero and
Villa, before going into exile (1915-1920). Upon his return to Mexico he was appointed Rector of the National
University of Mexico and between 1920 and 1924 served
as Minister of Education. He dedicated himself totally
to his work and was the driving force behind the renewed
emphasis on rural education and the general raising of
the literacy level in Mexico. Vasconcelos encouraged
muralists like Rivera and Orozco to paint on empty walls
all over the country, the results bringing world-wide fame
to many of Mexico's artists. In 1929 he ran for president, but was defeated. A prolific writer, his most famous work is La raza cósmica (The Cosmic Race), a
work in which he envisions a new, dynamic people being
formed out of the union of Indians and Europeans. His
autobiography, Ulises criollo, written in 1935, is still
widely read in Mexico.

VAZQUEZ DE CORONADO Y ALDES, FRANCISCO. 1510-
1554. Spanish explorer born in Salamanca. Arrived in
New Spain in 1535 and held various political posts before
embarking on his famous expedition (1540-1542) to find
the legendary Seven Cities of Cíbola and the Kingdom of
Quivira, reputed to possess great wealth. Although they
proved to be nothing more than a legend, Coronado did
make valuable discoveries, exploring from Arizona to
Oklahoma and reaching as far north as Kansas. Nevertheless, he returned to Mexico a disappointed man.

VAZQUEZ ROJAS, GENARO. 1931-1972. A school teacher
in San Luis, Guerrero, who organized an anti-government
Independent Campesino Federation (CCI) and a Civic Committee to organize student strikes throughout Guerrero in
1961, helping to force the federal government to remove
Caballero Aburto as Governor of Guerrero for not stop-
ping a break down of law and order. Vázquez was captured with other Marxist guerrillas at the National Liberation Movement headquarters in 1967 and imprisoned until 1968, when he escaped. He kidnapped the President
of the University of Guerrero, Jaime Castrejón Díaz. He
died on February 2, 1972, in an automobile accident in
Morelia while fleeing the police.

VELASCO, LUIS DE. 1511-1564. He was the second viceroy of New Spain and was well-loved because of his kind-

ness and generosity. He became viceroy in 1550, after
the great Antonio de Mendoza decided to become viceroy
in Peru. With the backing of the king, Velasco began a
policy of humane treatment of the Indians and gave many
of them their freedom. In 1553 he founded the University
of Mexico, extended the power of Spain into Durango and
opened up vast silver mines to add to the wealth of the
motherland. Velasco's vast accumulation of power and
authority was the reason why a viceroy was relegated to
only one six-year term of office, although he personally
always enjoyed a reputation of honesty. He was truly
mourned by the poor classes when he died.

VELAZQUEZ CARDENAS Y LEON, JOAQUIN. 1732-1786.
   Scientist and astronomer. He traveled to California to
   observe Venus passing across the sun. He also founded
   a school for mining engineers.

VELAZQUEZ SANCHEZ, FIDEL. Born on April 24, 1900,
   in Villa Romero, México. The best known, most powerful, and longest tenured labor leader in Mexican history.
   Secretary of the Union of Milk Industry Workers in 1921.
   Then head of the Milk Workers Union for the Federal
   District. Participated in the founding of the Federation
   of Mexican Workers (CTM) in 1936. Member of the Executive Committee of the CTM 1936-40. Elected the head
   or Secretary General of the CTM in 1946 for a six-year
   term, and re-elected by the CTM membership every six
   years since, in 1952, 1958, 1964, 1970, and 1976. The
   only head of a Labor Federation in Latin America to be
   in office more than 33 years. An inner-circle adviser
   on labor for Mexican Presidents, for the labor sector of
   the Institutional Revolutionary Party (PRI), and for Ministers of Labor.

VERACRUZ (CITY). The largest port in the republic, on the
   Gulf of Mexico, 200 air miles east of Mexico City. Its
   harbor is protected by breakwaters built on reefs and
   small islands. In the age before air flight and automobiles, it was Mexico's front door, where visitors from
   abroad entered by sea, then took horses or wagons to the
   interior. It is the terminal of Mexico's first railroad,
   connecting to Mexico City and to lines north and south.
   In the harbor is the San Juan de Ulúa Fort, an island
   prison before 1914 and nearby the colonial Santiago Fortress. It is Mexico's major port for shipping or receiving exports. Its 1976 population totaled 278,000. It was

the site of the first Spanish colonial headquarters in Mexico, built in 1519 by Hernán Cortés as his base for the conquest of Mexico. He called it Villa de la Vera Cruz or Town of the True Cross. The original settlement was moved down the coast but re-established in 1599. It was pillaged by pirates in 1653 and in 1712. It was captured by United States troops under General Winfield Scott on March 29, 1847, in the U.S.-Mexican War. It was captured by the French army occupying Mexico in 1861 to install Maxmilian as Emperor, until 1866. In 1914 when Mexican President Victoriano Huerta challenged the right of U.S. naval forces to be offshore, U.S. troops occupied Veracruz and remained for several months, leading to Huerta's resignation. It has Mexico's major manufacturers of cigars, liquors, and chocolate.

VERACRUZ (STATE). A state in eastern Mexico bordering the Gulf of Mexico along a 400-mile coastline from the Tamesí River in the north to the Isthmus of Tehuantepec to the southeast, extending 100 miles inland for an area of 72,815 square kilometers. Its 1976 population totaled 4.9 million. Its state capital is Jalapa. Veracruz is a mountainous state with a narrow, humid coastal plain cut off by the Sierra Madre Oriental in its central and western regions. Mexico's highest peak, the extinct volcano Orizaba rises 18,700 feet above sea level. The state has several rivers, the chief navigable one being the Coatzacoalcos in the southeast. Heavy rainfall yields tropical vegetation. Veracruz has more oil wells producing petroleum than any other state and the republic's largest concentration of oil reserves. It produces rubber, chicle, sugar cane, coffee, tobacco, rum, chocolate, liquors, cattle, and wood. In pre-Hispanic times, the state had the Olmec Indian civilization, and is the home of the Totonaca Indians famous for their "Flying Dancers" who descend from a pole whirling from ropes tied to their ankles. Veracruz originated the tropical folk music known as "La Bamba" songs, featuring a harp, violin, and small guitars. Folk singers and dancers often wear peaked straw hats and white cotton jackets and trousers, known as "jarocho" clothes. Women folk dancers use white fans and wear lace and embroidered white dresses.

VICARIO, LEONA. 1789-1842. A heroine of the independence movement, she married Andrés Quintana Roo. Among her personal sacrifices was the donation of all her jewelry to the cause of independence. After Mexico became inde-

pendent she worked closely with her husband in various
political and intellectual pursuits.

VICENCIO TOVAR, ABEL. Born in 1925 in Mexico City.
An attorney who has been a leader of the National Action
Party (PAN) since the 1950's. A Deputy in Congress
1963-67 and 1973-76. A PAN district, then regional
chairman. PAN Secretary General. Since 1978 he has
been PAN president.

VICTORIA, GUADALUPE. 1786-1843. Independence leader
and president, he was born in Durango and his real name
was Juan Manuel Félix Fernández. He changed it to
Guadalupe Victoria to show his dedication to the cause
of Mexican independence. After Morelos's death he stayed
in the mountains around Veracruz and waged guerrilla
war against the Spaniards, carrying on for years even
after his own men had abandoned him. After Iturbide
came to power he worked with him, but became disillu-
sioned and joined Santa Anna's successful revolt against
Iturbide in 1823. Guadalupe Victoria served as president
from 1824 to 1828, becoming more conservative during
the last years of his administration. He was the only
Mexican president in many years to serve out his full
term.

VILLA, PANCHO (FRANCISCO). 1877-1923. His real name
was Doroteo Arango. As a child he worked as a peon on
a hacienda in northern Mexico, but had to flee for his
life when he defended his sister against the advances of
one of the hacienda's owners. He then began his life as
a bandit leader, showing skill as a soldier, organizer and
administrator. Even though he lacked a formal education,
he did teach himself to read and write. His strongest
trait was his ability to cast fear into his opponents and
when necessary he was known to practice extreme cruelty.
    Villa supported Madero against Díaz and later fought
against Huerta and Carranza. The high point of his success was in 1914, when for five months he and Zapata
occupied Mexico City and took turns sitting in the presidential chair. However, from 1915 on his fortunes began
to wane and he finally lost out to Carranza, the División
del Norte sharply diminishing in numbers as Villa's defeats mounted. It is purported that at one time the División, the name given to Villa's forces, numbered 50,000.
In an effort to discredit Carranza, he raided Columbus,
New Mexico, the result being that General Pershing

mounted a punitive expedition to either kill or capture
him. Curiously enough, the people of Columbus erected
a statue to the bandit leader in their town square. While
he was never captured by Pershing's forces, indications
are that he was badly wounded. Villa retired to a hacienda in 1920 and was assassinated in 1923.

VILLARREAL, ANTONIO I. 1879-1944. A normal school
professor from Nuevo León who was seriously considered
as a presidential candidate three times, the last time in
1934 before the Revolutionary coalition decided on Lázaro
Cárdenas. He headed the Mexican Liberal Party in 1906
in exile in the U.S. He opened the Casa del Obrero in
1914 to revive Mexican labor unions. As a 1912 general,
he was Governor of Nuevo León. Then a key envoy of
President Madero in Europe. Minister of Agriculture
in 1920.

VIZCAINO MURRAY, FRANCISCO. Born in 1935 in Guaymas,
Sonora. A certified public accountant. Ph.D. in admin-
istrative sciences from the National Polytechnic Institute
(IPN). Secretary General of the Social Security system
(IMSS) 1970-72. As Assistant Minister of Health and
Welfare 1972-76 he became Mexico's and Latin America's
first Director of Environmental Protection, formulating
and administering pioneer regulations against pollution of
Mexico's air, water, and other resources. He initiated
emissions control testing for trucks and automobiles in
Mexico and emissions controls for factories.

VOTAN. An early Mayan ruler who founded the Kingdom of
Xibablá, which comprised parts of what are today the Mexican states of Tabasco, Campeche and Yucatán.

- W -

WALKER, WILLIAM. 1824-1860. Born in Nashville, Ten-
nessee. Although this American soldier of fortune is famous principally for his intrusions into Central America,
he did invade Lower California in 1853 and proclaimed
this region and Sonora an independent nation. Shortly
afterwards he was driven out of Mexico.

WARD, H. G. British chargé d'affaires in Mexico during the
1820's, he was a supporter of the conservative Scottish
Rite Masons who won out in influence over the liberal

York Rite Masons championed by Gerald Poinsett. Ward's greatest accomplishment was the negotiation of a trade treaty in 1827 between Mexico and England, years before the United States negotiated a similar one.

WATER RESOURCES. On January 9, 1926, the federal Law of Irrigation created the Commission of Irrigation, bringing modern administration of water resources to Mexican government. After his inauguration as President of Mexico on December 1, 1946, Miguel Alemán sent a bill to Congress which was promptly enacted, creating the Ministry of Hydraulic Resources. This entity remained autonomous until December 1976, when newly-inaugurated President José López Portillo merged this ministry with an older one, creating the Ministry of Agriculture and Hydraulic Resources. All hydroelectric dam projects are primarily the concern of the federal government, as well as the administration of usage and conservation of rivers, streams, and lakes within the national territory. Only 7 percent of Mexico's territory can be cultivated with natural rainfall. With the extensive building of hydroelectric dams since the 1940's, an additional 7 percent of the national territory has been brought under cultivation. A subministry, the Bureau of Environmental Protection within the Ministry of Health and Welfare, also concerns itself with potable water and with anti-pollution programs. The Boards for Water and Drainage found within each municipality are federal, and coordinate with state and local officials for operations involving sanitation and household and personal use of water.

WILSON, HENRY LANE. 1857-1932. Born in Indiana. American diplomat and ambassador to Mexico, 1910-1913. He was an opponent of Madero and a supporter of Huerta, believing that Madero's government was incapable of maintaining order. He strongly defended American business interests and is universally condemned for not trying to prevent Madero's murder at the hands of Huerta's assassins. President Woodrow Wilson demanded and obtained his resignation in July of 1913.

WILSON, WOODROW. President of the United States from 1912 to 1920. He authorized a punitive expedition into Mexico in 1916 in an effort to capture Pancho Villa because of the latter's raid on Columbus, New Mexico. In 1914, he authorized the occupation of Veracruz by the United States marines in an effort to topple the Huerta

government, a move which contributed greatly in bringing
this about. Wilson followed a foreign policy towards
Mexico based greatly on the concept that if a government
was immoral, then it should be punished. Nowhere was
this more evident than in the case of Huerta.

WORLD WAR TWO. Mexico broke diplomatic relations with
the Axis powers in February 1942 and declared war on
them on May 28, 1942, after German submarines sank
Mexican tankers. A treaty with the United States further
allowed farm workers (braceros) to harvest crops in the
U.S. Mexico also sent army and air force units to fight
in the Philippines and Italy.

- X -

XIBABLA, KINGDOM OF see VOTAN

XICALANCAS. A tribe of pre-Hispanic, pre-Aztec Indians
who roamed eastern central Mexico before 1200 A.D.

XICAPEXLI. A painted gourd bowl used by Indians and rural
peasants all over Mexico.

XICOTENACATLE, SANTIAGO FELIPE. From the city of
Tlaxcala, he was the commander of the famous Batallón
de San Blas and died in 1847 while defending Chapultepec
Park from the Americans. The popular belief is that instead of allowing a Mexican flag to fall into the hands of
the American invader, he wrapped it around himself and
was killed defending this flag, which can be seen today
in Chapultepec Castle.

XOCHIMILCO. Approximately 15 miles southeast of downtown
Mexico City are the "floating gardens of Xochimilco." A
tourist attraction, they are not really floating but are
small plots rooted into the Xochimilco Lake bed, forming
numerous canals. In pre-Hispanic times, the Xochimilco
Indians were vassals of the Aztecs. They filled huge
wicker baskets with earth, planted flowers and crops,
tied sections together to make floating tiny farms on their
lake. Over the centuries, the plots became permanently
rooted in the lake bottom. Flat-bottom launches with ven-
dors of flowers, food, and souvenirs now follow boatloads
of tourists up and down the canals, especially on week-
ends. At certain hours, mariachi folk bands serenade

from their own launches, for a fee. In addition to flowers, for many centuries the Xochimilcos basically cultivated vegetables in their garden plots, which they used as tribute for the Aztecs and as the basis for trade among themselves.

- Y -

YAÑEZ, AGUSTIN. Born on May 4, 1904, in Guadalajara, Jalisco. Law degree from the University of Guadalajara. Ph. D. in literature from the National Autonomous University (UNAM). A professor at preparatory and normal schools in Guadalajara. Governor of the state of Jalisco 1953-58. Minister of Education under President Díaz Ordaz 1964-70. One of Mexico's leading novelists since the publication in 1947 of his Al filo del agua, which became a classic throughout Latin America. It depicts small town Mexican life just before the 1910 Revolution. His 1959 novel La creación was widely read throughout Mexico. His 1962 Las tierras flacas is the classic portrayal of Jalisco's regional life-styles.

YAÑEZ, JOSE MARIA. 1803-1880. A military figure who was active against the Spaniards at Tampico in 1829 and in the defense of Veracruz against the French in 1838. His most notable achievement was the defeat at Guaymas of the French adventurer, Raousset de Boulbón, who was attempting to occupy the state of Sonora and turn it into an independent country.

YAQUI. The Yaqui Indians of Sonora through the centuries have refused to assimilate and as late as the 1920's were battling Mexican army troops to have their villages remain outside federal government regulations. Famous as deer hunters, they have folk dances celebrating the hunting of wild game.

YORKINOS. Members of the York Rite, a liberal wing of free masonry which the American Minister, Joel Poinsett brought to Mexico. He encouraged the development of this Masonic lodge in Mexico, as opposed to the conservative, British-supported Scotch Rite. However, internal dissension nullified any chance that the yorkinos would be an important influence in Mexican politics.

YUCATAN DISCOVERY. The first Europeans to land in the

Yucatán peninsula in the southeastern corner of Mexico
were shipwrecked Spaniards in 1512. Sailing from Cuba,
in 1517 Francisco de Córdoba explored the Yucatán coast,
as did Juan de Grijalva in 1518. Their contacts with the
Maya Indians soon spread the tale of that legend of the
white gods coming from the east, which had also been
part of Aztec mythology. Hernán Cortés touched the Yucatán coast in 1519 before launching his conquest from
Veracruz. Francisco Montejo the Elder and the Younger,
father and son, in the 1530's subdued the Maya Empire,
completing the conquest in 1540. In 1542 Montejo the
Younger founded Mérida.

YUCATAN PENINSULA. A projection of southeastern Mexico
between the Gulf of Campeche on the west, the Gulf of
Mexico on the north, and the Caribbean Sea on the east.
Its area of 70,000 square miles comprises three Mexican
states: Yucatán taking up a triangular northern third,
Campeche taking up the southwestern third, and Quintana
Roo taking up the southeastern third of the peninsula.
Mostly a dry flat plain with underground rivers, mes-
quite, cedar, and mahogany trees.

YUCATAN (STATE). It takes up the northern third of the
Yucatán peninsula, with a coastline on the Gulf of Mexico.
The state's area is 39,340 square kilometers and its 1976
population totaled 904,000. Its capital is Mérida. A
range of hills less than 500 feet high run along its border
with the state of Campeche. A dry plain with meager
topsoil. Rainfall occurs from May to September, seeping
through the surface and is collected in underground rivers
and wells called cenotes. Windmills pump water for irrigated cultivation of henequen, corn, and sugar. The
main industries relate to the sisal hemp from henequen
in the manufacture of rope, cord, fiber bags and hats
and shoes. Tourism depends on the ruins of the Maya
Empire at Chichén Itzá, Uxmal, Izamal, and Labná. The
chief port is Progreso. Mérida connected to Mexico City
by railroad in 1950 and by highway in 1961. The state
traditionally has been isolationist and somewhat politically
independent of the federal capital.

YUREN AGUILAR, JESUS. Born on January 1, 1901, in
Mexico City and died there on September 22, 1973. One
of the most influential labor leaders in modern Mexican
history and a close associate of Fidel Velázquez, whose
pro-government position attracted Yurén in 1941, after

his earlier activities with anti-establishment Marxist labor leader Vicente Lombardo Toledano. Head of the Sanitation Workers Union of the Federal District in 1922.
He was one of the founders of the Mexican Workers Federation (CTM) in 1936. Chief Mexican delegate to the
International Labor Conference in Geneva in 1938. Became a member of the executive committee of the CTM
in 1952. He was Secretary General of the CTM for the
Federal District 1949-73. He was Secretary for Labor
Action of the dominant Institutional Revolutionary Party
(PRI) 1958-64, and a longtime member of the PRI central
executive committee. A Deputy in Congress 1943-46. A
Senator during 1952-58 and 1964-70. He was the voice
of organized labor in the Senate. In the 1920's, he organized the drivers of vehicles for federal government
entities into a Chauffeurs Union in the Service of the
State. During the period 1941-48, he kept numerous key
labor leaders solidly in the CTM and away from smaller
rival anti-establishment unions and federations.

- Z -

ZABLUDOWSKY, MOISES. Born in Mexico City in 1959.
One of the most promising Mexican young artists. In
1977 he had his first one-man show and from that time
on has participated in many exhibitions, among them one
being held at the Bronx Museum of Arts in New York
City. Representative of his works are "Bicicleta" and
"Muro de los lamentos."

ZACATECAS (CITY). The capital of the state of Zacatecas,
at an elevation of 8,050 feet above sea level in the Sierra
Madre Occidental, with steep, narrow streets. It is surrounded by six peaks, including El Grillo and La Bufa.
Its 1976 population totaled 98,000. It was founded in 1548
by Juan de Tolosa, who discovered rich silver deposits
mined by the Zacateco Indians. He and another explorer,
Cristóbal de Oñate with the silver mines became the
richest men in Mexico. By 1832, the mines had produced bullion valued at 667 million pesos. In this century, its mining activity has decreased. In 1914 General
Francisco Villa won a Revolutionary battle here, celebrated in the popular song "Marcha Zacatecas," the official
march of the Mexican army. Colonial buildings include
the Cathedral built in 1612 and the Municipal Palace.
On La Bufa mountain peak is the Los Remedios Chapel,
the shrine of the Huichol Indians of the area.

ZACATECAS (STATE). A state in the central plateau of Mexico, with an area of 75,040 square kilometers. Its 1976 population totaled 1.1 million. It is bounded on the north by Coahuila, on the east by San Luis Potosí, on the south by Aguascalientes, and on the west by Jalisco and Durango. The Sierra Madre Occidental runs northwest to southeast across the state. There are valleys with temperate climate and even rainfall and there are deserts with cactus and mesquite. The rivers are tributaries of the Río Grande de Santiago, which empties into the Pacific Ocean. Silver, copper, gold, and lead are mined. Cattle, sheep, and mules are raised. Mining centers are Zacatecas city, Mazapil, Fresnillo, Concepción, Sombrerete, and Ojocaliente.

ZAMNA. One of the very first known Mayan leaders, he probably lived in the latter part of the seventh century. Legend has it that he was a priest and a scientist who specialized in plants and medicine. However, his greatest work was the naming of the many geographical sites on the Yucatán Peninsula, such as the lakes, plains and forests.

ZAMORA, ADOLFO. Born in 1902 in Nicaragua. Studied at the Sorbonne, Paris, 1926-30. Law degree from the National Autonomous University (UNAM). Professor of social welfare at UNAM. Professor of administration at the National Polytechnic Institute (IPN). He was the author of the 1943 Social Security Law which began the system in the republic.

ZAPATA, EMILIANO. 1880-1919. Born in Morelos. Indian leader and revolutionary, he sponsored the Plan of Ayala, which called for immediate land reform, the land to be given to peasants who had none. He was probably the most idealistic of all the leaders of the Mexican Revolution. Originally sided with Madero, but turned against him when he failed to carry out needed land reforms. He and Villa captured Mexico City in 1914 and shared the presidential chair. At one time during the Revolution he controlled most of southern Mexico and was staunchly supported and idealized by his men. He was assassinated by agents of Carranza, having been led into an ambush in which he never suspected foul play. The Mexican government considers him to be one of the greatest heroes of the Mexican Revolution and erected a statue to his memory, placing it on the Calzada de Tlalpan in Mexico City during the administration of Adolfo Ruiz Cortines.

ZAPATA LOREDO, FAUSTO. Born in 1940 in San Luis Po-
tosí. A reporter, then an editor for the daily newspaper
La Prensa in Mexico City. Assistant Minister of the
Presidency 1970-76. Press secretary for the National
Campesino Federation (CNC) 1968. Press secretary for
President Luis Echeverría, then for President José López
Portillo, since 1970.

ZAPOTEC. The Zapotec Indians of Oaxaca, related to the
Mixtec Indians of the same region, in the 14th century
built a civilization with pictograph writing and huge temples at Monte Albán and Mitla. Today in Oaxaca the
Zapotecs and Mixtecs number several hundred thousand.

ZARAGOZA, IGNACIO. 1829-1862. Mexican general and national hero. Born in Texas when it was still a part of
Mexico. A strong supporter of Juárez, he served as
Minister of War in his cabinet, but resigned after less
than a year to devote himself full time to his military
career. His forces dealt the French army a crushing
defeat at the Battle of Puebla on May 5, 1862, and for
this victory still commands the respect and admiration
of his countrymen. The Fifth of May (El Cinco de Mayo)
is celebrated as a national holiday in Mexico and it set
back by two years the French occupation of Mexico and
the establishment of Maximilian and the Second Empire.
Unfortunately, shortly after this victory Zaragoza contracted typhoid fever and died. Puebla was renamed
Puebla de Zaragoza in his honor.

ZAVALA, LORENZO DE. 1788-1836. Born in Yucatán, he
was a politician who held several high posts in various
governments after Mexican independence. After a falling
out with Santa Anna, he settled in Texas and fought for
its independence, losing his Mexican citizenship. When
Texas declared its independence in 1836, he became that
country's first vice-president. Mexicans generally regard
him as a traitor.

ZEA, LEOPOLDO. Born in 1912 in Mexico City. The longtime Dean of philosophy and letters at the National Autonomous University (UNAM) who became one of Mexico's
leading non-fiction authors and essayists. His 1943 book
El positivismo en México won the annual Book Fair
award. In his 1955 América en la conciencia de Europa
he stressed the future role of Latin America as a bridge
between Old World and New World cultures.

ZEMPOALTEPETL. The highest mountain peak in the state of Oaxaca, reaching 11,148 feet.

ZEPEDA, ERACLIO. Born in 1937 in Chiapas. He studied and taught literature at the University of Veracruz and since the 1950's has become nationally known as a short story writer in magazines ranging from Situaciones to Revista Mexicana de Literatura.

ZERMEÑO, MANUEL. Born in 1901 in Guadalajara, Jalisco. Graduated from the Naval Academy at Veracruz. Rose through the officer ranks to Admiral. Commander of the Fleet 1952-55. Minister of the Navy 1958-64. He modernized Mexico's naval ships by equipping them with missiles.

ZIHUATANEJO. A fishing port on the Pacific Ocean in the state of Guerrero, about 150 miles northwest of Acapulco. In the 1970's it has become a fashionable tourist resort.

ZOCALO. The main square of Mexico City, it is officially known as the Plaza de la Constitución and is one of the largest in the world.

ZORRILLA MARTINEZ, PEDRO. Born in 1933 in Monterrey, Nuevo León. Law degree from the National School of Law 1955. Ph.D. in economics from the University of Paris 1958. Professor at the National Autonomous University (UNAM), then at Ibero-American University. Attorney General of the Federal District 1972-73. Governor of Nuevo León 1973-79. He helped develop the National Border Industrial Program. In the 1960's, he developed an Institute of Political Training for the dominant Institutional Revolutionary Party (PRI).

ZULOAGA, FELIX. 1813-1876. Born in Sonora. General, political leader and President of Mexico. Originally a liberal who supported Comonfort, but he turned against him and forced him into exile, becoming President in 1858 and serving until December of that year. He repealed the Laws of Reform and was himself forced into exile by Miramón. This may have saved his life, for he lived out the French Intervention in Cuba, returning to Mexico afterward.

ZUMARRAGA, JUAN DE. 1468-1548. The first bishop of Mexico City and one of the greatest to ever occupy this

key post. Carlos V came to know Zumárraga personally,
spending Holy Week in the same Spanish monastery where
the future bishop of Mexico lived. When residents of New
Spain asked for a bishop, Carlos V asked Rome to send
Zumárraga. He was also authorized to use the title,
"Protector de los Indios." He was known as a great
benefactor of the Indians and among his major accomplishments were the building of the Cathedral of Mexico City,
the introduction of the printing press in Mexico and the
founding of a school for Indian noblemen, el Colegio de
Santa Cruz de Tlatelolco. However, the most dramatic
event during his governance was the appearance of the
Virgin of Guadalupe to Juan Diego, a poor Indian laborer.
After Bishop Zumárraga demanded proof of the Virgin's
apparition, Juan Diego presented him with fresh roses and
a painting of the Virgin inside his cloak, after which he
recognized the sincerity of Juan Diego. Bishop Zumárraga is buried in the Cathedral of Mexico City.

ZUÑIGA, ARMANDO. A painter born in 1948. He studied
at the Escuela Nacional de Arquitectura of the Universidad
Nacional Autónoma de México and is known primarily in
Mexico.

ZUÑIGA, FRANCISCO. Contemporary painter. One of his
most famous works is "Desnudo."

BIBLIOGRAPHY

PRE-1910 ERA

Adams, Richard E. W., ed. The Origins of Maya Civilization. Albuquerque: University of New Mexico Press, 1977.

Altman, Ida and James Lockhart, eds. The Provinces of Early Mexico. Los Angeles: Latin American Center Publications, University of California, 1976.

Andrews, George F. Maya Cities: Placemaking and Urbanization. Norman: University of Oklahoma Press, 1975.

Anton, Ferdinand. Ancient Mexican Art. New York: Putnam, 1969.

Bakewell, P. J. Silver Mining and Society in Colonial Mexico: Zacatecas. Cambridge: Cambridge Press, 1974.

Bancroft, Hubert H. History of Mexico. 6 Volumes. San Francisco: The History Company, 1883-1888.

Bannon, John F. The Spanish Conquistadores: Men or Devils? New York: Holt, Rinehart and Co., 1960.

Bauer, K. Jack. The Mexican War, 1846-1848. New York: Macmillan, 1974.

Bazant, Jan. A Concise History of Mexico from Hidalgo to Cardenas. Cambridge: Cambridge University Press, 1977.

Beals, Carleton. Porfirio Díaz, Dictator of Mexico. Philadelphia: J. B. Lippincott, 1932.

Benítez, Fernando. The Century After Cortés. Joan MacLean, translator. Chicago: University of Chicago Press, 1965.

Benson, Elizabeth P. The Maya World. New York: Crowell, 1977.

Benson, Nettie Lee, ed. Mexico and the Spanish Cortes, 1810-1822. Austin: University of Texas Press, 1966.

Bernal, Ignacio. Mexico Before Cortez: Art, History and Legend. Garden City, New York: Doubleday and Co., 1963.

237

Bibliography   238

_____. Museo Nacional de Antropología de México. México,
D. F.: Aguilar, 1967.

_____. The Olmec World. Doris Heyden and Fernando Horcasi-
tas, translators. Berkeley: University of California Press, 1969.

Blancke, W. Wendell. Juárez of Mexico. New York: Praeger,
1971.

Blumberg, Arnold. The Diplomacy of the Mexican Empire, 1863-
1867. Philadelphia: American Philosophical Society, 1971.

Bobb, Bernard E. The Viceregency of Antonio María Bucareli in
New Spain, 1771-1779. Austin: University of Texas Press, 1962.

Bolton, Herbert E. Rim of Christendom. A Biography of Eusebio
Francisco Kino, Pacific Coast Pioneer. New York: Russell and
Russell, 1960.

_____. The Spanish Borderlands. New Haven: Yale University
Press, 1921.

Brundage, Burr Cartwright. A Rain of Darts: The Mexican Aztecs.
Austin: University of Texas Press, 1972.

Brunhouse, Robert L. Sylvanus G. Morley and the World of the Ancient Mayas. Norman: University of Oklahoma Press, 1971.

Burland, Cottie Arthur. Montezuma, Lord of the Aztecs. New
York: Putnam, 1973.

_____ and Werner Forman. Feathered Serpent and Smoking Mirror. New York: Putnam, 1975.

Caballero, Romeo Flores. Counterrevolution: The Role of the
Spaniards in the Independence of Mexico, 1804-1838. Jaime E.
Rodríguez, translator. Lincoln: University of Nebraska Press,
1974.

Calderón de la Barca, Frances Erskine. Life in Mexico. Garden
City, New York: Doubleday, 1966.

Callcott, Wilfrid H. Santa Anna. Hamden, Conn.: Archon Books,
1963.

Cantu, Caesar C. Cortés and the Fall of the Aztec Empire. Los
Angeles: Modern World Publishing Co., 1966.

Carasco, Pedro, Johanna Broda, et al. Estificación social en la
Mesoamérica Prehispánica. México, D.F.: Centro de Investigaciones Superiores Instituto Nacional de Antropología e Historia,
1976.

Carbia, Romulo D. Historia de la leyenda negra hispanoamericana. Buenos Aires: Patagonia Press, 1943.

Caruso, John A. The Liberators of Mexico. Gloucester, Mass.: Peter Smith Press, 1967.

Caso, Alfonso. The Aztec: People of the Sun. Lowell Dunham, translator. Norman: The University of Oklahoma Press, 1958.

Castaneda, Carlos E., editor and translator. The Mexican Side of the Texas Revolution by the Chief Mexican Participants. Dallas: P. L. Turner Company, 1956.

Castro Leal, Antonio, ed. La novela del México colonial, 2 Volumes. México, D. F.: Aguilar, 1969.

Chamberlain, Robert S. The Conquest and Colonization of Yucatan, 1517-1550. New York: Octagon Books, 1966.

Chapman, Charles E. A History of California: The Spanish Period. New York: MacMillan, 1921.

Charlot, Jean. Mexican Art and the Academy of San Carlos, 1785-1915. Austin: University of Texas Press, 1962.

Chevalier, François. Land and Society in Colonial Mexico: The Great Hacienda. Berkeley: University of California Press, 1970.

Clavijero, Francisco Javier. Historia antigua de México. México, D. F.: Editorial Porrúa, S. A., 1958.

Coe, Michael. The Jaguar's Children: Pre-Classic Central Mexico. New York: The Museum of Primitive Art, 1965.

_____. The Maya. New York: Praeger, 1966.

_____. Mexico. New York: Praeger, 1962.

Cook, Warren. Flood Tide of Empire, Spain and the Pacific Northwest, 1543-1819. New Haven: Yale University Press, 1973.

Cortés, Hernán. Five Letters of Cortés to the Emperor, 1519-1526. J. Bayard Morris, translator. New York: W. W. Norton & Co., 1962.

Cosío Villegas, Daniel, ed. Historia moderna de México, 7 Volumes. México D. F.: Editorial Hermes, 1955-1966.

_____. The United States Versus Porfirio Díaz. Nettie Lee Benson, translator. Lincoln: University of Nebraska Press, 1963.

Costeloe, Michael P. Church Wealth in Mexico: A Study of the Juzgado de Capellanias in the Archbishopric of Mexico, 1800-1856. Cambridge: The Harvard University Press, 1967.

Davies, Nigel. The Aztecs: A History. New York: Putnam, 1973.

_____. The Toltecs, Until the Fall of Tula. Norman: University of Oklahoma, 1977.

Day, A. Grove. Coronado's Quest. Berkeley: University of California Press, 1964.

Díaz del Castillo, Bernal. The Discovery and Conquest of Mexico, 1517-1521. Edited from the original manuscript published in Mexico by Genaro García and translated by A. P. Maudslay. New York: Farrar, Straus, and Cudahy, 1956.

Durán, Fray Diego. The Aztecs: The History of the Indies of New Spain. Doris Heyden and Fernando Horcasitas, translators. New York: Orion Press, 1964.

Egan, Ferol. The El Dorado Trail. New York: McGraw-Hill, 1970.

Enciso, Jorge. Design Motifs of Ancient Mexico. New York: Dover Publications, 1953.

Faulk, Odie B. and Joseph A. Stout Jr., editors. The Mexican War: Changing Interpretations. Chicago: The Swallow Press, 1973.

Flynn, Gerard C. Sor Juana Inés de la Cruz. New York: Twayne Publishers, 1971.

Foster, Elizabeth Andros, translator and editor. Motolinia's History of the Indians of New Spain. Albuquerque: University of New Mexico, 1950.

Gardiner, Clinton Harvey. The Constant Captain, Gonzalo de Sandoval. Carbondale: Southern Illinois University Press, 1961.

Geiger, Maynard J. The Life and Times of Fray Junípero Serra. Richmond: William Byrd Press, 1959.

Gerber, Paul Neff. The Gadsden Treaty. Gloucester, Mass.: P. Smith, 1923.

Gerhard, Peter. México en 1742. México, D. F.: Porrúa, 1962.

Gibson, Charles. The Aztecs Under Spanish Rule. Stanford: Stanford University Press, 1964.

_____. Spain in America. New York: Harper & Row, 1966.

Gillmor, Frances. Flute of the Smoking Mirror: A Portrait of Nezahualcóyotl, Poet-King of the Aztecs. Albuquerque: University of New Mexico Press, 1949.

Gorenstein, Shirley. Not Forever on Earth. New York: Scribner, 1975.

Greenleaf, Richard E., ed. The Roman Catholic Church in Colonial Latin America. New York: Alfred A. Knopf, 1971.

_____. Zumárraga and the Mexican Inquisition, 1536-1543. Washington, D.C.: Academy of American Franciscan History, 1961.

Gruening, Ernest. Mexico and Its Heritage. New York: Century, 1928.

Hamill, Hugh M. The Hidalgo Revolt: Prelude to Mexican Independence. Gainesville, Florida: University of Florida Press, 1966.

Hanke, Lewis. The Spanish Struggle for Justice in the Conquest of America. Philadelphia: University of Pennsylvania Press, 1949.

Hanna, Alfred Jackson and Kathryn Abbey. Napoleon III and Mexico: American Triumph over Monarchy. Chapel Hill, North Carolina: University of North Carolina Press, 1971.

Harding, Bertita. Phantom Crown: The Story of Maximilian and Carlotta of Mexico. New York: Blue Ribbon Books, 1939.

Harris, Charles. A Mexican Family Empire: The Latifundio of the Sanchez Navarros, 1765-1867. Austin: University of Texas Press, 1975.

Haslip, Joan. The Crown of Mexico: Maximilian and his Empress Carlota. New York: Holt, Rinehart and Winston, 1971.

Helfritz, Hans. Mexican Cities of the Gods: An Archaeological Guide. New York: Praeger, 1970.

Hemming, John. The Conquest of the Incas. New York: Harcourt Brace Jovanovich, 1970.

Horgan, Paul. Conquistadors in North American History. New York: Fawcett World Library, 1963.

Innes, Hammond. The Conquistadors. New York: Knopf, 1969.

Ivanoff, Pierre. Maya. New York: Madison Square Press, 1973.

Jones, Oakah L., Jr. Santa Anna. New York: Twayne Publishers, 1968.

Lansing, Marion Florence. Liberators and Heroes of Mexico and Central America. Freeport, New York: Books for Libraries Press, 1941.

Bibliography   242

León-Portilla, Miguel. Aztec Thought and Culture: A Study of the
Ancient Nahuatl Mind. Jack Emory Davis, translator. Norman:
University of Oklahoma Press, 1963.

_____, ed. The Broken Spears: The Aztec Account of the Con-
quest of Mexico. Boston: Beacon Press, 1966.

Leonard, Irving A. Baroque Times in Old Mexico. Ann Arbor:
University of Michigan Press, 1959.

Lieberman, Mark. Hidalgo: Mexican Revolutionary. New York:
Praeger, 1970.

Liss, Peggy K. Mexico Under Spain, 1521-1556. Chicago: University of Chicago Press, 1975.

López de Gómara, Francisco. Cortés. The Life of the Conqueror
by his Secretary. Lesley Byrd Simpson, editor and translator.
Berkeley: University of California Press, 1964.

McAndrew, John. The Open-Air Churches of Sixteenth-Century Mexico. Cambridge: Harvard University Press, 1965.

McWhiney, Grady and Sue McWhiney, eds. To Mexico with Taylor
and Scott, 1845-1847. Waltham, Mass.: Blaisdell, 1969.

Madariaga, Salvador de. Hernán Cortés: Conqueror of Mexico.
Garden City, New York: Doubleday, 1942.

Magner, James Aloysius. Men of Mexico. Freeport, New York:
Books for Libraries Press, 1942.

Maza, Francisco de la. La Ciudad de México en el siglo XVII.
México, D. F.: Fondo de Cultura Económica, 1968.

Menéndez Pidal, Ramón. El Padre Las Casas. Su doble personali-
dad. Madrid: Espasa Calpe, 1963.

Morley, Sylvanus G. The Ancient Maya. Stanford: Stanford University Press, 3rd edition revised by George W. Brainerd, 1972.

Motolinía, Toribio. Memoriales e historia de los indios de la Nueva
España. Madrid: Atlas, 1970.

Nance, Joseph Milton. After San Jacinto, The Texas-Mexican Frontier, 1836-1841. Austin: University of Texas Press, 1964.

New York City Museum of Modern Art. Twenty Centuries of Mexican
Art. New York: Arno Press, 1972.

Nicholson, Irene. Mexican and Central American Mythology. London: Paul Hamlyn Ltd., 1967.

243 Bibliography

O'Connor, Richard. The Cactus Throne: The Tragedy of Maximilian and Carlota. New York: Putnam, 1971.

Peterson, Frederick A. Ancient Mexico: An Introduction to the Pre-Hispanic Cultures. New York: Capricorn Books, 1962.

Piña Chan, Román. Ciudades arqueológicas de México. México, D.F.: Instituto Nacional de Antropología e Historia, 1963.

Pletcher, David M. Rails, Mines and Progress: Seven American Promoters in Mexico, 1867-1911. Ithaca: Cornell University Press, 1958.

Porter, Muriel Noe. Tlatilco and the Pre-Classic Cultures of the New World. New York: Wenner-Gren Foundation for Anthropological Research, Inc., 1953.

Potash, Robert. El banco de avío en México. El fomento de la industria, 1821-1846. México, D.F.: Fondo de Cultura Económica, 1959.

Prescott, William H. History of the Conquest of Mexico, and History of the Conquest of Peru. New York: The Modern Library, 1936.

Price, Glenn W. Origins of the War with Mexico: The Polk-Stockton Intrigue. Austin: University of Texas Press, 1967.

Rabasa, Emilio. La evolución histórica de México. México, D. F.: Porrúa, 1972.

Ramírez, José Fernando. Mexico During the War with the United States. Walter V. Scholes, editor; Elliott B. Scherr, translator. Columbia, Missouri: University of Missouri, 1950.

Read, John Lloyd. The Mexican Historical Novel, 1826-1910. New York: Russell and Russell, 1973.

Reed, Alma M. The Ancient Past of Mexico. New York: Crown Publishers, 1966.

Reed, Nelson. The Caste War of Yucatan. Stanford: Stanford University Press, 1964.

Ricard, Robert. The Spiritual Conquest of Mexico: An Essay on the Apostolate and the Evangelizing Methods of the Mendicant Orders in New Spain, 1523-1572. Lesley Byrd Simpson, translator. Berkeley: University of California Press, 1966.

Rivet, Paul. Maya Cities. Miriam and Lionel Kochan, translators. London: Elek Books, 1960.

Robertson, William Spence. Iturbide of Mexico. Durham: University of North Carolina Press, 1952.

Bibliography   244

Roeder, Ralph. Juárez and His Mexico: A Biographical History.
New York: The Viking Press, 1947.

Roys, Ralph L. The Book of Chilam Balam of Chumayel. Norman:
University of Oklahoma Press, 1967.

Ruiz, Ramón Eduardo, ed. An American in Maximilian's Mexico
1865-1866: The Diaries of William Marshall Anderson. San Marino, California: The Huntington Library, 1959.

_____. The Mexican War: Was It Manifest Destiny? New York:
Holt, Rinehart and Winston, 1964.

Sahagún, Fray Bernardino de. General History of the Things of New
Spain. Florentine Codex. Arthur J. O. Anderson and Charles E.
Ibble. Santa Fe, New Mexico: School of American Research and
the University of Utah, 1950-1957.

Santa Anna, Antonio López de. The Eagle: The Autobiography of
Santa Anna. Ann Fears Crawford, editor. Austin: Pemberton
Press, 1967.

Sierra, Justo. Evolución política del pueblo mexicano. México,
D. F.: Fondo de Cultura Económica, 1950.

Simpson, Lesley Byrd. The Encomienda in New Spain. Berkeley:
University of California Press, 1950.

Smith, Gene. Maximilian and Carlotta: A Tale of Romance and
Tragedy. New York: William Morrow and Co., 1973.

Smith, Justin H. The War with Mexico. 2 Volumes. Gloucester,
Mass.: Peter Smith, 1963.

Soustelle, Jacques. Arts of Ancient Mexico. London: Thames and
Hudson, 1967.

_____. The Daily Life of the Aztecs on the Eve of the Spanish
Conquest. Patrick O'Brien, translator. Stanford: Stanford University Press, 1970.

Spores, Ronald. The Mixtec Kings and Their People. Norman:
University of Oklahoma Press, 1967.

Spratling, William. More Human Than Divine. México, D. F.: Universidad Nacional Autónoma de México, 1960.

Thompson, John Eric Sidney. Maya Archaeologist. Norman: University of Oklahoma Press, 1963.

_____. Maya History and Religion. Norman: University of Okla-
homa Press, 1970.

_____. The Rise and Fall of the Maya Civilization. Norman: University of Oklahoma Press, 1954.

Timmons, Wilbert H. Morelos: Priest, Soldier, Statesman of Mexico. El Paso, Texas: Texas Western Press, 1970.

Tischendorf, Alfred Paul. Great Britain and Mexico in the Era of Porfirio Díaz. Durham: Duke University Press, 1961.

Turner, John Kenneth. Barbarous Mexico. Austin: University of Texas Press, 1969.

Vaillant, George C. Aztecs of Mexico. Garden City, New York: Doubleday, 1962.

Verrill, A. Hyatt and Ruth Verrill. America's Ancient Civilization. New York: Capricorn Books, 1967.

Von Hagen, Victor W. The Aztec: Man and Tribe. New York: The New American Library, Mentor Books, 1962.

_____. World of the Maya. New York: The New American Library, Mentor Books, 1960.

Wagner, Henry Raup. The Life and Writings of Bartolomé de las Casas. Albuquerque: University of New Mexico Press, 1967.

Weaver, Muriel P. The Aztecs, Mayas and Their Predecessors. New York: Seminar Press, 1972.

Webster, Edna Robb. Early Exploring in the Lands of the Maya. Sherman Oaks, California: Wilmar Publishers, 1973.

Westheim, Paul. The Art of Ancient Mexico. Ursula Bernard, translator. Garden City, New York: Doubleday, 1965.

White, Jon Manchip. Cortés and the Downfall of the Aztec Empire: A Study in a Conflict of Cultures. New York: St. Martin's Press, 1971.

Wilgus, A. Curtis. The Historiography of Latin America. A Guide to Historical Writing, 1500-1800. Metuchen: The Scarecrow Press, 1975.

_____. Histories and Historians of Hispanic America. New York: Cooper Square Publishers, 1965.

Wolf, Eric. R. The Indian Background of Latin American History, The Maya, Aztec, Inca, and Their Predecessors. Robert Wauchope, ed. New York: Alfred A. Knopf, 1970.

_____. Sons of the Shaking Earth. Chicago: University of Chicago Press, 1959.

Zavala, Silvio. The Colonial Period in the History of the New World. México, D. F.: 1962.

Zorita, Alonso de. Life and Labor in Ancient Mexico. Benjamin Keen, translator. New Brunswick, New Jersey: Rutgers University Press, 1963.

MODERN ERA

Adie, Robert F. "Cooperation, Cooptation, and Conflict in a Mexican Peasant Organization," Inter-American Economic Affairs, Winter 1970, pp. 3-25.

Aguilar, Gustavo F. Los presupuestos mexicanos. México, D. F.: Editorial GFA, 1947.

Aguilar, Manuel G. La derrota de un régimen. Hermosillo, Sonora: Imprenta Regional, 1971.

Aguirre Beltrán, Gonzalo. El proceso de aculturación. México, D. F.: Universidad Nacional Autónoma de México, 1957.

_____ y Ricardo Poazas. Instituciones indígenas en el México actual. México, D. F.: UNAM, 1954.

Alba, Victor. Las ideas sociales contemporáneas en México. México, D. F.: Fondo de Cultura Económica, 1960.

_____. The Mexicans: The Making of a Nation. New York: Praeger, 1967.

_____. Politics and the Labor Movement in Latin America. Stanford, Calif.: Stanford University Press, 1968.

Alessio Robles, Miguel. Historia política de la revolución. Mexico, D. F.: Editorial Botas, 1946.

Alisky, Marvin. "Airlines: Makers of Modern Mexico," Mexican-American Review, October 1967, pp. 19-22.

_____. "Budgets of State Governments in Mexico," Public Affairs Bulletin, Vol. 5, No. 2, 1966, pp. 4-8.

_____. "CONASUPO: A Mexican Agency," Inter-American Economic Affairs, Winter 1973, pp. 37-59.

_____. "Early Mexican Broadcasting," Hispanic American Historical Review, November 1954, pp. 515-526.

_____. Government of the Mexican State of Nuevo León. Tempe, Az.: ASU Center for Latin American Studies, 1971.

_____ . The Governors of Mexico. El Paso, Tex.: University of Texas at El Paso Southwestern Studies Monograph 12, 1965.

_____ . "Growth of Newspapers in Mexico's Provinces," Journalism Quarterly, Winter 1960, pp. 75-82.

_____ . Guide to the Government of the Mexican State of Sonora. Tempe, Az.: ASU Center for Latin American Studies, 1971.

_____ . "Jazz in Mexico City," Metronome, April 1955, pp. 26, 44-45.

_____ . "Mexican-Americans Make Themselves Heard," The Reporter, February 9, 1967, pp. 45-48.

_____ . "Mexican Newscasts Link a Nation," The Quill, September 1953, pp. 12-14.

_____ . "Mexico City's Competitive Radio Market," Inter-American Economic Affairs, Winter 1953, pp. 19-27.

_____ . "Mexico: Perspective from India," Mexican-American Review, October 1978, pp. 26-28.

_____ . "Mexico Versus Malthus," Current History, May 1974, pp. 200-203, 227-230.

_____ . "Mexico's Federal Betterment Boards," Public Affairs Bulletin, Vol. 9, No. 4, 1970, pp. 1-6.

_____ . "Mexico's Investigations Ousts High-Level Bureaucrats," USA Today, January 1979, pp. 11-12.

_____ . "Mexico's National Hour on Radio," Nieman Reports, October 1953, pp. 17-18.

_____ . "Mexico's Population Pressures," Current History, March 1977, pp. 106-110, 131-134.

_____ . "Mexico's Rural Radio," Quarterly of Film, Radio, and Television, Summer 1954, pp. 405-417.

_____ . "Mexico's Steel Industry," Intellect, March 1976, pp. 462-465.

_____ . "Mix of Many Ministries," Mexican-American Review, June 1976, pp. 10-16.

_____ . "Radio's Role in Mexico," Journalism Quarterly, Winter 1954, pp. 66-72.

_____ . State and Local Government in Sonora, Mexico. Tempe, Az.: ASU Bureau of Government Research, 1962, 2nd edition 1966.

_____. "Surging Sonora," Arizona Highways, November 1964, pp. 17-37.

_____. "Tranquility: The Colegio de México," Intellect, April 1974, pp. 445-447.

_____. "U.S.-Mexican Border Conflicts," South Eastern Latin Americanist, September 1973, pp. 1-6.

_____. "U.S.-Mexican Relations," Intellect, February 1978, pp. 292-294.

_____. Who's Who in Mexican Government. Tempe, Az.: ASU Center for Latin American Studies, 1969.

Anguiano, Arturo. El estado y la política obrera del Cardenismo. México, D.F.: Ediciones Era, 1975.

Arreola, Juan J. Confabulario and Other Inventions. Austin: University of Texas Press, 1974.

Ashby, Joe C. Organized Labor and the Mexican Revolution Under Cárdenas. Chapel Hill, N.C.: University of North Carolina Press, 1967.

Azuela, Mariano. The Underdogs. Translated by E. Munguía. New York: New American Library, 1963.

Bailey, David C. Viva Cristo Rey: The Cristero Rebellion and the Church-State Conflict in Mexico. Austin: University of Texas Press, 1974.

Beals, Ralph L. "Anthropology in Contemporary Mexico" in James W. Wilkie, Michael C. Meyer, and Edna Monzón de Wilkie, eds., Contemporary Mexico: Papers of the IV International Congress of Mexican History. Berkeley: University of California Press, 1975.

Beezley, William H. Insurgent Governor: Abraham Gonzales and the Mexican Revolution in Chihuahua. Lincoln: University of Nebraska Press, 1973.

Bernstein, Marvin D. The Mexican Mining Industry, 1890-1950. Albany, N.Y.: State University of New York Press, 1964.

Beteta, Ramón. Pensamiento y dinámica de la Revolución Mexicana. México, D.F.: Editorial México Nuevo, 1950.

Blaisdell, Lowell. The Desert Revolution: Baja California, 1911. Madison: University of Wisconsin Press, 1962.

Brady, Haldeen. Pershing's Mission in Mexico. El Paso: University of Texas at El Paso Press, 1966.

Brandenburg, Frank. The Making of Modern Mexico. Englewood Cliffs, N.J.: Prentice-Hall, 1964.

Brenner, Anita. Idols Behind Altars. Boston: Beacon Press, 1970.

Briggs, V. M. and Wendell Gordon. "United States Border Policy," Social Science Quarterly, December 1975, pp. 476-491.

Brown, Lyle C. The Mexican Liberals and Their Struggle Against the Díaz Dictatorship. México, D.F.: Mexico City College Press, 1956.

_____ and James W. Wilkie. "Recent United States-Mexican Relations," in John Braeman, ed., Twentieth Century Foreign Policy. Columbus: Ohio State University Press, 1971.

Brushwood, John S. Mexico in Its Novel: A Nation's Search for Identity. Austin: University of Texas Press, 1966.

Bustamante, Jorge. Espaldas mojadas. México, D.F.: El Colegio de México, 1975.

Call, Tomme C. The Mexican Venture. New York: Oxford University Press, 1963.

Calvert, Peter. The Mexican Revolution, 1910-1914. Cambridge, England: Cambridge University Press, 1968.

_____. Mexico. London: Ernest Benn, 1973.

Camp, D. A., Jr. "Autobiography and Decision-making in Mexican Politics," Journal of Inter-American Studies and World Affairs, May 1977, pp. 275-283.

Camp, Roderic Ai. "Education and Political Recruitment in Mexico: The Alemán Generation," Journal of Inter-American Studies and World Affairs, August 1976, pp. 310-315.

_____. The Education of Mexico's Revolutionary Family. Tucson: University of Arizona Press, 1979.

_____. "Mexican Governors Since Cárdenas," Journal of Inter-American Studies and World Affairs, November 1974, pp. 454-481.

_____. Mexican Political Biographies, 1935-75. Tucson: University of Arizona Press, 1976.

_____. "The Middle-Level Technocrat in Mexico," Journal of Developing Areas, July 1972, pp. 571-581.

_____. "The National School of Economics and Public Life in Mexico," Latin American Research Review, Fall 1975, pp. 137-151.

_____. "A Reexamination of Political Leadership ... in Mexico, 1934-73," Journal of Developing Areas, January 1976, pp. 193-211.

Carlos, Manuel L. Politics and Development in Rural Mexico. New York: Praeger, 1974.

Charlot, Jean. The Mexican Mural Renaissance. New Haven: Yale University Press, 1967.

Chavira, Carlos. La otra cara de México. México, D. F.: Editorial La Nación, 1966.

Clark, Marjorie. Organized Labor in Mexico. Chapel Hill, N. C.: University of North Carolina Press, 1934.

Clendenen, Clarence C. The United States and Pancho Villa. Ithaca, N. Y.: Cornell University Press, 1961.

Cline, Howard. Mexico: Revolution to Evolution, 1940-1960. New York: Oxford University Press, 1963.

_____. The United States and Mexico. New York: Atheneum, 1963.

Cochrane, James D. "Mexico's New Científicos: The Díaz Ordaz Cabinet," Inter-American Economic Affairs, Summer 1967, pp. 67-72.

Cockcroft, James D. Intellectual Precursors of the Mexican Revolution, 1900-1913. Austin: University of Texas Press, 1968.

Cole, William E. Steel and Economic Growth in Mexico. Austin: University of Texas Press, 1967.

Coleman, Kenneth M. Diffuse Support in Mexico. Beverly Hills, Calif.: Sage Publications, 1976.

_____ and John Wanant. "On Measuring Mexican Presidential Ideology Through Budgets," Latin American Research Review, Spring 1975, pp. 77-88.

Córdova, Arnaldo. La formación del poder político en México. México, D. F.: Ediciones Era, 1975.

Cornelius, Wayne A. Politics and the Migrant Poor in Mexico City. Stanford: Stanford University Press, 1975.

Cosío Villegas, Daniel. El estilo personal de gobernar. México, D. F.: Joaquín Mortiz, 1974.

_____. Historia moderna de México. 8 Volumes. México, D. F.: Editorial Hermes, 1948-1965.

_____. El sistema político mexicano. México, D. F.: Joaquín
Mortiz, 1972.

_____. La sucesión: desenlace y perspectivas. México, D. F.:
Joaquín Mortiz, 1975.

_____. La sucesión presidencial. México, D. F.: Joaquín Mor-
tiz, 1974.

_____. The United States Versus Porfirio Díaz. Lincoln: Uni-
versity of Nebraska Press, 1963.

Creelman, James. Díaz: Master of Mexico. New York: Appleton,
1916.

Cronon, E. David. Josephus Daniels in Mexico. Madison: University of Wisconsin Press, 1942.

Cumberland, Charles C., ed. The Meaning of the Mexican Revolution. Boston: D. C. Heath, 1967.

_____. Mexican Revolution: Genesis Under Madero. Austin:
University of Texas Press, 1952.

_____. Mexican Revolution: The Constitutionalist Years. Austin:
University of Texas Press, 1972.

_____. Mexico: The Struggle for Modernity. London: Oxford
University Press, 1968.

Davis, C. L. "Mobilization of Public Support: Case of the Lower
Class in Mexico City," American Journal of Political Science,
November 1976, pp. 653-670.

Dillon, E. J. President Obregón: A World Reformer. London,
England: Hutchinson, 1923.

Dulles, John W. F. Yesterday in Mexico: A Chronicle of the Revolution. Austin: University of Texas Press, 1961.

Eckstein, Susan. The Poverty of Revolution: The State and the Urban Poor in Mexico. Princeton, N.J.: Princeton University
Press, 1977.

Espinoa de los Reyes, Jorge. La distribución del ingreso nacional.
México, D. F.: Escuela Nacional de Economía, 1958.

Fagen, Richard. "Realities of U.S.-Mexican Relations," Foreign
Affairs, July 1977, pp. 685-700.

_____ and William Touhy. Politics and Privilege in a Mexican
City. Stanford: Stanford University Press, 1972.

Fernández, Julio A. Political Administration in Mexico. Boulder: University of Colorado Bureau of Governmental Research, 1969.

Fernández, Justino. A Guide to Mexican Art. Chicago: University of Chicago Press, 1969.

Flores, Edmundo. Tratado de economía agrícola. México, D. F.: Fondo de Cultura Económica, 1961.

_____. Vieja revolución, nuevos problemas. México, D. F.: Joaquín Mortiz, 1970.

Fuentes, Carlos. A Change of Skin. New York: Farrar, Straus and Giroux, 1968.

_____. Where the Air Is Clear. New York: Farrar, Straus and Giroux, 1960.

_____. The Death of Artemio Cruz. New York: Noonday Press, 1966.

García Cantú, Gastón. La hora de los halcones. Puebla, México: Universidad Autónoma de Puebla, 1976.

García Rivas, Heriberto. Breve historia de la revolución mexicana. México, D. F.: Editorial Diana, 1964.

Garza, David T. "Factionalism in the Mexican Left," Western Political Quarterly, September 1964, pp. 447-460.

Gill, Clark C. Education in a Changing Mexico. Washington, D. C.: U. S. Office of Education, 1969.

Glade, William P., Jr., and Charles W. Anderson. The Political Economy of Mexico. Madison: University of Wisconsin Press, 1963.

González Casanova, Pablo. Democracy in Mexico. New York: Oxford University Press, 1970.

González Morfín, Efraín. El cambio social y el PAN. México, D. F.: Ediciones de Acción Nacional, 1975.

Greenberg, Martin. Bureaucracy and Development: A Mexican Case Study. Lexington, Mass.: Heath Lexington, 1970.

Grieb, Kenneth J. The United States and Huerta. Lincoln: University of Nebraska Press, 1969.

Griffiths, B. B. Mexican Monetary Policy and Economic Development. New York: Praeger, 1972.

Grindle, Merilee S. Bureaucrats, Politicians, and Peasants in Mexico: A Case Study in Public Policy. Berkeley: University of California Press, 1977.

Guerra Utrilla, José. Los partidos políticos nacionales. México, D. F.: Editorial América, 1970.

Guzmán, Martín Luís. The Eagle and the Serpent. Garden City, N. Y.: Doubleday and Company, 1965.

_____. Memoirs of Pancho Villa. Austin: University of Texas Press, 1965.

Haddox, John H. Vasconcelos of Mexico. Austin: University of Texas Press, 1967.

Hale, Charles A. and Michael C. Meyer. "Mexico: The National Period," in Roberto Esquenazi-Mayo, ed., Latin American Scholarship Since World War II. Lincoln: University of Nebraska Press, 1971.

Hansen, Roger D. The Politics of Mexican Development. Baltimore: Johns Hopkins Press, 1971.

Hayner, Norman. New Patterns in Old Mexico. New Haven: College and University Press, 1966.

Hellman, Judith A. Mexico in Crisis. New York: Holmes and Meier, 1978.

Hualuja, Mario and José Woldenberg. Estado y lucha política en el México actual. México, D. F.: Ediciones El Caballito, 1976.

Hundley, Norris, Jr. Dividing the Waters: Controversy Between the United States and Mexico. Berkeley: University of California Press, 1966.

Infield, H. F. and Koka Freir. People in Ejidos. New York: Praeger, 1954.

Innes, John S. "Universidad Popular Mexicana," The Americas, Vol. 30, No. 1, 1973, pp. 110-122.

Iturriaga, José. E. La estructura social y cultural de México. México, D. F.: Fondo de Cultura Económica, 1951.

James, Daniel. "Sears, Roebuck's Mexican Revolution," Harper's, June 1959, pp. 1-6.

Johnson, Kenneth F. Mexican Democracy: A Critical View. Boston: Allyn and Bacon, 1971; revised edition, New York: Praeger, 1978.

Bibliography   254

Johnson, William Weber. Heroic Mexico. Garden City, N.Y.:
Doubleday, 1968.

Kautsky, John H. Patterns of Modernizing Revolutions: Mexico and
the Soviet Union. Beverly Hills, Calif.: Sage Publications, 1975.

King, Timothy. Mexico: Industrialization and Trade Policies Since
1940. New York: Oxford University Press, 1970.

Kirk, Bett. Covering the Mexican Front. Norman: University of
Oklahoma Press, 1942.

Kneller, George F. Education of the Mexican Nation. New York:
New York University Press, 1951.

Langford, Walter. The Mexican Novel Comes of Age. Notre Dame,
Indiana: University of Notre Dame Press, 1971.

Lanz Duret, Miguel. Derecho constitucional mexicano. México,
D. F.: Editorial L. D. S. A., 1947.

Leaming, George F. and W. H. Delaplane. "An Economy of Contrasts," in R. C. Ewing, ed., Six Faces of Mexico. Tucson:
University of Arizona Press, 1966.

Lewis, Oscar. The Children of Sánchez. New York: Vintage
Books, 1961.

_____. Five Families. New York: Mentor Books, 1959.

_____. Life in a Mexican Village: Tepoztlán Restudied. Urbana:
University of Illinois Press, 1951.

_____. Pedro Martínez: A Mexican Peasant and His Family.
New York: Vintage Books, 1967.

Lieuwen, Edwin. Mexican Militarism. Albuquerque: University of
New Mexico Press, 1968.

Looney, Robert E. Mexico's Economy. Boulder, Colorado: Westview Press, 1978.

López Aparicio, Alfonso. El movimiento obrero en México. México, D. F.: Editorial Jus, 1952.

López y Fuentes, Gregorio. El Indio. New York: Frederick Ungar
Publishing Company, 1961.

Mabry, Donald J. Mexico's Acción Nacional. Syracuse, N.Y.:
Syracuse University Press, 1973.

Machado, Manuel A. An Industry in Crisis: ... Foot-and-Mouth Disease. Berkeley: University of California Press, 1968.

Maldonado, Braulio. Baja California: comentarios políticos. México, D. F.: Costa-Amic, 1960.

Meyer, Michael C. Huerta: A Political Portrait. Lincoln: University of Nebraska Press, 1972.

_____. "Isidro Fabela's documentos históricos," Hispanic American Historical Review, February 1972, pp. 123-129.

_____. Mexican Rebel: Pascual Orozco and the Mexican Revolution, 1910-1915. Lincoln: University of Nebraska Press, 1967.

_____ and William L. Sherman. The Course of Mexican History. New York: Oxford University Press, 1979.

Michaels, Albert L. "The Crisis of Cardenismo," Journal of Latin American Studies, Vol. 2, No. 1, 1970, pp. 51-79.

Millan, Verna C. Mexico Reborn. Boston: Houghton Mifflin, 1939.

Millon, Robert P. Mexican Marxist: Vicente Lombardo Toledano. Chapel Hill, N. C.: University of North Carolina Press, 1966.

Mora, Juan Miguel de. Por la gracia del señor presidente. México, D. F.: Editores Asociados, 1975.

Mosk, Sanford A. Industrial Revolution in Mexico. Berkeley: University of California Press, 1950.

Muñoz, Hilda. Lázaro Cárdenas. México, D. F.: Fondo de Cultura Económica, 1976.

Needleman, Carolyn and Martin. "Who Rules Mexico?" Journal of Politics, November 1969, pp. 1011-1034.

Needler, Martin C. Political Systems of Latin America. Princeton, N. J.: Van Nostrand Reinhold, 1970.

_____. Politics and Society in Mexico. Albuquerque: University of New Mexico Press, 1971.

Niemeyer, E. Victor, Jr. Revolution at Queretaro: The Mexican Constitutional Convention of 1916-1917. Austin: University of Texas Press, 1974.

O'Donnell, Guillermo A. Modernization and Bureaucratic Authoritarianism. Berkeley: University of California Press, 1973.

Padgett, L. Vincent. The Mexican Political System. Boston: Houghton Mifflin, 2nd edition, 1976.

Paz, Octavio. El arco y la lira. México, D. F.: Fondo de Cultura Económica, 1972.

_____. The Labyrinth of Solitude: Life and Thought in Mexico. New York: Grove Press, 1961.

_____. The Other Mexico: Critique of the Pyramid. New York: Grove Press, 1972.

Pellicer de Brody, Olga. "Mexico in the 1970's," in Julio Cotler and Richard Fagen, eds., Latin America and the United States. Stanford: Stanford University Press, 1974.

Pérez López, Enrique. Mexico's Recent Economic Growth. Austin: University of Texas Press, 1967.

Piñeda, Hugo. José Vasconcelos. México, D. F.: Harper and Row Latinoamericana, 1975.

Poleman, Thomas T. The Papaloapan Project. Stanford: Stanford University Press, 1964.

Poulson, Barry W. and T. Noel Osborn, eds. U. S.-Mexico Economic Relations. Boulder, Colo.: Westview Press, 1979.

Powell, J. R. The Mexican Petroleum Industry, 1938-1950. Berkeley: University of California Press, 1956.

Price, John A. Tijuana. Notre Dame, Indiana: University of Notre Dame Press, 1974.

Purcell, Susan Kaufman. "Decision-making in an Authoritarian Regime," World Politics, October 1973, pp. 28-54.

_____. The Mexican Profit-Sharing Decision: Politics in an Authoritarian Regime. Berkeley: University of California Press, 1975.

Quirk, Robert E. An Affair of Honor: Woodrow Wilson and the Occupation of Veracruz. New York: W. W. Norton, 1967.

_____. The Mexican Revolution and the Catholic Church, 1910-1929. Bloomington: Indiana University Press, 1973.

_____. The Mexican Revolution, 1914-1915. New York: Citadel Press, 1963.

Ramos, Samuel. Profile of Man and Culture in Mexico. Austin: University of Texas Press, 1962.

Reed, Alma. Orozco. New York: Oxford University Press, 1956.

Reyes Heroles, Jesús. Discursos políticos. México, D. F.: Editorial del CEN del PRI, 1975.

Reyna, José Luis and R. S. Weinert. Control político. México, D. F.: Colegio de México, 1976.

Reynolds, Clark. The Mexican Economy. New Haven: Yale University Press, 1970.

Romanell, Patrick. Making of the Mexican Mind. Lincoln: University of Nebraska Press, 1952.

Ronfeldt, David. Atencingo. Stanford: Stanford University Press, 1973.

Ross, Stanley R., ed. Francisco I. Madero, Apostle of Mexican Democracy. New York: Columbia University Press, 1955.

_____. Is the Mexican Revolution Dead? Philadelphia: Temple University Press, 2nd edition, 1975.

_____, ed. Views Across the Border. Albuquerque: University of New Mexico Press, 1977.

Ruiz, Ramón E. Labor and the Ambivalent Revolutionaries. Baltimore: Johns Hopkins University Press, 1976.

_____. Mexico: Challenge of Poverty and Illiteracy. San Marino, Calif.: Huntington Library, 1963.

Rutherford, John. Mexican Society During the Revolution. New York: Clarendon Press, 1971.

Schmitt, Karl M. Communism in Mexico. Austin: University of Texas Press, 1965.

_____. Mexico and the United States, 1821-1973. New York: John Wiley and Sons, 1974.

Scott, Robert E. Mexican Government in Transition. Urbana: University of Illinois Press, revised edition, 1964.

Shafer, Robert Jones. Mexican Business Organizations. Syracuse, N.Y.: Syracuse University Press, 1973.

Siller Rodríguez, Rodolfo. La crisis del partido revolucionario institucional. México, D.F.: Costa-Amic, 1976.

Silva Herzog, Jesús. Breve historia de la Revolución mexicana. 2 Vols. México, D.F.: Fondo de Cultura Económico, 1972.

_____. Lázaro Cárdenas. México, D.F.: Editorial Nuevo Tiempo, 1975.

_____. La Revolución mexicana en crisis. México, D.F.: Cuadernos Americanos, 1944.

Simmons, Merle E. The Mexican Corrido. Bloomington: Indiana University Press, 1957.

Simpson, Eyler N. The Ejido: Mexico's Way Out. Chapel Hill, N. C.: University of North Carolina Press, 1937.

Simpson, Lesley B. Many Mexicos. Berkeley: University of California Press, 1960.

Sommers, Joseph. After the Storm. Albuquerque: University of New Mexico Press, 1968.

Stevens, Evelyn P. Protest and Response in Mexico. Cambridge, Mass.: MIT Press, 1974.

Stevenson, Robert. Music in Mexico. New York: Thomas Y. Crowell, 1971.

Tannenbaum, Frank. Mexico: The Struggle for Peace and Bread. New York: Alfred A. Knopf, 1956.

_____. Peace by Revolution. New York: Columbia University Press, 1966.

Taylor, Philip B. "The Mexican Elections of 1958," Western Political Quarterly, September 1960, pp. 722-744.

Townsend, William C. Lázaro Cárdenas. Ann Arbor, Mich.: George Wahr Publishing Company, 1952.

Tucker, William P. Mexican Government Today. Minneapolis: University of Minnesota Press, 1957.

Turner, Frederick C. The Dynamic of Mexican Nationalism. Chapel Hill, N. C.: University of North Carolina Press, 1968.

_____. Responsible Parenthood: Politics of Mexico's New Population Policies. Washington, D. C.: American Enterprise Institute, 1974.

Ugalde, Antonio. Power and Conflict in a Mexican Community. Albuquerque: University of New Mexico Press, 1970.

Vasconcelos, José. A Mexican Ulysses. Bloomington: Indiana University Press, 1963.

Vernon, Raymond. The Dilemma of Mexico's Development. Cambridge, Mass.: Harvard University Press, 1963.

_____, ed. Public Policy and Private Enterprise in Mexico. Cambridge, Mass.: Harvard University Press, 1964.

Von Sauer, Franz. The Alienated "Loyal" Opposition. Albuquerque: University of New Mexico Press, 1974.

Warman, Arturo. Los campesinos. México, D. F.: Editorial Nuestro Tiempo, 4th edition, 1975.

Wilkie, James W.   The Mexican Revolution: Federal Expenditure and
Social Change Since 1910.   Berkeley: University of California
Press, 2nd edition, 1970.

_____ and Albert L. Michaels, eds.   Revolution in Mexico: 1910-
1940.   New York: Alfred A. Knopf, 1969.

_____ and Edna Monzón de Wilkie, eds.   México visto en el siglo
XX.   México, D. F.:   Instituto Mexicano de Investigaciones Eco-
nómicas, 1969.

Williams, Edward J.   "Oil in Mexican-U.S. Relations," Orbis,
Spring 1978, pp. 210-211.

Wolfe, Bertram D.   The Fabulous Life of Diego Rivera.   New York:
Stein and Day, 1969.

Womack, John, Jr.   Zapata and the Mexican Revolution.   New York:
Alfred A. Knopf, 1969.

Yates, Paul L.   El desarrollo regional de México.   México, D. F.:
Banco de México, 1961.

Zea, Leopoldo.   Del liberalismo a la revolución en la educación
mexicana.   México, D. F.:   Biblioteca del Instituto Nacional de
Estudios Históricos, 1956.